Strategy without Design

Strategy exhibits a pervasive commitment to the belief that the best approach to adopt in dealing with affairs of the world is to confront, overcome and subjugate things to conform to our will, control and eventual mastery. Performance is about sustaining distinctiveness. This direct and deliberate approach draws inspiration from ancient Greek roots and has become orthodoxy. Yet there are downsides. This book shows why. Using examples from the world of business, economics, military strategy, politics and philosophy, it argues that success may inadvertently emerge from the everyday coping actions of a multitude of individuals, none of whom intended to contribute to any pre-conceived design. A consequence of this claim is that a paradox exists in strategic interventions, one that no strategist can afford to ignore. The more single-mindedly a strategic goal is sought, the more likely such calculated instrumental action eventually works to undermine its own initial success.

ROBERT C. H. CHIA is Professor of Management at the University of Strathclyde Business School.

ROBIN HOLT is Reader at the University of Liverpool Management School.

Strategy without Design

The Silent Efficacy of Indirect Action

Robert C. H. Chia and Robin Holt

CAMBRIDGE
UNIVERSITY PRESS

CAMBRIDGE UNIVERSITY PRESS
Cambridge, New York, Melbourne, Madrid, Cape Town,
Singapore, São Paulo, Delhi, Tokyo, Mexico City

Cambridge University Press
The Edinburgh Building, Cambridge CB2 8RU, UK

Published in the United States of America by Cambridge University Press, New York

www.cambridge.org
Information on this title: www.cambridge.org/9780521189859

First published 2009
Reprinted 2010
First paperback edition 2011

A catalogue record for this publication is available from the British Library

Library of Congress Cataloguing in Publication data

Chia, Robert C. H., 1949–
   Strategy without design : the silent efficacy of indirect action / Robert
C. H. Chia, Robin Holt.
      p.   cm.
ISBN 978-0-521-89550-7
      1. Strategic planning–Social aspects.   2. Planning–Social aspects.
3. Strategy (Philosophy)   I. Holt, Robin, 1966–   II. Title.
   HD30.28.C4953 2009
   658.4′012–dc22

                                                            2009024546

ISBN 978-0-521-89550-7 Hardback
ISBN 978-0-521-18985-9 Paperback

For our wives
Jeanny – RCCH
and
Jenny – RH

[T]he motive of success is not enough. It produces a short-sighted world which destroys the sources of its own prosperity... [A] great society is a society in which its men of business think greatly about its function. Low thoughts mean low behaviour, and after a brief orgy of exploitation, low behaviour means a descending standard of life.

Alfred North Whitehead, 1933

Contents

Preface

This book arose out of a vague suspicion that much of what we call 'strategy' involves retrospective sense-making: that there is a tendency to impute purposefulness design and deliberate forethought to what are often locally embedded coping initiatives in which the primary concern is the alleviation of immediate pressing problems, with little thought about broader eventual outcomes. The tendency is rife. Strategy-making is typically assumed to be a deliberate, planned and purposeful activity. Conscious choice, instrumental rationality and goal-directed behaviour are supposed to underpin strategic action. Successful outcomes are attributed to the systematic carrying out of a pre-thought programme of actions while failure is, conversely, attributed to the lack of proper planning. Clearly, this view of strategy as being something consciously designed prior to practical engagement with the world helps to explain many instances of individual and organizational success, particularly under stable, predictable conditions and in the short term. Nonetheless, the possibility that successful strategies may also *emerge* inadvertently as unintended consequences of human action and interaction remains. In what is now considered a seminal contribution to the strategy debate, Henry Mintzberg and James Waters[1] distinguish between *deliberate* and *emergent* strategies and maintain that, in the case of the latter, an *'unintended'* strategic order may arise even in the clear absence of deliberate planning and design. Mintzberg and Waters, however, do not go on to explore or elaborate on *how* it might be that, notwithstanding such lack of intention, strategy could still emerge spontaneously in practice.

In this book, we propose to investigate how it is that collective social good and organizational accomplishments may result from local actions and adaptations without the oversight or pre-authored design of 'big' strategists. Many established social phenomena and institutions that we take so much for granted and that enable modern society to function, including political structures, language, money and legal systems, have all emerged unplanned and undirected. Notwithstanding their obvious complexity, the regularity and orderliness we encounter in the social sphere of everyday life are often a consequence of the cumulative efforts of countless individuals acting over long periods of time, none of whom intended to contribute to any preconceived plan. In other words, *in seeking to explain individual, corporate and societal accomplishments there is no need to invoke deliberate intention, conscious choice and purposeful intervention. Collective success need not be attributable to the pre-existence of a deliberate planned strategy.* Rather, such success may be traced indirectly as the cumulative effect of a whole plethora of coping actions initiated by a multitude of individuals, all seeking merely to respond constructively to the predicaments they find themselves in.

A corollary of this emphasis on the non-deliberate emergence of strategy is a heightened awareness of the surprising efficacy of indirect action: action that is oblique or deemed peripheral in relation to specified ends can often produce more dramatic and lasting effects than direct, focused action. Throughout this book we make mention of a paradox in human affairs: *that the more directly and deliberately a specific strategic goal is single-mindedly sought the more likely it is that such calculated actions eventually work to undermine and erode their own initial successes, often with devastating consequences.* Planned strategic interventions may regularly produce initially impressive results, but their spectacular achievements are often unsustainable in the long term because they are bought at the expense of the life projects of others. At times they may even generate catastrophic consequences that spill over well beyond the scene of local initiation. Witness the current global economic turmoil initiated by the offering of risky sub-prime mortgages that, in disguised form, created a toxic credit system that eventually fouled entire economies. The finance houses' strategy of originating and distributing credit risk was deliberate, fixated on achieving bigger and more impressive short-term profits and justifying an extravagant bonus culture. Its advocates were sure it worked; money was being earned and clients appeared happy, borrowers and lenders alike. During 2008, however, some of the most respected US investment banks out of whose innovative grand strategies these toxic products emerged – Bear Stearns, Lehman Brothers and Merrill Lynch – disappeared entirely under a rising tide of worthless positions. Many of the banks that survive have sought sanctuary in the regulated shallows of state care, effectively becoming extensions of public treasuries. Hedge funds are trying to plug huge holes in their listing ship, whilst others that have been singular in their preparedness for a rising tide of toxicity have risen gleefully on the foaming, chaotic swell. Insurance giants have become mired in unfathomable, muddied depths of potential liability. National economic systems are becoming engulfed in this financial swell as their hastily erected bulwarks of trading suspensions and publicly funded pump-priming fail to hold back the reflux of collective, commercial delirium. All this originated in deliberate, strategic intent. As we shall show, the '*entire realm of strategy is pervaded by a paradoxical logic*', which requires 'an entirely different mode of comprehension and engagement from that of linear instrumental rationality'.[2]

This different mode of engagement is the corollary of designed intervention. It is a less spectacular, more understated and *oblique* strategic approach that appears to be more compatible with the attainment of longer-lasting success – one in which seemingly insignificant small gestures, which often go unnoticed, are recognized for the overall effect they eventually produce. In other words, there may be greater wisdom in approaching a strategic situation more modestly and elliptically and allowing strategic priorities to emerge spontaneously through local ingenuity and adaptive actions taken *in situ*. Here, strategy, instead of being something explicitly and boldly stated upfront, emerges organically, takes shape and infuses itself into the everyday actions of individuals and institutions. Understood thus, strategy is not so much about the act of *navigation* as it is about a process of *wayfinding*. We only *know as we go*. This implies that, rather than focusing on the pre-fixing of strategic priorities and positions, we would do well to adopt a more humble and nimble stance, which we call 'strategic blandness'; one that itself may be paradoxically characterized as a strategy-less strategy. It entails a will-o'-the-wisp endurance that invites no opposition and assumes no domination; it exists only in the plenitude of as yet unrealized possibilities. To exemplify a strategic blandness is to abandon positions, to withdraw from grandiosely stated preferences, to shy away from once fervid ambition and stringently held commitments and, instead, nurture a curiosity whose meandering enquiry moves through infatuation, temperance and indifference with equal passion. It is to appreciate the subtlety and cumulative efficacy of small gestures and indirect actions as the founding basis for progressive and sustainable social and economic endeavours. The idea of strategic design informed by rational assessment and realized in clear execution becomes a conceit of those unable to appreciate the potential of a life lived outside the confines of the intellect and unwilling to acknowledge the debilitating emptiness of always seeing the world head-on. It is, we suspect, time for strategy without design.

Our book itself may be thought of as an outcome of small gestures and indirect actions, often surprising us both in the direction in which it has evolved and the shape that it has taken over the past eighteen months. It is a book of small, not big, ideas. It is written in a way that incorporates obliqueness, circuitousness and detours in order to exemplify as well as articulate this much-neglected aspect of strategic reality. This writing would have been impossible without our immersion in conversation with a wealth of people from whose insights and practical-mindedness we have drawn considerable sustenance. In particular, Robert Chia would like to thank Bob Cooper for his inspiration and guidance over the years, David Eastwood for his critical and constructive comments and suggestions, his golfing 'mates' at Grange Golf Club, Monifieth, for their refreshing canniness and home-brewed wisdom, and his siblings, especially Thomas and Roselie, for their love, encouragement and support. Robin Holt's thanks go to his family, friends and bike, in whose presence he has become aware of a world far richer than any over which he might have any influence.

Introduction

Large streams from little fountains flow,
Tall oaks from little acorns grow.
Old English proverb

Boundless – this vast heap earth,
this bottomless heaven,
how perfectly boundless.[1]
T'ao Ch'ien, Elegy for Myself *(translated by David Hinton)*

In this introductory chapter we document several instances of successful accomplishments in a number of business and social spheres and show how we recognize the emergence of a coherent strategy even though the people involved may not have deliberately intended it to be so. This leads us to justify our belief in the plausibility of what we call here 'strategy without design', in which invisible coordinating forces appear to work to bring together fruitful outcomes indirectly and circuitously through a plethora of local coping actions. We also show that, conversely, when well-intentioned attempts to deliberately design and engineer a desired strategic outcome dominate concerns they are frequently ineffective and at times may even unexpectedly produce disastrous consequences. Paradoxically, the more direct and deliberate the effort applied the less sustainable the eventual outcome. Conversely, systematic, sustainable, longer-term accomplishments are often a consequence of attending to small, seemingly insignificant details through local, everyday coping actions.

Reaching for the ground

In 1974 the country of Bangladesh experienced a severe famine that threatened the livelihood of thousands in the rural villages. Amidst this chaos and human catastrophe, a Bangladeshi professor at the University of Chittagong was so touched by the plight of the families affected by the famine that he decided to make a small personal loan of US$27 to a group of forty-two local households so that they could

1

begin the process of self-help by producing small items for sale, hence earning much-needed income without the burdens associated with predatory lending. The overwhelming success of this seemingly insignificant and spontaneous human gesture led to the eventual formation of Grameen Bank (literally 'Bank of the Villages', in Bangla) two years later to support and help alleviate the plight of local residents living around the university, beginning with the village of Jobra and then spreading rapidly further afield, almost like a virus, to other districts in Bangladesh and beyond to countries as distant as Indonesia, the Philippines, Latin America, sub-Saharan Africa, China and even the United States. By November 2007, in a relatively short space of some thirty-one years, the bank had 2,468 branches in Bangladesh alone, covering 80,257 villages and employing a total staff of 24,703. Its total loans distributed amounts to some US$6.55 billion, more than 98 per cent of which has been repaid.[2] Its founder, Muhammad Yunus, and Grameen Bank were publicly recognized for their efforts to create economic and social development from below and jointly awarded the Nobel Peace Prize in 2006. More importantly, more than a half of the 7 million borrowers, mostly women, are reported to have successfully extricated themselves and their families from acute poverty, as measured by such basic standards as the ability to provide schooling for their children, eating three meals a day and having proper sanitation, rainproof housing, clean drinking water and the ability to maintain regular repayment of a US$8.00-a-week loan charge.

The unexpected and remarkable success of Grameen Bank is attributable to the spontaneous reactions of a concerned individual who found it incomprehensible that a matter of US22 cents could be the threshold barrier between a life of poverty and the liberating possibility of extricating oneself from the debilitating credit trap in which villagers around his university in Chittagong found themselves. Yunus, who was the head of the economics department at that time and who had done his PhD at Vanderbilt University in the United States, speaks of this sense of incredulity and exasperation in his recent book *Banker to the Poor*. His encounter with Sufia Begum, a twenty-one-year-old local old mother of three, was a significant moment in his intellectual awakening to the sterility and impotence of grand theory in classical economics. Sufia, like many other women in the village, borrowed an amount equivalent to US22 cents from 'paikars' (lender-middlemen) to buy strips of bamboo, which she then used to make stools for sale. Each day, as a result of a whole day's labour, she made a 'profit' of US2 cents, which was barely enough to feed her family.

I had never heard of anyone suffering for a lack of 22 US cents... Should I reach into my pocket and hand Sufia the pittance she needed? That would be so simple, so easy... Why had not my university, my economics department, all the economics departments in the world for that matter, and the thousands of intelligent economics professors, why had they not tried to understand the poor and to help those who needed help the most?[3]

For Yunus, this was a moment of rude awakening to the harshness of economic reality. As a student of economics he had been mesmerised by the neatness and persuasiveness of economic theories and how they appeared to provide comprehensive answers to economic problems. This stark encounter with the struggle for survival at his very doorstep, however, radically changed his whole attitude.

What good were all these elegant theories when people died of starvation on pavements and on doorsteps... Where was the economic theory which reflected their real life? I felt I had to escape from academic life. I wanted to discover the real-life economics that were played out every day in the neighbouring villages... I opted for what I called the *'worm's eye view'*.[4]

It was this shock and reaction to the helplessness and resignation of the villagers to the effects of that devastating 1974 famine that led him to recognize the vast chasm existing between textbook 'solutions' and economic 'realities': between designed strategic interventions initiated from the top and the everyday practical coping actions of locals. This acute awareness, rendered by the immediacy and urgency of the situation, led him to gather some of his students and colleagues to help with alleviating the plight of those around him. It was this spontaneous initiative and not some deliberate planned strategy that generated the impetus for his search for a novel way of helping the villagers to 'bootstrap' themselves out of the poverty trap they had, through no fault of their own, found themselves in. The outcome of the unexpected success of his cumulative efforts, together with those of his students and colleagues, was Grameen Bank.

Grameen Bank is novel, in that it contradicts in a number of ways the dominant logic of banking practice. Principally, in conventional banking wisdom, credit is extended only to a person who is able to satisfy the bank that he/she possesses some form of 'collateral': thus the more you have the more you are likely to be able to borrow. This, of course, means that if you have little or nothing you get nothing: you are invariably caught in a 'poverty trap'. Grameen Bank operates on a radically reversed philosophy, which starts from the predicament an individual finds him- or herself in, and hence the immediate needs to be met, rather than from the traditional bank's priority to its shareholders. There are four main aspects to Grameen Bank's approach: first, it maintains that credit is a human right, so that those who do not have any possessions are those most in need and hence must be given the highest priority in acquiring loans to help improve their lot, provided they are first able to demonstrate their reliability; second, it holds that most people can be trusted to make their weekly repayments diligently, particularly if their failure to do so is tied to material consequences for the rest of the community of which they form a part (in Grameen Bank, there are no binding contracts between the borrower and the bank); third, Grameen Bank systematically encourages borrowers to focus their efforts on health, social and educational development to improve their own living conditions rather than on material trappings; fourth, it views poor people as human 'bonsais' – stunted in their growth not though their own fault but through a lack of proper support and nourishment. These fundamental principles contradict the very logic of modern capitalism, with its emphasis on maximizing material gains, self-interested exchange and the survival of the fittest through direct, highly focused competition. Nevertheless, they have led to this most unlikely but remarkable growth and success in micro-credit banking.

It is not merely the notion of micro-credit itself that is particularly definitive about Yunus's remarkable achievement but, rather, the under-lying counter-intuitive logic of practice associated with it, which goes against the grain of some of the deepest-held assumptions about how to achieve economic progress. The accrual of material wealth is, we assume, an outcome of clarified insight, careful planning, hard work, the diligent and often singular pursuit of known goals, and so on. The associated trading actions are believed to follow from deliberate choices, and choices, in turn, are seen to emanate from the prior anticipation of outcomes intended to fulfil individual desires. This form of 'conse-quentialist reasoning' provides the underlying premise for the social and behavioural sciences in general and for the field of economics in particular.[5] Nonetheless, this presumption of a deliberate and calcula-tive goal-oriented logic of action fails to account adequately for the emergence and success of Grameen Bank, whose formation and rise to prominence owed much more to the local initiatives of a single individ-ual and his students and colleagues who were merely seeking to deal with the immediate problems they saw around them. Despite the even-tual spectacular success of Grameen Bank, Yunus had no initial grand designs for creating a bank of such immense scale. That did not prevent it from becoming a reality, however. His cumulative constructive actions gradually took on global significance not through any deliber-ately planned course of action, or even any initial desire to do so, but through the gradual gathering of momentum of the small initiatives undertaken locally to cope with the immediate business of securing the basic material conditions to sustain human life.

The key point we wish to make here is that strategy and consistency of action can emerge non-deliberately through a profusion of local interventions directed towards dealing with immediate concerns. These local coping actions may actually give rise to a strategic consistency even in the absence of prior specified goals. In other words, *attending to and dealing with the problems, obstacles and concerns confronted in the here and now may actually serve to clarify and shape the initially vague and inarticulate aspirations behind such coping actions with sufficient consistency that, in retrospect, they may appear to constitute a recognizable 'strategy'.* We often act and react knowing what we do not want rather than in response to any predefined goals. In other words, strategy may evolve from knowing what we do *not want* or what *not to do* rather than what we want or what to do; a 'negative' or *latent* form of coping strategy may exist without us being ever conscious of it. In this sense, strategy does not necessarily imply something deliberately planned or pre-thought. Indeed, strategically favourable outcomes may even emerge serendipitously as a consequence of an individual's actions or the actions of a small group of individuals, who unintentionally trigger a movement or trend shift through their local choices and interests where no overall coordinated initiative is involved. Sir Richard Branson's Virgin Airways, for instance, was born serendipitously as a consequence of him and his girlfriend being stranded on one of the Virgin Islands during a holiday in the Caribbean in the late 1970s. When they got to the local airport on the island to return home, they found, together with other waiting passengers, that their flight to Puerto Rico had been cancelled.

[P]eople were roaming about, looking lost. No one was doing anything. So I did – someone had to. Even though I hadn't a clue what I was really doing, with a great deal of aplomb I chartered a plane for $2,000 and divided that by the number of passengers. It came to $39 a head. I borrowed a blackboard and wrote on it: VIRGIN AIRWAYS: $39 SINGLE FLIGHT TO PUERTO RICO. All the tickets were snapped up by grateful passengers. I managed to get two free tickets out of it and even made a small profit! The idea for Virgin Airways was born, right there in the middle of a holiday.[6]

This spontaneous coping action, born of necessity given the negative circumstances he found himself in, provided the embryonic start to the idea of running a transatlantic airline so much so that, when the idea was suggested to him some years later, he found the proposition difficult to resist. 'I can make up my mind about people and ideas in sixty seconds. I rely more on gut instinct than thick reports. . . I've always said that you don't need to do a lot of expensive research, or produce vast files and reports to know that something is a good idea and will work.'[7] Today Virgin Airways flies to over 300 destinations all over the world, and Branson has even started Virgin Galactic, which offers short suborbital flights into space.

The dangers of deliberate planning

Skiing in Bavaria toward the end of World War II, an orthopaedic specialist, Dr Klaus Maerten, fell and hurt his foot. Normal shoes were too painful for him to wear for long and post-war restrictions meant that there were very few bespoke options available in any event, so, together with his friend Dr Herbert Funck, Maerten designed his own shoe using layered rubber taken from used tyres. These soles were lightweight and the layers sandwiched with heat-sealed or welted pockets of cushioning air. After guiding Maerten to a full recovery, the doctors set up shop and began selling the boots to others, emphasizing the virtues of comfort to those who found walking difficult. Their market seemed to consist mainly of older women. Despite setting up a factory in Munich during the early 1950s, expansion was proving difficult, with many potential manufacturing partners in Germany thinking the air-cushioning a bit of a gimmick. Maerten and Funck decided to look further afield, and placed advertisements in the trade press.

One of these was read by Bill Griggs of shoe- and bootmakers R. Griggs and Son of Wollaston, England, who had been making the 'Bulldog' boot for the British army. Griggs bought the worldwide rights, refined the design a little using yellow stitching and patterned soles, anglicized the name to 'Dr Martens' and launched the boot on the world on 1 April 1960 – hence the boot's name, the 1460. The 1460's intended users were peripatetic workers such as postmen and the police. The addition of steel toecaps and lengthened uppers extended the appeal to others, such as construction workers. It was the unassuming utility of the boot that generated burgeoning interest amongst the mods during the mid-1960s. Notorious not only for perfecting a smart and distinctive look but for their seasonal migratory bust-ups with the old-school rockers or Teddy boys, mods found the aggressive-looking, hard-working boot ideal as both a statement of distinction and a ready-to-hand weapon. It was also something that could be polished; bright shoes were no longer the preserve of the officer classes – they had been appropriated.

The fact that it was comfortable to wear simply added to its adamantine appeal amongst a youth culture whose world was so strikingly shot in the film *Quadrophenia*. As the mods morphed into factional tribes during the early 1970s, so the boot, especially in its original ox-blood leather guise, became a sort of badge for the most aggressive and hostile of these, the skinheads. This association with male and often right-wing violence was never total and did not prevent other, often opposing groups from adopting different versions of the seemingly infinitely adaptable boot. Punks wore them during the late 1970s, and during the 1980s they were adopted by doleful, cardigan-wearing students angsting over the shallowness of an all-encompassing neoliberal economic revolution. By the end of the 1980s the boot had become an icon of counterculture in Britain and abroad, an emblem of dissatisfaction only intensified by the geriatric posturing of the last guardians of old-empire hierarchy as they blustered on about the boot being threatening and disrespectful.

Appropriately enough for an icon of iconoclasm, however, this image as a symbol of youthful disdain was always itself in some state of tension. The boots had an openness of character that was no better demonstrated when they ended up on the feet of such a motley as: the British Member of Parliament Tony Benn; an SAS (Special Air Service) unit of the British army; and even Pope John Paul II. This rise in popularity was not planned for nor stimulated; at no point did the Griggs decide to target or resist a specific group of wearers. Indeed, their strategy, insofar as they had one, was simply to produce as many good-quality boots as were wanted, and when expansion was required they organically merged with other local firms steeped in their local region's shoemaking patterns of life.

During the 1990s the insouciance of Dr Martens (DM) boots began to wane. As with many things radical, as soon as they became chic, purred over by the arbiters of fashion and aped by designers the world over, they lost what had made them novel. In a kind of object-based version of Robert Michels' 'iron law of oligarchy', they betrayed their spirit.[8] It is perhaps no coincidence that the steady demise of their appeal coincided with the deliberate massive expansion of production. By 1994 the company had 2,700 employees and sales of £170 million and was making 10 million boots and shoes a year. The company began opening Dr Martens shops. The first was in London's Covent Garden and was spread over six floors, selling everything from watches to food. The classic boot was just an anchor point for a burgeoning array of branded goods. Griggs' simple operation was being sharpened by a deliberate and sophisticated top-down strategy. More large stores were opened and yet more were planned. The DM-wearing grunge movement in the United States had seemingly opened a huge new market. The appeal was simply assumed to be a growing given. Russia and China lay in wait. The strategists had it all worked out.

It was the strategic activities designed to exploit the appeal that actually detracted from it, however. Prior to this expansion, the lasting appeal of Dr Martens came from their being a *tabula rasa*, a welcome, indefinable open space in a world of consumption plagued with manipulated tastes and targeted placements. As a brand they were worthless, because as a brand they became subject to the vagaries of fashion; they became 'a something', and therefore something that could be used up and discarded. Of course, other factors, such as competition spurred by cheap, outsourced labour, threatened demand, but why Dr Martens perhaps suffered more than other brands and failed to adapt was because what was forgotten was how the prior success had simply been about the boots being whatever people wanted to make of them. The fortunes of Griggs deteriorated rapidly; in three years the company lost £100 million, and by 2003 the only way of saving it was to close most of the retail outlets, shut the factory in Wollaston and move production to the Far East. Dr Martens boots are still produced, but the presence of an object that had, for decades, blossomed of its own accord and found its own way has been eroded. They are now one amongst many purchase options.

Like the fortuitous circumstances that gave rise to Virgin Airways and the unexpected success of Muhammad Yunus and Grameen Bank, a cluster of interlocking local events and actions can unexpectedly gather momentum, spread like a contagious disease and generate a trend and movement that eventually leads to the spectacular outcomes that no one single person, or even groups of persons, could have envisaged or be held accountable for. Dr Martens boots flourished in the case of their users. Paradoxically, the subsequent attempt to strategically articulate and then influence the use of the product backfired and led to near-failure.

This is not an uncommon experience in business, warfare or life generally: the more that directly and deliberately action is taken the more it tends to eventually undermine its own aspirations. Such an insight has led the military strategist Basil Liddell-Hart to suggest that a direct approach tends to provoke a stubborn resistance because of the conflict of wills that is the inevitable result of confrontation.[9] Thus, in the case of Griggs, the later attempt to deliberately leverage the Dr Martens brand through its explicit commodification led to the eventual loss of its uniqueness as an expression of defiance to social categorization.

On the other hand, and as the story of Dr Martens boots also shows, highly favourable outcomes may emerge and evolve quite spontaneously through local perturbations and interactions without there being any need for planned and coordinated strategic action. This is as true for business growth and social change as it is for urban development. The Nobel-Prize-winner Herbert Simon points out that an absence of deliberate centralized planning in urban development does not necessarily imply an ineffective outcome.

> I retain vivid memories of the astonishment and disbelief expressed by...students whom I taught...when I pointed to medieval cities as marvellously patterned systems that had mostly just 'grown' in response to myriads of individual human decisions. To my students a pattern implied a planner in whose mind it had been conceived and by whose hand it had been implemented. The idea that a city could acquire its pattern as naturally as a snowflake was foreign to them.[10]

The city of London, for instance, developed spontaneously from early hamlet settlements around three hills: Tothill, Penton Hill and Tower Hill. Tracks and footpaths wound their way between them, and these gradually became roads and lanes, encouraging further dwellings to grow up around them so that these clusters of hamlets became villages, towns and eventually what we now know as London. It is, therefore, the interactional and iterative process of local actions that feeds urban growth and regeneration. The small, evolving actions of the city's denizens are what creates and sustains the complex and organic urban expansion that gives cities their often vivid character, the melange of smallness and influence making them, at one and the same time, 'so thrilling and terrifying, so liable to swallow [their] inhabitants. London, Tokyo, Delhi...pulsate, they groan and sigh and spread their many tendrils.'[11]

Grameen Bank, Virgin Airways and the unexpected and almost epidemic-like popularity of Dr Martens, as well as the unplanned growth of cities, all point towards a relatively unacknowledged phenomenon in business strategy research and theorizing: that strategic success may very well be an indirect and unintended outcome of everyday coping actions and embedded local opportunism. Conversely, the more that direct and deliberate strategic action is taken the more it eventually spawns negative unintended consequences. It is the persistence of both these observations across a wide variety of natural and social circumstances that has led to the realization that, in order to appreciate and explain strategic success fully, we must begin to acknowledge the prior existence of a *latent* strategic impulse, which provides the momentum and direction of development such that spectacular success may actually be attained without there being any deliberate intention involved on the part of actors.

Take care of the pennies. . .: strategy from the 'bottom up'

Malcolm Gladwell's *The Tipping Point* describes how, in the mid-1980s, the New York City Transit Authority decided to revamp the subway system, which had suffered a loss of control on the part of the authorities and was on the verge of collapse because of the numerous incidents of serious crime taking place within its premises. In the effort to clean up and make safe the subway system, an unusual approach was adopted, thanks to the insights of the newly appointed subway director David Gunn. Instead of directly addressing the problem of serious crimes being committed and the problem of subway reliability, Gunn decided to focus his attention on diligently removing the graffiti from the train cars, despite the advice of his peers. For Gunn, the extensive presence of graffiti on the train cars symbolized the loss of control and an impending collapse of the system of law and order in the subway system, and the battle against graffiti was in fact a battle against the insidious forces of disorder, which had become rampant in the subway. This indirect way of addressing the problem of social order by attending to local details resonates with what two criminologists, James Q. Watson and George Kelling, have called the 'broken window' theory of crime. The argument is that if a broken window along a street is left unrepaired the overall impression it leaves is that no one cares and that no one is in charge. It therefore serves as a magnet attracting further acts of vandalism, crime and destruction within the area. Very soon more windows nearby are broken, and this spreads till an overall state of dissolution exists, sending a clear message that anything goes in that area. Thus, in a city and in urban spaces what appear to be relatively minor problems, such as graffiti, vandalism, small-scale public disorder and so on, serve as an indirect invitation to the commission of more serious crimes.

Muggers and robbers, whether opportunistic or professional, believe they reduce their chances of being caught or even identified if they operate on streets where potential victims are already intimidated by prevailing conditions.[12]

This controversial 'broken windows' perspective on crime, despite its questionable status at that time, was, nevertheless, employed to deal with the problems encountered in the New York subway, and with great effect. Gunn decided to set up a highly efficient system for dealing promptly and almost religiously with the graffiti, train by train and line by line. If a carriage came in with graffiti it was either removed from service or the graffiti was cleaned off immediately. Each time new graffiti appeared it was immediately dealt with. What this did was to send an unequivocal message to the vandals responsible for the graffiti that it was not worth their while investing energy and time drawing and colouring their 'artwork' only to see it disappear almost straight away in the cleaning process. The whole 'clean-up' initiative, which took several years to generate the desired effect, was a resounding success; it was followed by a similar campaign revolving around another minor and related problem of 'fare-beating', and again this proved to be highly successful. The real point behind this episode, however, was less to do with the success with graffiti and 'fare-beating' than with the subsequent dramatic fall in felonies that accompanied this clean-up; a drop of some 75 per cent in serious crime rates by the end of the decade was recorded.[13]

What the 'broken window' theory suggests is that it is not so much attending to the major issues of law and order and relying on high-profile, spectacular interventions that helps generate a more lasting, desirable outcome but, rather, small, sustained local initiatives aimed specifically at dealing with immediate concerns. This kind of thinking resonates deeply with a piece of popular wisdom that still applies as far as the older generation in Britain is concerned: 'Take care of the pennies and the pounds will take care of themselves.' Indirectly attending to the small, seemingly marginal and insignificant aspects of a situation can often lead to surprisingly wider ramifications. A *detour* or diversion of attention away from the overall concern to the minutiae of concrete situations frequently triggers an upward-spiralling sequence of outcomes that are often unrecognizable from their apparently insignificant source of initiation. As Magora Maruyama shows in his seminal contribution to *American Scientist* entitled 'The second cybernetics', in which people typically grant a privileged status to processes that seemingly restore equilibrium or balance, what Gunn is showing is an awareness of 'deviation-amplifying' processes that have the potential to generate strategically beneficial changes. Seemingly mundane, small and repetitive activities can produce dramatic transformations over a period of time. Take, for example, the weathering of rocks. A small crack in the rock collects water. When the water freezes the crack is enlarged. This, in turn, collects more water, which then makes the crack even larger. Eventually, there is sufficient water to support organic life. The accumulation of organic matter leads to the growth of a tree, and so on. Thus, what began with a small deviation and persistent repetitive activity amplifies itself to support the growth of vegetation and the eventual dramatic transformation of the landscape.[14] Gunn was advocating something similar. He didn't get any thanks initially. His actions were deemed too unspectacular, neither dramatic nor bold.

They had a lasting effect, though – much like the way that Muhammed Yunus's small gesture eventually led to the success of Grameen Bank, Branson's opportunistic action led to the formation of Virgin Airlines, and the persistent cleaning of the graffiti and the sustained efforts against fare-dodging unexpectedly led to a dramatic fall in serious crime rates. The same epidemic-like spread of a phenomenon from small but sustained local efforts at improvement can be employed to explain the latent and emergent strategy of a globally successful company such as the Toyota Motor Corporation.

Strategy through self-cultivation

On 23 December 2006 *The New York Times* reported that the Japanese auto manufacturer Toyota was poised to supplant General Motors (GM) as the world's largest carmaker after seventy-five years of domination by GM. In April 2007 both the BBC and MSNBC News reported that Toyota had indeed overtaken GM to become the top vehicle seller in the world. In the period from January to March 2007 Toyota sold 2.35 million vehicles worldwide, surpassing the 2.26 million sold by GM. Furthermore, whilst GM suffered a loss of some US$3 billion in 2006, Toyota made a profit of US$11.8 billion in the same year. Similarly, Ford lost US$12.6 billion in 2006 while DaimlerChrysler lost US$1.5 billion. The Detroit 'big three' (GM, Ford and Chrysler) continued their downward spiral of losses despite massive efforts to restructure, reduce costs and engineer a turnaround. In 2006 alone the US auto manufacturers laid off some 150,000 workers and all three had further plans to downsize significantly, reducing their workforce and closing down several plants in the process. In 2007, whilst Toyota's market capitalization was in excess of US$200 billion, the combined value of the big three had shrunk to something like US$35 billion. In 2006 the Toyota Camry, the number one seller in the United States, was outselling GM's number one car, the Chevy Impala, by some 35 per cent. Its fuel-efficient cars, such as the Corolla, the Yaris and the hybrid Prius, had also become increasingly popular as fuel prices began to surge, and its flagship, top-of-the-range Lexus was recording the fastest-growing sales of any in the luxury car sector. Whilst Detroit's cars were piling up on dealer lots, Japanese cars were being snapped up by customers in much less time. In 2007 GM, Ford and Chrysler cars sat on dealer lots for anything from eighty-two to 103 days whilst Japanese cars such as Toyota and Honda makes were being driven off within twenty-seven to thirty-two days, respectively. These sales translated into revenue, with Toyota enjoying double-digit margins well into 2007 and being consistently placed in the top three revenue-per-employee earnings of the major car makers.[15] In the face of imploding demand, this success has become hard to sustain, given the structural constraints associated with a relatively high domestic manufacturing base and a strong currency, yet 2008 saw Toyota maintain its dominance, selling nearly 9 million vehicles to GM's 8.3 million, and Toyota's losses in 2009 have been eclipsed by the bankruptcy of GM.

It has taken Toyota the best part of fifty years to reach its global status. Since the introduction of the tinny, 60 horsepower Toyopet Crown in the United States in the mid-1950s (with initial annual sales of only 288) Toyota has built a rock-solid reputation for quality, reliability and performance, and, more latterly, unsurpassed luxury in the form of the best-selling Lexus. What accounts for this remarkable success of Toyota, however, from its modest foundation in 1937 by the Toyoda family, whose members remain intimately involved in the company and symbolize the values and emotional unity of the company? What gives it its competitive edge over other auto manufacturers? A multitude of reasons have been proffered, including: the Bank of Japan's active pursuit of and support for a weak yen; the learning from and copying of manufacturing techniques and quality control from the United States; the debilitating influence of strong unions in the big three; the huge legacy costs that form part of the US manufacturers' employment package compared to Toyota's much leaner provision; better and more efficient manufacturing techniques, such as the now famous just-in-time approach to production; the use of highly skilled workers; and the changing US market, which up until the 1990s especially had been dominated by larger, higher-margin cars and pick-ups.

So far so orthodox. The Toyota story appears like the rise of a consistently dominant firm versed in a well-designed and well-executed strategy of selling the right cars in the right places at the right time. According to Sergio Marchionne of Fiat, Toyota is 'an execution machine': it does everything better, faster and with fewer errors, thanks to a determined and loyal workforce and a relentless management style.[16] The rewards have been well deserved. We might look a little deeper, though. Woven throughout any telling of Toyota's success story has been the much-vaunted Toyota production system (TPS). This originated in the aftermath of World War II, when all the means of production in Japan (capital; young, active labour; resources; and even space) were scant. The constraints imposed by a war-torn environment meant that Toyota – originally a cotton-spinning machine producer based in the largely rural region of Nagoya – had, out of necessity, to produce long-lasting cars with limited material resources in small batches using labour-saving methods. Critical to its expansion was an internationally minded executive, Taichi Ohno, who visited the United States and studied the mass production methods to which the TPS might be applied. It was not just mechanical operations either; Ohno believed all activities, from the shop floor to the boardroom, could be subjected to the TPS. The mantra is doing more with less by standardizing processes, breaking activities down into their constituent parts and requiring employees to contribute to improvements rather than passively relying upon managerial initiative. Celebrated elements of the system include the elimination of waste (*muda*); fail-safe error-fixing (*poka-yoke*) and continuous improvement (*kaizen*). The emphasis remains pragmatic: it is the manufacturing engineers who sign off design decisions and who determine budgets and production gateways. Things are kept simple and the emphasis is always on producing simply (far fewer options and gadgets and design additions and very low inventory levels), quickly (consistently one of the lowest man-hours per unit) and well (high on satisfaction rankings and very low warranty claims).

In many of these accounts, however, what is often overlooked is the underlying philosophical attitude and predisposition of the Japanese mentality. Whilst *kaizen* is often equated with the idea of 'continuous improvement', what is often missed or glossed over in this (mis)interpretation is the notion of continuous soul-searching and relentless *self-criticism* associated with the rejection of large-scale dramatic change in favour of a strategy of painstakingly accumulating *small gains*. As the commentator Kiichi Shimokawa, a business professor at Tokai Gakuen University, maintains, 'Winning didn't happen overnight... Japanese makers built their business, slowly but surely, accumulating technology and developing good cars.'[17] Instead of trumpeting the company's achievements in overtaking GM – a status that the 2008/9 recession makes all the more stark – Toyota's president, Katsuaki Watanabe, chose to thank the customers, maintaining that the company's results are 'wholly thanks to the support of our customers in every region around the world'. When further pressed about his view on Toyota's accomplishment, Watanabe is reported to have said that Toyota had to continue to improve its quality in order to remain a leader in the field. For him, 'no growth can come without improving quality'. Moreover, he said: 'We are still developing in many regions in the world. I don't regard that [surpassing GM] as success yet.'[18] There was an unusual reluctance to crow about the company's hard-won status. 'Our goal has never been to sell the most cars in the world. We simply want to be the best in quality. After that, sales will take care of themselves.'[19] The global recession of 2008/9 has brought this attitude into yet further relief: the firm made a loss for the first time since 1950, and in early 2009 had what was the only triple-'A' rating for a non-financial, non-governmental Asian corporation down-graded.

Surely something has to give? Nevertheless, the newly installed chief executive, Akio Toyoda, is promising to concentrate on the founding spirit of a firm versed in customer satisfaction and an unwavering attention to the minutiae of the factory floor.[20] This reflects what the firm's managers feel to be the success of the 'indirect approach' to strategy identified by Liddell-Hart. Even in times of austerity there is a reluctance to embrace a big vision, and instead a willingness to continue with what Takahiro Fujimoto, in his book on Toyota, recognizes as an enduring and slightly obsessive concern with the apparently smallest of things.[21] To concentrate on quality, Toyota hires its workers as young graduate engineers and keeps them to retirement, only reluctantly employs non-Japanese workers and maintains executive turnover at virtually zero. When this status is threatened as the firm struggles to sell new models, therefore, Toyota remains reluctant to issue redundancy notices, deflecting the ire of its regular workers by treating the more distant 'part-time' contract staff relatively casually and encouraging in-house savings through wage and bonus reductions and yet more unwavering attention to the possibilities for minor improvements. Such an emphasis on getting and keeping the right kind of people and attitude exemplifies the modest and low-keyed management philosophy underpinning Toyota.

What, we suggest, remains the lodestone of Toyota's success – and why it is so hard to replicate despite Toyota being very open about its production system – is this humble and ingrained attention to fine details and to continuous improvement in the most mundane and, hence, seemingly unimportant aspects of business operations. As Simon Caulkin remarks, the production system is less a set of replicable procedures than an emergent living thing, a formidable organism rather than the product of grand design.[22] *Kaizen*, as understood in the Japanese context, is more intimately linked to an individual's sense of identity and reflects an internalized disposition more than a matter of instrumental efficacy.[23] *Kaizen* is inextricable from what has come to be known as the 'five Ss' of the Japanese attitude in manufacturing. The five Ss are:

(i) *seiro* – remove unnecessary work tools, materials, equipment or paperwork;
(ii) *seiton* – organize and classify work items and documents to ensure easy locatability;

(iii) *seiso* – keep the work environment spotlessly clean;

(iv) *seiketsu* – standardize operations and activities whenever possible; and

(v) *shitsuke* – observe and respect rules regarding timeliness, safety, machine procedures and accepted practice.

Although these five Ss may initially appear tangential to the aspiration of manufacturing systems and excellence, for the Japanese they reflect a whole mental orientation and cultivated disposition for dealing with matters using the same thoroughness, attention and care that is expected in dealing with any state of affairs. Manufacturing practices and problems are no different. What Toyota well understands is how this meticulous personal demeanour and disposition expresses an innate quality of engagement that reflects the overall attitude and ethos for attending to fine details that is, in turn, strategically important to its business. It is not too far-fetched to attribute Toyota's success to the individual, purposive acts of self-cultivation and self-perfection undertaken daily by each and every one of its employees.

The limits of designed strategic intervention

As we have written them, and their protagonists experienced them, the stories of Grameen Bank, Virgin, Dr Martens and even Toyota start with a radically reversed philosophy in which it is the predicament an individual finds him- or herself in that makes sense of the ensuing wealth-creating activity. We have also touched on how, once these activities become successful, pressures to initiate procedures and fix goals using the tools of orthodox strategy start to emerge, often with detrimental effect. Take the case of Grameen again. Yunus tells of the numerous overtures and attempts by the World Bank to impose its 'multilateral donor's style of doing business', with its overwhelming reliance on panels of 'smart economists', on the Grameen operation, which he had to resist constantly because these cut across the core values espoused by Grameen Bank.

I think the growth of the consultancy business has seriously misled international donor agencies. The assumption is that the recipient country needs to be guided at every stage of the process... Donors and the consultants they employ tend to be arrogant in their attitude towards the recipient countries. Furthermore, consultants have a paralysing effect on the thinking and the initiative of the recipient countries.[24]

What often starts out as a well-intentioned attempt to provide aid to the poor and needy is lost in the goal displacement that takes place at the level of disbursement decisions, when lending officers in such aid agencies become more interested in making their careers, by meeting target lending amounts to needy countries, than in addressing the actual concerns and priorities of the receiving countries themselves. The result is often the allocation of aid funds to high-profile projects rather than to areas where such funds could have been more productively employed. That this tendency is more widespread than is generally acknowledged accounts for much of the apparent ineffectiveness associated with many aid programmes, including those supported by the World Bank.[25]

Consider further an example related to Grameen Bank, this time the response of international aid agencies following the aftermath of the Asian tsunami disaster. In a Harvard Business School working paper analysing the attempt to bring aid to the region of Aceh in Indonesia following the devastation in December 2004, the authors Daniel Curran and Herman Leonard, both from Harvard Business School, maintain that the large-scale efforts of relief agencies to help rebuild the lives of local survivors were largely ineffective, even though the valuable aid they organized and provided unquestionably helped save many lives in the immediate aftermath of the tsunami. Within hours of the unfolding tragedy many responded generously, and experienced aid agencies, the United Nations (UN) and international non-governmental organizations (NGOs) rushed to the scene of the devastation to help deal with the hundreds of thousands of displaced, traumatized people, many of whom had lost their homes and loved ones and now had no sources of food, clean water, shelter and clothing. The social infrastructure was in ruins, and transport and communication were almost impossible in the most severely affected areas. Amidst this catastrophe, the agencies set about coordinating the rescue efforts.

Planeloads of people and supplies materialized. Headquarters were established, supply depots built, fleets of vehicles brought in or assembled to enable local distribution of relief commodities. In the face of an obvious and well-defined need, an organized, commensurate response – experienced, expert people with only a desire to help, providing resources to sustain life and health in the short run – was well targeted to the critical needs of affected communities.[26]

The scale and rapidity of the response had the effect of eventually overrunning the capacity of the fragile local infrastructure, however. 'Airports were almost instantly clogged. Relief supplies – from bags of rice to pallets of bottled water to boxes of antibiotics, tents and cooking supplies – rapidly began to pile up in depots and warehouses.' As the 'flow of aid continued unabated', 'stacks of basic supplies continued to pile up'. Curran and Leonard maintain that this 'top-down', large-scale, coordinated response, although clearly effective in dealing with the immediate needs of the emergency situation, was nevertheless largely ineffective in helping the locals to rebuild their lives in the longer term, because it was more preoccupied with grand-scale and high-profile interventions. In so doing, it overlooked the more ongoing practical needs of the local farmers, fishermen and shopkeepers, who were trying to get on and rebuild their shattered lives and who needed not so much the advice of fishery and farming experts, for instance, but small amounts of money, disbursed directly to help them reconstruct their houses, drain their fields, build their boats and restock their shops. The priorities of the aid agencies increasingly became disconnected from the more pressing priorities of the affected communities, who showed, despite the shock and trauma they had experienced, sufficient resilience, resourcefulness and capability to deal with the situation they found themselves in but who needed some practical financial help to get their lives back to some semblance of normality.

What Grameen Bank and the large-scale, coordinated response to the Asian tsunami disaster reveal is the eventual inadequacy of our conventional ways of thinking and dealing with the longer-term, multifarious practical needs of everyday real-life situations. Whilst these direct, wide-ranging, planned responses may have an immediate visible impact, they can eventually become ineffective in the longer term. Ambitious strategic plans, the 'big picture' approach that seeks a lasting solution or competitive advantage through large-scale transformations, often end up undermining their own potential effectiveness because they overlook the fine details of everyday happenings at 'ground zero' level. In contrast to the Grameen Bank experience, and similarly to what was observed to be needed in the Aceh situation, the design and formulation of large-scale planned interventions and the concentrated mobilization and application of capabilities and resources to the attainment of predefined ends unwittingly generate outcomes that prevent the effective execution of otherwise well-intentioned initiatives.

Such an observation of the negative unintended consequences of large-scale strategic planning is well documented and analysed in James Scott's *Seeing Like a State*, in which he writes about the centrally planned attempt to introduce a scientific approach to German forestry in the eighteenth and nineteenth centuries and the disastrous consequences that ensued. The plan was to plant and harvest monocrop forests of either Norwegian spruce or Scottish pine. Initially this resulted in a highly profitable forestry industry. The productivity of the new forests 'reversed the decline in the domestic wood supply..., provided more useable wood fibre, raised the economic return of forest land, and appreciably shortened rotation times... Little wonder that the German model of intensive commercial forestry became standard throughout the world.'[27] What the foresters did not fully appreciate, however, was the more complex and balanced ecological system they had unwittingly destroyed through their deliberate monocrop strategy. The wider ramifications of a 'stripped-down' forest became 'painfully obvious [only] after the second rotation of conifers had been planted'. Clearing of the underbrush, deadfalls and standing dead trees, to make it easier for access for management and extraction of the crop by lumberjacks, 'greatly reduced the diversity of insect, mammal and bird population so essential to soil-building processes'. The increasing absence of wildlife and of rotting wood on the forest floor, in turn, greatly reduced the replenishment of the soil with the necessary nutrients to sustain crop growth, and in addition made the trees more vulnerable to storms. 'Same-age, same-species forests not only create a far less diverse habitat but were also more vulnerable to massive storm-felling.'[28] Moreover, the very uniformity of the species provided a favourable habitat for pests, which quickly built themselves up to epidemic proportions, inflicting severe losses on crop yield and making the foresters incur considerable outlays for the insecticides, fungicides and rodenticides necessary to contain their destructive effects.

The same paradox of (non-)intervention in woodland management also occurred in the United Kingdom. In October 1987 the typically benign and temperate region of south-eastern England was cut through by winds of up 120 miles per hour. Overnight, wide swathes of woodland were left flattened, prompting a massive clear-up and replanting effort. So widespread was the damage that some areas were passed over and left to their own devices. It was the neglected woodland that fared best, however. The gaps in the tree canopy allowed light to stimulate the growth of once stunted shrubs, and the rotting wood and leaf litter began to enrich the humus. Newly resurgent plants and better soil catalysed diverse flora and fauna as well as affording a good environment for the slow regeneration of the trees. The areas of planned intervention fared less well. The clearing of fallen trees and undergrowth stripped the land of fecund organic material. Despite being diverse, the new plants, often alien to the immediate locale, found themselves in similar growth cycles, competing for the same, inevitably scarce, nutrients and space. The resulting woods became very fragile, requiring yet more management. It would have been better, easier and far cheaper to let regeneration take its own course. The strategic goal of regaining the lost woodland was literally negated by the strategic interventions deemed necessary to realize it. Woods, it seems, thrive on indifference.

The world is not nice

The word 'nice' was originally an architectural term referring to a building being proportional, ordered, stable. Its subsequent spread in the English language to cover virtually any state of affairs we find welcome or pleasant is suggestive. We see the world as a place of order, and where there is no order we attempt to create it. In his book, Scott goes on to document the many instances in which the allure of planned, centralized interventions to improve the human condition by creating nicety have failed spectacularly. The supreme confidence of 'high modernism', with its reliance on instrumental rationality, root-tree logic and social engineering, has gone far in making a dystopia of what were potentially promising situations. We have tried to prescribe a niceness upon the world, and in doing so have unwittingly brought about much disorder. It is manifestly plain to see that the central planner with a map of the territory does not always know best: the nicely ordered blueprint is not how the world is. We all know this well. Nevertheless, the tendency to want to understand the world as potentially nice is overwhelmingly pervasive, and nowhere is this more evident than in the business strategy literature, for it is this mentality that underpins the notion of strategic planning and design. The writer Nassim Nicholas Taleb calls this tendency 'Platonicity'.

What I call *Platonicity*...is our tendency to mistake the map for the territory, to focus on pure and well-defined 'forms', whether objects, like triangles, or social notions, like utopias... When these ideas and crisp constructs inhabit our minds, we privilege them over less elegant objects, those with messier and less tractable structures... Platonicity is what makes us think we understand more than we actually do.[29]

Somewhat ironically, given Plato's metaphysical leanings, in its modern guise the tendency towards Platonicity, in turn, hinges on our propensity to attend to the manifest and the superficial: 'The cosmetic and the Platonic rise naturally to the surface.'[30] We might not be able to order the meaning of life nicely, but we can more easily order our material conditions. So we look for niceness in immediate appearance, and enquire after instances in which this niceness breaks down. 'It is why,' argues Taleb, 'we fall for the problem of induction, why we *confirm*... We love the tangible, the confirmation, the palpable..., the visible, the concrete, the known, the seen, the vivid, the visual..., the official, the scholarly-sounding verbiage..., pompous Gaussian economists, the mathematicized crap...'[31] Because of this overwhelming tendency, we construct our own role as detached observers, analysts and strategists, moving people, assets and resources around the 'territory' as if on a chessboard. Indeed, associating the idea of chess with the idea of strategic positioning and manoeuvres of resources provides the quintessential exemplar of a planned and designed strategy. The covers of strategy textbooks are adorned with images of chess pieces, with navigational tools, with well-defined, graphic curves. Strategy is presumed to be an exercise in making things visible and controllable so that the good can be separated from the bad. Strategists therefore look to portray their organization as it is, as it might be, and then rationally judge the available means by which the organization can be guided from its existing condition to a desired one.

The intention is to use managerial calculation and control to effect planned movement over a predictable but fast-moving environment in order to realize well-designed aims. What gets emphasized, however, is a caricature, a picture that can never be whole (for where are we to draw boundaries?), and the accompanying strategic narrative remains more fairy tale than gritty realism. No matter how standardized and simplified the activities and procedures are, no matter how well defined the arenas of these activities are and no matter how rigorous the logic of performance is by which activities and outcomes are assessed, there are always exceptions, outliers and unpredictable forces that upset the niceness of the generalities. The neat, well-defined spaces defined by a formalized strategy appear like the perfectly framed objects called up on the screen of Captain Kirk's Starship Enterprise; they hang there, devoid of idiosyncratic, contextualizing relief, and threatening some kind of improbable future. The world is not all nice, and attempts to make it nicer often result in its becoming more nasty.

In the realm of political economy, for instance, instead of democracy, capitalism and wealth creation leading to a more equitable world, we now find that the gap between rich and poor is greater than ever before even in the most developed countries of the world. A world of unprecedented opulence sits side by side with one of remarkable deprivation and destitution. Even in the United States, arguably one of the most successful economies in the world, the 'longevity of substantial groups is no higher than that in much poorer economies of the so-called third world'.[32] African-American men, who form much of the lower-income bracket in the United States, but who are much richer in income terms than their male counterparts in India and China, have significantly lower survival prospects. So much so that 'it is not only the case that American blacks suffer from *relative* deprivation...; they are *absolutely* more deprived than the low-income Indians in Kerela...and the Chinese...in terms of living to ripe old age'.[33] Whilst there are clearly problems of interpretation associated with such forms of research on issues related to perception, the surprising nature of these findings should spur us to reflect on the possibilities regarding the failure of the mode of reasoning that underpins policy-making and strategic planning at all organizational levels.

In the realms of politics and international relations, despite the achievements of democracy, economic progress and the spread of globalization to many parts of the world, and hence the new-found opportunity to participate in expanding degrees of freedom through such economic development, the world seems to be increasingly engaging in what Samuel Huntington has provocatively termed the 'clash of civilizations', pitting a monumental collision of deep religious values and beliefs between 'the West and the Rest'.[34] Whilst a sense of millennial despair is nothing new, and whilst a pervading sense of threat has accompanied nearly every boast that we are indeed at 'the end of history', what remains particularly troubling about our current sense of turmoil is that the forces of potential destruction have arisen as much out of our so-called civilized endeavour as they have from opposition to it. Terrorism is a case in point. The apparent pre-emptive interventions, following the events of 9/11, seem to have exacerbated rather than eliminated the threat of terrorism. As a recent 148-page report by the Oxford Research Group maintains, the aggressive foreign policy adopted by the United States and United Kingdom has actually played into the hands of Al-Qaeda and other militant groups.[35] According to the report, every aspect of the strategy has been counterproductive, from the loss of civilian life through to the controversial mass detentions without trial at Guantanamo Bay. Once again, here we see that well-intentioned strategies and efforts to impose peace through spectacular interventions from without seem to have failed spectacularly. The United States and United Kingdom seem to be rediscovering the truism that Liddell-Hart articulated so clearly some time ago when he condemned the notion of 'total war' as a method, and 'victory' as a war aim, as 'out-of-date concepts'.[36] Liddell-Hart realized that winning a war, bringing it to an end and achieving lasting peace, as we are now discovering in post-Saddam Iraq, are entirely different things.

Rediscovering strategy without design

Against the pervasive and dominant belief that strategy has to be a product of deliberate conscious design and purposeful implementation from the top, we argue here that frequently what appears to be the outcome of pre-thought and pre-designed interventions may be more attributable to unconsciously acquired, culturally shaped habits of acting; a modus operandi that, though latent and invisible, nevertheless plays an active role in shaping individual choices and strategic action. The French social theorist Pierre Bourdieu calls this modus operandi 'habitus'; a 'durable transposable set of dispositions'[37] that is the source of a series of moves that may be construed as 'strategies without being the product of a strategic intention'.[38] What this suggests is that attributing authorship of strategic decisions solely to autonomous, consciously choosing, intentional agents understates the ever-present moderating effects that invisible historical and cultural forces immanent in situations have on the eventual choices made.

Specifically, we argue that the dominant mode of theorizing strategy that configures actors (whether individual or organizational) as distinct entities deliberately engaging in purposeful, visible strategic activities aimed at neatly ordering and controlling a surrounding environment overlooks the existence of this more pervasive and latent tendency, which ensures the internal consistency of action necessary for strategy to emerge through uncoordinated local actions. Such an emergent strategy is actively materialized through each instance of seemingly insignificant and mundane practical coping action. Whereas, from the conventional design perspective, strategy is predicated upon the prior conception of plans that are then orchestrated and coordinated to realize desired outcome, from an emergent strategy perspective there is no presupposition of deliberate intention and purposeful goal-oriented behaviour involved: every adaptive action taken in the course of coping with exigencies instantiates the actualizing of this latent strategy. Hence, observed consistencies in actions are explained not through deliberate choices taken but through an internalized disposition to act in a manner congruent with past actions and experiences. Explaining strategy in these terms enables us to understand how it is that actions may be consistent and organizationally effective without (and even in spite of) the existence of explicit strategic plans.

Our objective here is to show that, in order to have a fuller and more complete grasp of how strategy is experienced in the everyday lives of ordinary practitioners as they go about effectively dealing with the issues that crop up and require attention, we need a more adequate reconceptualization of human agency, action and practice and how they interrelate. We argue that the dominant observer-centred approach, which conceptually elevates individuality, purposefulness and goal-directed behaviour as the founding basis for explaining strategic behaviour, underestimates the extent of the influence of an unconscious, socially internalized and culturally shaped predisposition on strategic decision-making. In theorizing strategy, there is no inherent need to have recourse to the presumption that the starting point for understanding strategic action is the meaning and purposefulness ascribed by an autonomous agent (whether individual or organizational) in which the prior mental representation of a strategic situation provides the necessary opening for any meaningful engagement with it. Furthermore, we maintain that emphasizing the non-deliberate character of much of strategy-making enables us to see how it is that a 'bottom-up', more 'indirect' or *circuitous* approach to strategy that emphasizes the importance of attending to the small and seemingly peripheral details and concerns of a strategic situation can often prove more efficacious in the long run than dealing directly with the more 'spectacular' focal concerns. In other words, everyday actions that appear to address only tangentially the overall concern may frequently prove more efficacious than a direct approach: better access and advantage can often be achieved indirectly and elliptically than through direct confrontation and engagement.

These two interpenetrating claims – first, that strategy may emerge non-deliberately through the exercise of local coping actions, and, second, that actions that are inconspicuous and may appear peripheral or tangential to the primary concerns of a strategic situation can often turn out to be more efficacious in bringing about desirable and sustainable outcomes – provide the underlying basis for the argument developed in this book. This is what we mean by 'strategy without design': *a latent and retrospectively identifiable consistency in the pattern of actions taken that produces desirable outcomes even though no one had intended or deliberately planned for it to be so.* In this regard, this book departs substantially from much of the current mainstream literature on business strategy.

1 Spontaneous order: the roots of strategy emergence

Every step and every movement of the multitudes...are made with equal blindness to the future; and nations stumble upon establishments, which are indeed the result of human action, but not the execution of any human design.

Adam Ferguson, An Essay on the History of Civil Society, *p. 122*

Fools only strive
To make a great and honest hive.

Bernard Mandeville, The Grumbling Hive, *pp. 409–410*

In the introduction we entered a world of counter-intuitive, paradoxical and even ironic experiences in which human assumptions regarding the orderliness of the world, and their control over that world, have both been shown to be wanting. Of course, there are many instances when what was designed and intended have predictably come to pass. Individuals have found status, battles have been won, firms have earned profits and even souls have been saved. It is also clear, however, that there are numerous instances when very productive orders, patterns of regularities, and consistencies in behaviour have emerged quite non-deliberately. What we investigate in this chapter is just how such strategic ordering may arise spontaneously through social interactions without any singular agency intending for it to be so. What we call 'strategy' is so intimately linked to intentionality, purposefulness and goal orientation that assumptions we make about the world around us remain essentially unquestioned; assumptions regarding regularity, separability and malleability, in which a mute and mutable world is slowly harnessed and transformed through human endeavour into a vast and silent warehouse of well-ordered productive resources and outcomes.

We suggest, however, that, where this order does exist, it is often far from being the outcome of deliberate human design. Indeed, it is often unplanned, a spontaneous expression of an unpredictable and inherently chaotic world with whose warp and weft we humans are inextricably woven. Though we might behave as though the world may be tamed by our singular and rational power, we are in experience less god-like, and the nicely defined systems that we believe illustrate our civilizing, god-like power are, in experience, less well-authored blueprints than the unwitting flowering of a myriad of under-labourers, all absorbed in their own life worlds.

25

Pattern, order and predictability in the socio-political and economic realms have been central preoccupations of philosophers, social scientists and political economists throughout the ages. That there is some kind of order in social life may seem obvious, but how it has come to be so remains an enigma. From where does structural regularity, pattern and consistency of behaviour and action originate? What makes the socio-political and economic worlds function with a degree of predictability despite the obvious multiplicity and complexity involved? On encountering such apparent orderliness and patterned regularity, the default explanatory setting is to attribute their existence to a deliberate design authored by reasoning human beings. This tendency is age-old, and finds dramatic and stark expression in the explanatory device of the social contract whose exponents have thought to cast themselves into a condition of social nudity. If we can envisage what we would be like were we stripped of all social mores and the accidents of birth, left only with our innate human capabilities, what kind of cultural, political and economic orders would it make sense for us to create?

The English philosopher Thomas Hobbes took this thought experiment to dramatic heights. He believed life in such a primordial, stripped-down condition would be 'solitary, poor, nasty, brutish and short'. All that was left in this state of nature were individuals driven by a motivational admixture of vainglory and fright, and lacking in sufficient pre-eminence to subdue others permanently. This base physiological and psychological soup of impotency, insatiable want and anxiety found public expression in a 'warre of all against all' in which there were only ever losers. Hobbes felt himself peculiarly qualified to understand this condition. Born in 1588, he often recalled how it was upon hearing news of the sighting of the Spanish Armada come to try and lay waste the English nation that his mother went into labour; he was, he believed, twinned with 'fear'. His sibling proved instructive, because it was from fear, particularly our *summum malum*, a fear of death, that Hobbes found bedrock upon which we might build our own salvation. Self-interested enough to do whatever it takes to avoid this absolute bad, Hobbes supposed people rational enough both to contemplate alternative lives to those lived in the raw and to design systems by which they might realize such alternatives. The most persuasive of these – because it was the most certain or peaceable – was a covenant whereby all of us would cede our right to act as we felt fit to a third party, the leviathan, who became the sole source of power (an authority over the people) but remained indebted to others (authored by us, the covenanting people). It was the strictures and blandishments of the leviathan that provided the framework of clear and consistent relations that characterize a well-governed society. Where naturally there was only absence, the architecture of the leviathan brought a restricting and ordering presence.[1] Hobbes' idea has been a bewitching one; unable to generate sufficient eminence in our natural condition, we must partially relinquish our autonomy to some form of externally imposed design, whether it is a parliament, a constitution, an empire or a council of elders, out of whose conscious direction and authority we author our own institutionally bound peace.

This kind of externally imposed order in which the *state* or some overarching authority becomes responsible for planning and orchestrating desired outcomes was called a 'made' order by the political economist Friedrich Hayek, in contrast to the kind of 'spontaneous order' he envisaged as the proper basis for understanding economic and social phenomena. In the former case, order originates from a social architecture that is designed and then applied so as to manage people and their relations better. It is, like the leviathan, artificially constructed and consciously directed. The world of engineering and construction relies substantially on this form of deliberate made order, out of which come cars, modern buildings, silicon chips and the like, each of which bears the imprint of a consciously conceived, definite and distinct outline. Society is just one more production, one more artefact whose lineaments are to be detailed by the conscious direction of over-lookers and watchmen. Spontaneous social order, on the other hand, as the term suggests, occurs non-deliberately and undesigned, emerging serendipitously through the actions and interactions of the multitude of individuals, who 'mindlessly' coordinate their actions with each other solely for the purpose of attaining their own *self-interested* outcomes and satisfying immediate needs. They have not developed because people foresaw their likely collective benefits and deliberately constructed them, but arose as an unintended consequence of each pursuing his or her own sense of specific need in the company of others doing likewise. Spontaneous orders give rise to the emergence of cultural traditions, social practices, rules and economic and social institutions. Indeed, advocates of spontaneous order claim that the most important human institutions and phenomena we have today – language, markets, law, money, communities – have all arisen not from any deliberate centrally planned and designed initiatives but through the unpremeditated cooperation of members of society interacting amongst themselves on a day-to-day basis. Much of what we call 'society' is a complex network of these essentially voluntary and spontaneous associations. Such spontaneous orders are not made but emerge, and are grown and regrown from within the embedded context of changing social relations and interactions. For

Hayek, these social, political and economic phenomena are *endogenous* self-generated patterns of order, in contrast to the deliberately designed *exogenous* impositions associated with made order.

That such spontaneous social orders are more common and pervasive is not generally acknowledged. So much of everyday experience seems to assure us that, wherever order and patterned regularity exist and persist, they must have been the result of deliberate, planned intervention. Undesigned order is all around us though. Societies and civilizations emerged and flourished, quite spontaneously displaying some semblance of social order, long before any form of modern centralized planning existed and long before philosophers, political theorists, sociologists and anthropologists came along to investigate and explain their existence. Indeed, the whole discipline of economics originated with a kind of clinical curiosity as to what had given rise to the experience of evidently successful commercial systems. The first economists, such as Richard Cantillon, Adam Smith, Frédéric Bastiat and Carl Menger, did not set out to investigate *whether* there existed something that could be called an economic order. Rather, they *noticed* economic order and wondered how that had come about without any deliberate design and purposeful intervention on the part of the state. They puzzled as to how it was that, through a strange quirk of nature, people seemingly acting in their own self-interest actually helped to promote the benefits of trade (Smith), how it was that 'Paris is fed' without anyone deliberately ensuring that that was the case (Bastiat) or how 'money' came to be the common medium for economic exchange (Menger). These stark facts alone suggest that any theory that denies the prior existence of undesigned order is built on a self-contradiction and, hence, is self-refuting.

The same claim can be made for social systems and institutions. As Ronald Hamowy maintains:

> Social structures come into being as a consequence of the aggregate of numerous discrete individual actions, none of which aims at the formation of coherent social institutions. Society is not the product of calculation but arises spontaneously, and its institutions are not the result of intentional design.[2]

For Hamowy, it was the Scots, especially Adam Ferguson, David Hume and Adam Smith, amongst others in the Scottish Enlightenment, who adumbrated the idea that favourable outcomes and institutions often came from the skein of actions and experiments that were aimed at dealing with more mundane and immediate practical concerns. The Scots maintained an idea of undesigned beneficial order that extended far beyond the theory of markets. They inferred 'invisible hands' that extended to the realms of morality, culture and the evolution of political institutions, and, conversely, warned of the shortcomings of overzealous planning; something well encapsulated in the poet Robert Burns' admonishment that '[t]he best laid schemes o' Mice an' Men,/Gang aft agley'.

As is patently clear in the work of these Scottish thinkers, and subsequently elaborated upon by the Austrian political economists such as Menger and Hayek, and most recently by complexity theorists, the emphasis on spontaneous order prompts enquiry into three arenas of human experience: first, the limits of human consciousness and instrumental reason; second, the inarticulate and tacit nature of much of human knowledge; and, third, the evolution of social institutional arrangements to facilitate and overcome the limitations previously noted. As is the way with much in the world of ideas, whilst these enquiries were ascribed as being original to the West, the relatively vague notion of an invisible force moving things and shaping situations regardless of human intention and design has been an abiding preoccupation of the ancient worlds of both the West and the East. In what follows we very briefly attempt to trace the lineage from those ancient intimations to modern thought.

Heraclitus, *Lao Tzu* and the ever-changing world order

The sixth and fifth centuries BC were a time of philosophical ferment both in the West and in the East, spawning thoughts as various as those of the *Lao Tzu* in China, Zarathustra in Iran, the Upanishads in India and the pre-Socratic thinkers in ancient Greece. Within the Western intellectual tradition, the pre-Socratic Greek thinker Heraclitus was arguably one of the first to recognize the pervasiveness of a spontaneously ordered universe. Plato called Heraclitus the 'dark philosopher', on account of his frequently obscure pronouncements. For Heraclitus, the universe was in constant flux, so much so that 'all things come to pass through the compulsion of strife'.[3] Conflict, struggles and temporary reconciliations are the stuff of life. Were there no conflicts, struggle and strife, all things would cease to exist. Thus the universe flows along of its own accord, shaping its own destiny. Human interventions simply fall in with this flow; they are less distinct than we would imagine. As Wheelwright observes, 'To say that the universe flows along as it is destined. . . or that counters are moved arbitrarily and by chance, are different ways of asserting that the major occurrences in the universe lie outside the range and power of any man.'[4]

Heraclitus recognized the spontaneous and self-organizing nature of the universe and emphasized the need to appreciate this underlying hidden order, even though many people appear to be totally unaware of it, naively believing in their own ability to control their own destiny. 'This world order, the same for all, no god made or any man, but it always was and is and will be an ever-living fire, kindling by measure and going out by measure.'[5] Thus, for those with this metaphysical awareness, 'the world order is one, common to all', yet the majority remain asleep, 'each in a world of his own'. Because of this ignorance, Heraclitus advocated seeking out the invisible and inarticulate in the order of things. As Graham Parkes writes, quoting Heraclitus, '*Harmoniê aphanê phranerê kreittôn*...the hidden harmony is deeper, the invisible connection stronger, the inconspicuous correspondence more interesting than the apparent.'[6] Clearly, Heraclitus was an unlikely precursor to this tradition of recognizing spontaneous order in the West. Similarly, the East had its own advocates of spontaneous order during that same period.

Chinese civilization and culture would have been utterly different had the *Lao Tzu* or *Tao Te Ching*, a collection of wise aphorisms dating back to the fifth century BC, not been documented and disseminated over the course of the last 2,000 years or so. Its influence is so subtle and pervasive and yet sublime that, despite the elevation and promotion of Confucianism as the proper way of life, the thinking and philosophical attitude to life promoted by the *Lao Tzu* remains ever-present and influential, albeit implicitly and hence less widely acknowledged. Contrary to popular understanding, Taoism, in its advocacy of an existential stance, is a severe critic of Confucianist ideology. Whilst Confucianism emphasizes the primacy of social order and the roles and obligations imposed on individuals in society in order for social cohesion, progress and prosperity to occur, the *Lao Tzu* teaches the abandonment of protocol. It advocates concentration on perfecting and cultivating individual lives and achieving harmony and tranquillity through a sympathetic alignment with the universe of things and with others. Whilst Confucianism advocates the importance of *nice* orders, the *Lao Tzu* constantly alludes to the primacy of an ever-present, non-directed *natural* order; a paradoxically unnameable *Tao* or Way that underlies and spontaneously moves all things and situations. 'The Tao that can be named is not of the eternal Tao... The Nameless is the origin of Heaven and Earth.'[7]

Tao alludes to the internal propensity of things, the *latent* force contained within situations themselves, which provides the impulse and momentum for change and which thereby gives rise to the emergence of pattern and orderliness. In this regard, the *Lao Tzu* champions the 'natural' way and opts for non-design and 'non-interference' on the part of authorities. Thus:

The best rulers are those whose existence is [merely] known by the people,
The next best are those who are loved and praised,
The next are those who are feared,
And the next are those who are despised.[8]

Too much interference on the part of formal authorities will ruin the situation. Hence: 'Ruling a big country is like cooking a small fish.' It is easy to overdo or 'overcook' a situation with artificial impositions and unnecessarily generated rules, systems and protocol. It is preferable to allow the situation to 'ripen' naturally and only then channel its internal forces and momentum, allowing them to fulfil their natural potential. Patience and non-interference is a virtue, for it is through small, seemingly insignificant but aggregative actions that mighty outcomes are quietly accomplished, often unnoticed. 'A tower of nine storeys begins with a heap of earth. The journey of a thousand *li* [about a third of a mile] starts from where one stands.'[9]

Similarly, Chuang Tzu, who followed in the same philosophical tradition of non-intervention, commented on the restrictive and oppressive nature of social and political institutions, which were incapable of responding to the diversity of needs and preferences of people. For him, good order was that which 'results spontaneously when thing are let alone'.[10] It is not difficult to see, then, that, despite the contemporary predominance of explicit Confucian values, which actively promote a state-imposed control and system of order and the social protocols associated with it, the legacy of naturalism still inherent in much of the Chinese psyche instinctively veers towards non-interference; apparent 'passivity' and the preference for spontaneous and ad hoc adaptive responses remain very much the prevailing attitudes amongst many traditional Chinese. Such an attitude towards social and economic order, as we have intimated, finds sympathy in the thought of the eighteenth-century Scottish Enlightenment thinkers.

The Scottish Enlightenment

This idea that social patterns and institutional order emerge spontaneously without the deliberate intentions of any singular agency or authority preoccupied eighteenth-century Scottish Enlightenment philosophers. Adam Ferguson is today perhaps the least known and appreciated of the Scottish Enlightenment thinkers but it is to him that we owe the first explicit articulation of the possibility of spontaneous ordering as a basis for explaining the emergence of social institutions. For Ferguson,

[m]ankind...in striving to remove inconveniences, or to gain apparent and contiguous advantages, arrive at ends which even their imagination could not

anticipate. . . Every step and every movement of the multitude, even in what are termed enlightenment ages, are made with equal blindness to the future, and nations stumble upon establishments, which are *indeed the result of human action, but not the execution of any human design.*[11]

In making this claim, Ferguson was reiterating and toying with what the Dutchman Bernard Mandeville had earlier observed in the *Fable of the Bees* (1714), itself based on his infamous 1705 poem *The Grumbling Hive (or Knaves Turn'd Honest)*. Mandeville, displaying a very Dutch trait of exposing the human underbelly for mannered inspection, suggested to his morally kempt readers that the envy, pride and greed they had regarded as sinful were not only natural feelings but the wellspring of collective social achievement. Far from being the outcome of sober and proper design, the commercial and material order of cities such as Amsterdam and London had formed without any appreciable intervention from God, God's representatives or God's rules: 'We often ascribe to the excellency of man's genius and the depth of his penetration, what is in reality owing to the length of time, and the experience of many generations.'[12] Order simply emerges. For Mandeville, the undoubted public benefits attached to wide pavements, navigable canals, elaborate gables, lofted spires and the rule of law were the gradually built-up residue of the energetic expression of private vice. Left to their own devices, their own enterprise, their own concerns with power, esteem and pleasure, the actions of people unwittingly created things of social value. Whilst Hobbes' thought experiment was simply wrong, and the evidence was there before us, good society – by which Mandeville meant commercially successful society – came from integrating, not suppressing, personal portfolios of greed, pride and envy. There was no need to author a leviathan, and the state of nature was just a gaudy bad dream exalted to the status of a treatise by an overanxious Englishman. The role of the social planner and politician was not to manage the creation of wealth but to co-opt and exploit its useful effects. Mandeville likened the role to trimming a 'dry, crooked and shabby vine' from which, when tied and cut, fruit and wine come aplenty. Try to interfere with the vine itself though, try to build a great society, and you erode the very vibrancy and strength by which such a society is made possible.

The denizens of northern Europe did not take their self-belief or religion so seriously as to deride thinkers such as Mandeville and Ferguson outright for suggesting that their society was simply an accident of their own selfish, even sinful, actions. Any culture that had, centuries beforehand, afforded recognition to the disorienting panoramas of sin painted by Hieronymus Bosch could absorb the suggestion that so-called sinful acts were contested territory. Where they might rightfully have queried Mandeville and Ferguson, however, is in the lack of any enquiry into *how* order may form itself rather than simply observing *that* it formed itself. Step forward Adam Smith and his 'invisible hand'. Unknown to Smith, an investigation into the positive unintended consequences of human action had already been undertaken by one Richard Cantillon, an Irishman living in France, who published his observations in his *Essai sur la Nature du Commerce en Général* around 1730. Nonetheless, it was Smith who armed himself with the pithy metaphor, and to whom we must be especially grateful for pursuing such an investigation with a sustained vigour that found expression in his *Theory of Moral Sentiments* (1759) and subsequent *Wealth of Nations* (1776).

Smith, writing in the *Theory of Moral Sentiments*, puzzles over the condition of the landowners. He observes how they are wealthy yet without the freedom to choose how that wealth might be expended. Any eighteenth-century landowner (typically a man) must necessarily feed and support all those who work for him; in the fields, in his house and in the production of the clothes and luxury goods he so badly wants, to assure himself of his standing. His well-being is dependent on his satisfying his dependents. As a result, the eventual distribution of goods tends, surprisingly, toward equality. The landlords are, willy-nilly,

led by an *invisible hand* to make nearly the same distribution of the necessaries of life, which would have been made, had the earth been divided into equal portions among all its inhabitants, and *thus without intending it, without knowing it, advance the interest of society, and afford means to the multiplication of the species.*[13]

Later, in his *Wealth of Nations*, Smith invokes the same metaphoric phrase in describing how merchants direct their capital according to their own sense of gain, and how there are good economic reasons why such capital tends to be employed domestically. An investor who has an equal option to invest either domestically or abroad will naturally tend to the former:

By preferring the support of domestic to that of foreign industry, he intends only his own security; and by directing that industry in such a manner as its produce may be of the greatest value, he intends only his own gain, and he is in this, as in many other cases, led by an *invisible hand* to promote an end which was no part of his intention. Nor is it always the worse for the society that it was not part of it.[14]

Investment activity seems to operate under some self-generated, self-organizing mechanism that eschews any need for grand themes or purpose as the basis of order; the maintenance of capital within a country is governed by prudent self-interest rather than overt government decree.

The resonance of Smith's metaphor reverberates through generations of analysis and policy-making relating to wealth-creating activity. It is almost a Platonic form of what we mean by an economy of material force; its affects are peerless. Efficiency, and the liberty and flourishing it brings, are manifest not in what is designed, or hoped for, but in what simply exists and exists well. Smith was not advocating selfishness or an atomized society here, however. His metaphor – which he used only sparingly – suggests connectivity, an organic unity whereby one commercial interest is woven into another without separation, and that such communion is most strongly felt domestically. There is an immediate, unspoken disposition to tend towards one's interests *in situ*, acknowledging one's immediate fellows, one's native place; thereby, in striving to improve one's own gains, the annual revenue of society as a whole is improved. Interfere with this immediate, collective sensibility and the associated bias of immediacy in the allocation of capital and effort and you interfere with those who, for the most part, are the best judge of their own circumstances.

Smith was, of course, alive to this being a somewhat idealized condition. In practice, government and regulation retains a role in the proper governing of economies. Enterprises deemed culturally significant or working in the interest of national security, for example, were accepted by Smith to be the province of state influence. Relatedly, Smith also recognized the importance of overseeing the activities of pivotal economic institutions such as banks, recommending, for example, laws requiring bankers to pay up when presented with notes by bearers. More widely still, he acknowledged that the steady hum of self-sustained trading between persistent, independent individuals and institutions would produce a materially wealthy and well-ordered society only if oligopolistic tendencies, malfeasance and the negative effects of externalizing activities are kept in check.[15]

Recognizing the importance of and need for oversight has led some of the more insightful commentators on Smith to lament the emphasis placed on the metaphor of the 'invisible hand' if by that metaphor is meant reference to some supernatural force.[16] Invisibility can also refer to something that exists but is necessarily concealed, however; something unnoticed, that goes without saying. It is not absent, but present in everyday drag, so to speak. On this reading, the metaphor is of some importance, because through figurative language Smith is setting this typically unnoticed presence in some kind of relief, showing his readers how the witting pursuit of collectively accepted personal projects leaves an unspoken, organized residue by which our public lives remain governed. Thus, rather than valorizing the absence of regulation, Smith is inviting us to acknowledge how such regulation is most efficient when it remains unseen, prompting us to lift the institutional stone. Underneath we find a basic moral order of reciprocity, by which what Smith calls our natural disposition to 'truck, barter and exchange one thing for another' finds shape. For the most part this reciprocity is invisible, a habit that we, all of us, acknowledge what is due when others provide for us. On occasion this habit is broken, and we require an explicit institutional architecture to compensate. The invisible hand describes how, ordinarily, we have a propensity to modify our actions so as to realize mutually beneficial outcomes without consciously directing those actions using explicit instruction.

Bastiat and the seen/unseen orders

In his classic essay entitled 'What is seen and what is not seen', in a collection entitled *Essays on Political Economy*, the French economist Claude Frédéric Bastiat, writing in the middle of the nineteenth century, explores the consequences of not attending to the unseen in our academic attempts to understand how the economy of a country works.[17] Admonishing economists for tending to preoccupy themselves only with the seen, Bastiat shows that true insight into an economic situation is achieved only by attending to that which is not obvious and often unseen, for therein lie the actual intricate workings of a political economy. In *Fallacies of Protection*, he ponders over the question of how it is that a million inhabitants of Paris are able to sleep peacefully without worrying about how they will feed themselves each day.

On entering Paris, which I had come to visit, I said to myself – Here are a million of human beings who would all die in a short time if provisions of every kind ceased to flow towards this great metropolis. Imagination is baffled when it tries to appreciate the vast multiplicity of commodities which must enter tomorrow through the barriers in order to preserve the inhabitants from falling prey to the convulsions of famine, rebellion and pillage. And yet all sleep at this moment, and their peaceful slumbers are not disturbed for a single instant by the prospects of such a frightful catastrophe. On the other hand, eighty departments have been labouring today without concert, without any mutual understanding, for the provision of Paris. How does each succeeding day bring what is wanted, nothing more nothing less, to so gigantic a market? What, then, is the ingenious and secret power which governs the astonishing regularity of movements so complicated, a regularity in which everybody has implicit faith, although happiness and life itself are at stake? This power is an *absolute principle*, the principle of freedom in transactions.[18]

He then goes on to contrast this smooth, unthinking and spontaneously cooperative efficiency with the more deliberate attempts to impose an order over these goings-on by asking rhetorically:

In what situation, I would ask, would the inhabitants of Paris be if a minister should take it into his head to substitute for this power the combination of his own genius, however superior we might suppose them to be – if he thought to subject to his supreme direction this prodigious mechanism, to hold the springs of it in his hands, to decide by whom, or in what manner, or on what conditions, everything needed should be produced, transported, exchanged and consumed? Truly, there may be much suffering within the walls of Paris – poverty, despair, perhaps starvation, causing more tears to flow than ardent charity is able to dry up; but I affirm that it is probable, nay, that it is certain, that the arbitrary intervention of government would multiply infinitely those sufferings, and spread over all our fellow-citizens those evils which at present affect only a small number of them.[19]

Two aspects of the unseen are highlighted here: the apparent ability of the political-economic system to coordinate itself without any form of centralized design or control or anyone being apparently in charge; and, second, even if this unseen aspect of everyday accomplishments is noticed, one would be hard put to explain how it has come about. The invisible made visible remains an enigma. Bastiat reminds us that for much of our lives we are generally unaware of the wider impact of our local actions and that, curiously, despite the apparent lack of any form of centralized coordination, favourable outcomes nevertheless ensue in much of human affairs. Much like the traffic round the Arc de Triomphe, somehow the kind of spontaneous urban cooperation noted by Herbert Simon seems to occur, which resists ordering but which nevertheless allows drivers to continue on their way, after a fashion. It was the architect Le Corbusier who planned for the elimination of such emergent Parisian order in his purist *plan voisin* of 1925. Swathes of what to many would seem already ordered streets and tenements were to give way to a chequerboard latticework of well-spaced towers and open, orthogonal roads. The plan remained just that, an impossibly comprehensive vision from an improbable crow's nest. Le Corbusier, the crow, flew on. His later city dioramas were steadily relieved of such overt regularity, as they admitted the meandering influence of myth, history and organic locale; oversight gives way to the expression of place.

This sense of place was inherently restless. Take the city of London again. By Mandeville's time it was an intricate and heaving nest of interlopers, traders, trendsetters, orphans, aristocrats, malcontents, n'er-do-wells, hypochondriacs and antiquaries. In his biography of the city, Peter Ackroyd describes how trades flocked to certain areas of the city almost like migrating birds, gathering awhile before moving on in accord with unspoken and undivinable lines of force.[20] So medics moved from Finsbury to Harley Street during the mid-nineteenth century for no apparent reason, and hatters shifted westwards from Bermondsey to

Blackfriars and furniture makers from Shoreditch to Camden. These trade patterns persist. Bookshops form an improbable colony clinging onto the costly tourist corridors around Charing Cross Road, before giving way to electronic goods stores further north along Tottenham Court Road. Soho retains its atmosphere of sleaze, which then permeates rather naturally into the media and film industry centred along Wardour Street and culminating with the BBC at its northerly tip. Throughout the history of the city trade pockets have flocked, roosted and dispersed. The resultant patterns are temporary, but have lasting influence in the form of street names, ethnic distributions, wealth distribution and cultural habits. Fleet Street no longer habours printers and journalists, but the pubs remain. The city's spontaneously grown order was, and still is, always interrupting, overwhelming and resisting deliberate attempts at control; the city is always moving, disrupting well-laid plans, opening new opportunities, threatening dissolution at the very moment of success.

Henry George, in his discussion of the merits of protection and free trade, gives these observations on the intricacy of civic order a homespun spin. Even in the most ordinary of events in the most ordinary of lives arises this phenomenon of the unseen but spontaneous cooperation characteristic of the 'invisible hand'. A rural family preparing for a meal of bread, fish and tea before a cheery fire may seem a very ordinary affair; yet it is the product of some invisible but accomplished achievements.

The settler cut the wood. But it took more than that to *produce* the wood. Had it been merely cut, it would still be lying where it fell. The labour of hauling it was as much a part of its production as the labour of cutting it ... [T]he journey to and from the mill was as necessary to the production of the flour as the planting and reaping of the wheat. To produce the fish the boy had to walk to the lake and trudge back again. And the production of the water in the kettle required not merely the exerting of the girl who brought it in from the spring, but also the sinking of the barrel in which it collected, and the making of the bucket in which it was carried... As for the tea, it was grown in China, was carried on a bamboo pole upon the shoulders of a man to some river village, and sold to a Chinese merchant, who shipped it by boat to a treaty port. There, having been packed for ocean transportation, it was sold to the agency of some American house and sent by steamer to San Francisco. Thence it passed by railroad, with another transfer of ownership into the hands of a Chicago jobber. The jobber, in turn, in pursuance of another sale, shipped it to the village storekeeper, who held it so that the settler might get it when and in such quantities as he pleased.[21]

George, like Bastiat and Smith, wants to pick away at the weave by which the ordinary is woven. That way we can marvel at the extent and pervasiveness of this unseen and unintended cooperation in order for our everyday lives to function, as well as appreciate more deeply how it is that each event and each context of each event carries with it the power to alter our life histories in significant yet unpredictable ways.

Decrying the overwhelming tendency to elevate the seen over the unseen, Bastiat writes that the difference between the good economist and the bad economist is that the latter confines himself to the *visible* effect whilst the good economist takes into account both the effect that can be seen and those effects that must be *foreseen*. Foresight is a wide-ranging skill, however, and claims to its possession continually beg the question as to the kind of phenomena being confined and the methods of confinement being employed. At its most general, however, Bastiat, like Smith, is suggesting that economics as a discipline ought to explain, rather than just report on, wealth-creating phenomena, and to do this economists have to get at how patterned orders of trade emerge in the way they do. Imputing these patterns to a spiritual force might be satisfactory for deists such as William Paley, whose 'God as blind watch-maker' argument had proved both appealing and convenient to spiritu-ally minded industrialists with little inclination for metaphysical speculation; but the phenomena of trade were surely more substantial than those of the afterlife, and so warranted something more pragmatic. After all, we are dealing with pin factories, not angels on pinheads.

Carl Menger and the phenomenon of money

What Smith and Bastiat had in mind was the kind of spirited argument delivered by the founding father of what has now come to be called the Austrian school of economics, Carl Menger. Menger happened upon the undesigned nature of the market system in the 1870s, when he examined how subjective human valuations set in motion the competitive discov-ery process of the market. Menger saw that market prices and other phenomena seem to emerge as unintended consequences of these sub-jective evaluation processes. In 1883 he published *Investigations into the Method of the Social Sciences with Special Reference to Economics*, and this caused a storm of reactions from his contemporaries, who derisively referred to his approach as the 'Austrian school' to emphasize its radical departure from the then dominant historical school of thought in eco-nomics. Menger, much like Smith and Bastiat, posed this question: 'How can it be that institutions which serve the common welfare and are extremely significant for its development come into being without a common will directed towards establishing them?'[22] Menger's famous theory of the origins of the economic phenomenon of money is often held up as an exemplary instance of 'spontaneous order' emerging as an unintended consequence of human actions.

As is to be found in standard textbook explanations, people wishing to trade and exchange will first begin with the process of bartering. The increasing absence of the necessary 'double coincidence' in goods desired makes barter difficult as a widespread practice of exchange, however. Eventually some individual actors begin to realize that they will be more likely to trade successfully if they happen to have goods that many other people desire. This begins a process of cultural adaptation, in which people increasingly attempt to anticipate the subjective preferences of others. Those who possess goods that have greater subjective value to others are likely to make more exchanges easily and hence become wealthier in the process. As they do, their choices are observed and imitated by others, who also begin to acquire those goods regarded as having greater subjective value as media of exchange. As the number of 'media' goods gets smaller the demand for each grows, making them each time more suitable as a medium for exchange. The process eventually converges to one (or possibly two) goods that become so highly subjectively desired that they become, for all intents and purposes, what we now call 'money'.

It is important to note the spontaneous elements in this account of the emergence of money. Money is basically a product of individual self-interested action, not of human design. Actors need never be conscious of the fact that they are helping to create money for it to happen. The institution of money is thus a positive unintended outcome of human exchange: something none of the individual actors could have intended or even imagined. Menger's approach to the notion of spontaneous, undesigned order begins with the subjective perceptions of individuals and ends with the establishment of social institutions, such as that of money, as thoroughly social phenomena. While Cantillon and the Scots, including Smith, understood this process of the invisible workings of the market in its broadest outlines, it was Menger who provided a much more detailed account of how such institutions can arise spontaneously. Menger thus set the stage for the seminal contribution of Friedrich Hayek.

Friedrich Hayek and 'spontaneous order'

Taking off from the contributions of Smith, Bastiat and Menger, Hayek's *Individualism and Economic Order* emphasizes that the division of labour has a counterpart: the division of knowledge. Because of the former, each individual comes to possess specialized and detailed knowledge in one specific aspect such that he or she alone fully appreciates its uses and limitations. If this happens as a consequence of the division of labour, however, a coordinating mechanism is required for all the participants of an economy. This is the pricing system. Prices not only serve as incentives to stimulate work, they also communicate information regarding opportunities worth pursuing. Thus: '[W]e must look at the price system as such a mechanism for communicating information... The most significant fact about this system is the economy of knowledge with which it operates, or how little the individual participants need to know in order to be able to take right action.' This crucial insight then leads him to maintain: 'The marvel is that in a case like that of a scarcity of one raw material, *without an order being issued, without more than perhaps a handful of people knowing the cause, tens of thousands of people whose identity could not be ascertained by months of investigation, are made to use the material or its products sparingly.*'[23] He therefore concludes that, if the price system were the result of deliberate design, rather than the unintended consequence of individual actions, 'this mechanism would have been acclaimed as one of the greatest triumphs of the human mind'.[24]

This realization that the price system was a quintessential exemplar of spontaneous order became the centrepiece of Hayek's writings. Hayek argued that virtually all forms of social practices and institutions, such as language, customs, traditions, rules and exchange relationships, have evolved and developed without any conscious design guiding them. This, in turn, means that any advanced, civilized society must of necessity be a 'planless' society where no single mind or group of minds controls or directs it. Civilization, as such and by necessity, advances through a spontaneous order.

In articulating this detailed argument for the existence of unplanned and undesigned order, Hayek extended the ideas of Ferguson, Smith, Bastiat and Menger in two interesting ways. First, he provided an epistemological justification for spontaneous order explanations. Second, he showed how economic institutions such as market prices were able to bring about spontaneous ordering processes without the need for any external interventions. For Hayek, there is a limit to humankind's ability to consciously and comprehensively design, direct and predict the nature of human institutions and their outcomes. The crucial problem facing any concerted attempts to impose an economic or social order externally stems from the fact that 'knowledge of the circumstances of which we must make use never exists in a concentrated or integrated form but solely as the dispersed bits of incomplete and frequently contradictory knowledge which all separate individuals possess'.[25] There is always an element of uncertainty regarding possible outcomes, precisely because of the fragmented and incomplete nature of such collective knowledge, which implies the unknowability of the future.

Hayek's acknowledgement of this unknowability of many future events was something that Bastiat's Enlightenment enthusiasm, despite his awareness of the importance of the unseen, could not fully comprehend or absorb. Bastiat argued that what went unseen was sufficiently patterned in its occurrence to warrant predictions being made as to future outcomes. Trends bleed through the present into the future, and the job of the good economist is to reveal these. The job of the social scientist and historian is to investigate these patterns in economic and social spheres in which activities, habits and institutionalized procedures produce both immediate, obvious effects and hidden and inchoate influences that linger and emerge unseen. Thus: 'Often, the sweeter the first fruit of a habit, the more bitter are its later fruits... When a man is impressed by the effect *that is seen* and has not yet learned to discern the effects *that are not seen*, he indulges in deplorable habits.'[26] For Bastiat, decorum is restored only when the unseen effects and repercussions are made visible, when there is a restoration of the kind of foresight in which the intricate bloom of future implications are laid bare, like a map of the estuarine deposits left at the mouth of a river as it plunges into the sea.

In this, Bastiat was being a good heir of the French *philosophes*: a man of pragmatic science for whom the meddlesome, patrician estates (*états*) of clerics and aristocrats ought to give way to the liberal sensibilities of commercial minds, who knew their way about the economic system. Hayek suggests that the sagacity of such a science, noble though its aspirations were, was always limited. Admittedly, commercial operators could reckon on events repeating themselves with different levels of probability. They could use statistical modelling to confine the future positing causal links between available options and likely consequences. This is the realm of risk management, judging the likelihood and impact of events. Risks describe outcomes and conditions in which knowledge of the frequency and nature of past events informs predictions concerning the frequency and nature of future events.[27] Of course, those who use such models are not so naive as to assume that our world unfurls in strict adherence to linear patterns; for every effect there are many possible causes, and from each event many possible effects may ensue. Using probabilistic reasoning is a pragmatic admission of the inevitability of surprise, of randomness and of the unforeseen. The logic employed uses terms such as 'error', 'outlier' and 'deviation', as well as sophisticated numeracy and computing power, to absorb the complex features of the world being mapped, on the assumption that, by and large, these disturbances are sufficiently infrequent and so patterns can still be discerned. For pragmatic scientists such as Bastiat, therefore, good economics is about understanding the risks associated with choosing to act in one way or another – risks that can often go unseen and are in need of analytic elaboration.

For Hayek, however, many acts – indeed, most acts – are not governed in this way; nor can they be. Rather than acting in risky situations, much of what goes by the practice of trade takes place in conditions of *uncertainty*. Uncertainty differs from risk, as it pertains when observation and judgement fail to yield sufficiently similar states of affairs for classification or even the assignment of weightings to stated preferences. *Uncertainty is what is left when probabilistic reasoning lies exhausted, unable to reveal meaningful patterns.* In uncertain states of affairs, only estimates can be made; events have propensities but no probabilistic direction. Estimates are followed creatively, or imaginatively; procedures collapse into hunches and patterns of aesthetic or habitual attraction. Here action occurs in the face of persisting vagueness and often rapid fluctuation. Understanding the world as a place of uncertainty rather than risk fundamentally alters our relationship with it. No longer are we separated, looking upon our situation and deciding how to respond to assessments of what we think has occurred, is occurring and will occur in the future. Rather, we are thrown into the world and by our actions we constantly strive to make sense of our condition; our acts are attempts to intervene and to clarify the ambiguous situations we naturally find ourselves in. As Hayek's contemporary Ludwig von Mises writes in *Human Action*, uncertainty is always 'implied in the very notion of action. . .to acting man the future is hidden, and that is why he acts; were he [*sic*] certain, there would be no need to act, action presupposes uncertainty'.[28] The distinction between risk and uncertainty follows through into what we have already introduced as Hayek's distinction between two kinds of order: made order and spontaneously grown order. Made orders occupy situations that have been confined by the probabilistic calculations associated with risk, and they are deliberately designed and imposed by some central authority, whilst spontaneous orders occupy uncertain situations, and are self-generated without any reliance on an overarching coordinating authority. Where firms or community groups were, for Hayek, examples of made orders, their institutional environments, such as markets and cities, were more spontaneous; their actions created urban and trading contexts without any sense of how such contexts were being designed.

For the economist George Shackle, however, made orders lead a precarious existence. The absence of any complete statement of underlying conditions in business life means that, irrespective of what is said of their decision-making, what business strategists do when they make decisions is to invoke 'imagined biographies of the future'. These biographies are versed in inductive familiarity; they envisage what might happen given discernible textures or patterns in the evolution of investment patterns, human behaviour and the like. This might yield some broad class groupings, which Shackle terms 'perfectly possible', 'slightly surprising', 'very surprising' and 'perfectly impossible'.[29] That is as far as they can venture into the realms of prediction, however; they present themselves with an incomplete set of plausible scenarios. What governs strategic judgement is not the likelihood of each (within each class they are indistinguishable, because uncertainty prevails) but their desirability (a ranking from bad to good – for example, the expected level of profitability). It is value, not truth, that enlivens strategic debate; the heated faculty of imagined gain and threat rather than the cool temper of reason predominates.

If made orders do exist, then they are very loose and fragile groupings based on possibilities under constant threat from the proliferation of knowledge and technology. Strategists do use statistics to identify a valid class of measurement, identify members of that class and look for variables of each member that might then be grouped in patterns leading to stereotypes and, hence, predictive laws. This enables them only to identify what might be possible, however; it gives them a grip on plausibility. For Shackle, what defines them as businesspeople, though, is not this pursuit of possibility but the exploitation of uncertainty, the ability to convey the desirability of one possible state of affairs over another that others have not recognized, using the faculty that Shackle calls a 'radial' rather than an 'axial' mind.

Today, in what the German sociologist Ulrich Beck calls the 'world risk society', this distinction between made and spontaneous order is becoming ever more blurred; the possible is becoming ever harder to contain. Contemporary firms, political associations, government departments and even clubs and cooperatives are increasingly organized in ways analogous to loose societal networks rather than fixed hierarchical systems. Clearly, top-down planning is still being undertaken, central coordinating authorities remain in power, and directives are still being issued and acted upon. Made orders are still with us but they are not as obvious or self-consciously well defined as when Hayek first labelled them. Current communication and distribution technologies have fostered faceless, instant relationships whose character and influence are notoriously difficult to control, as they transcend traditional boundaries such as nation states, gender or religion. Technological, financial, environmental and biological uncertainties permeate the globe, can move with great rapidity and yet linger for aeons. Human value systems and expectations are being constantly brought into question, creating often polarized and splintered social conditions. The world in which made orders act is hastening on along rapid and unpredictable lines of flight, constantly bringing into question the continued appropriateness of established hierarchies, goals, procedures and the like; events carry on almost regardless, and the expert strategists and designers are no longer the font of all knowledge and authority. In tracking and illustrating this growing exposure, Beck identifies a growing disjunction between the epistemological frameworks we use to calculate risks and our lack of ability to actually fix and control the events we presume ourselves to be capable of fixing and controlling.[30] This is because, no matter how much in the way of resources we have at our disposal to calculate 'risk', we create ever more unquantifiable uncertainties. Far from extending our control by expanding our awareness of risk and attendant decision-making, our capacity to influence the world wittingly is shrinking; the future is colonizing us rather than vice versa.

In this world risk society, the made orders of economic activity are becoming increasingly permeable, transient and interconnected as they look to survive. Firms are no exception. Managers are charged with producing more with less – this is their job: minimizing value-depleting waste – and so are constantly looking to find ways of externalizing costs from the firm by having them absorbed within the wider environment. Supermarkets' increasing use of self-service counters, for example, is one such simple attempt to pass on their overhead costs (of employing checkout cashiers) to their customers. Of course, the term 'value' is loaded. Amongst economic institutions it primarily means value to shareholders and customers, and so the waste being minimized often results in the imposition of costs elsewhere, whether it be the costs of pollution or training, or the provision of infrastructure – generally, the kinds of costs Adam Smith regarded as the preserve of public bodies. So incessant and pressing is the value requirement, however, that managers have little truck with the non-value-adding demands of public service provision. The more a firm can negotiate or even deny its presence, the more room managers have to elude cost claims, passing them over to other orders without guilt.

Corporate tax avoidance is a good case in point. Rather than persist with clear boundaries, many firms will look to unravel their order to avoid tax. In 2005/6 nearly a third of the United Kingdom's 700 largest firms avoided paying any corporation tax using a complicated array of debordering and offsetting techniques. Offshore firms set up in tax havens, for example, are used to allow managers to create alternative worlds, into which they move revenues, eroding the made order of the parent firm in order to lessen liabilities. In these attempts, managers are constantly working at the edges, exploiting temporary loopholes, hiding in systemic sconces awhile, before restlessly moving on. Just as the managers try to impregnate their wider environment with costs in this way, so the environment continues to impose costs upon firms, often without notice, requiring managers to respond. Uncertainties associated with *force majeure* events – terrorism, stock market volatility or viruses, for example – are being felt across the globe; there is less and less distance and immunity in the wake of shock events. Naomi Klein's *Shock Doctrine* describes in vivid prose the kinds of managerial responses made by some firms that have found new opportunities for trade amidst such disasters. Here firms become very loose agglomerations of accountable order that thrive in conditions of legal, moral and social instability, such as post-invasion Iraq. Rather than lament the erosion of made orders, these loose-knit alliances of interest relish this radicalization of market activity.

The eroding distinction between Hayek's made and spontaneous orders is also played out in Herbert Simon's suggestion that the artificial world of human things – machines, firms, norms, societies – never quite purrs with the kind of preordained hum aspired to by some of their designers. Artificial things only ever have an imperfect fit with their environment; their functional design is only ever satisfactory rather than optimal. The kind of firm that excites Klein's ire is one such artificial entity. On Hayek's terms, it is a consciously made order. According to Simon, however, this consciousness is not of the kind that is able to design and test responses to a found environment without first being amidst such an environment. Any made order exists only as an adequate but never fulsome response to environmental forces, and so evolves in an evolutionary, survivalist fashion as it struggles to secure a good fit with its surroundings.[31] This fit is never complete, because, first, the available amount of management time and attention is never sufficient to acknowledge, absorb and plan for all environmental contingencies and, second, the environment itself is inherently complex, meaning that even were managers afforded a global purview of their environment they could not confine it using probabilistic reasoning as Bastiat and others assumed. Instead, like Shackle, Simon suggests that firm strategists try to anticipate prospectively significant futures and the opportunities these might reveal, and that, once these are concentrated on, planned responses can be designed and then revisited and alternatives considered as events come to pass: 'In an uncertain world, forecasting must always be yoked to feedback so that as the passage of time squeezes out uncertainty attention can be focussed on issues that really matter and the timing of responses adjusted.'[32]

This suggests that made orders are reactive and so somewhat mute, but Simon's message is not so passive. To survive made orders requires the ingenuity and subtlety of human response, because in the world of made orders the system constraints are not enduring. As Klein's book makes clear, markets and firms can arise in the most hostile, morally dubious and unstable of contexts. In these situations there is no possibility of calculating risks, because the future is inherently unknowable, but there is the possibility of acting intelligently, of searching for novelty, of intervening in evolution in ways that influence that evolution, albeit without any prospect of reaching predefined goals. Though operating in apparently more stable conditions, the same might be said for all strategic interventions made by managers of firms, because what is of importance for continued survival is not so much that what is anticipated is exact, or even a good approximation of what comes to pass, but that as an anticipation it is more effective than the anticipations made by others.

Here Simon is introducing two related strains of thought. First, designing or making involves decision-makers creating opportunities rather than selecting from available choice sets. Contrary to common understanding, decision *produces* the choices available. A decision is fundamentally an act of what the philosopher Alfred North Whitehead called 'cutting off'; the creating of an 'incision' into the otherwise undifferentiated flow of reality, so much so that what is 'given' is separated from what, for that occasion, is 'not given'.[33] Decision-makers act from within a system, itself part of other systems, and in acting inevitably isolate and bestow significance upon one or other aspect of their environment, thereby creating rather than simply encountering the conditions and criteria by which their decisions are judged sensible and appropriate; they undertake what Shackle calls 'inceptive acts' that impose on the material chaos of our world a psychic order of our own making. The incisional operation acts as a form of judgemental orientation, so that what then appears as real and substantial does so in a manageable form because it is a form that we have created; it is an artifice.[34] Second, designing or making orders is inherently competitive. The survival of the system is a relative achievement. Whilst it is accepted that, *in extremis*, rapidly altering environmental conditions can affect everyone similarly (world drought, say), on the whole it is those systems or orders that are able to accept and react more quickly to their surroundings by actually being involved in those surroundings that will survive.

The artificial or made condition that both Hayek and Simon speak about is, then, less a stable entity than a relational one. Being able to cope with and flourish in changing environments means that systems have to react or adapt, yet maintain their own presence and identity. Simon finds inspiration in the devices used by biological systems, which include:

homeostasis (maintaining constant internal conditions using inventories of inputs to internal processes, such as fat stores or latent DNA); membranes (skins or borders that insulate systems from external conditions without making them ignorant of these conditions); specialization (reducing the number of tasks in which the system excels); and, finally, near-decomposability (the use of nested subsystems [stacked much like a Russian doll] whose own internal systems remain somewhat independent and insensitive of one another).[35] These capabilities for survival and flourishing are equally applicable to organizational systems.

Our example of a firm engaging in tax avoidance can be understood as an instance of a system showing all four of these capabilities. Insisting on a duty to shareholders is a form of homeostasis, using and replenishing stored income to pay dividends and reduce prices and so maintain internal clarity in the face of an ever more complex environment of constituent interests. Using alternative institutional status (say offshore accounts or company registration in a tax haven) creates an insulating membrane to avoid 'debilitating' demands upon its resources from external systems. The employment of tax and legal experts is an investment in specialized activities connected to other specialized units of its own system and subsystems. Finally, the avoidance of tax often requires systems to present themselves as a looser agglomeration of subsystems, each with its own affairs and responsibilities, to which any demands from external systems must make individual and tailored approaches.

Simon accepts, though, that, whilst these system responses preserve a sense of order, they carry their own costs of complexity; a system such as a firm faces the continual pressure of having to invest in new systems to cope with the burgeoning ebb and flow of wider systems of competition and regulation. The resultant experience is never stable. New technologies, shifting values and even personal morality intrude. It is inherently unstable, meaning that the made orders are never really at peace with themselves, as their members are always experimenting with ways of reinventing the system in order that the system flourishes: the more uncertain the environment of which the system is inevitably a part the more pressing, arduous and rapid this experimentation.

Open source

Computer software development offers a good example of the resurgence of spontaneous order within the made orders of human life. The emergence of software applications for computing activity has been characterized by an ebb and flow between what the hacker Eric Raymond has termed the different design architectures of the cathedral and the bazaar. The cathedral metaphor describes how software design is the job of an expert elite hermetically sealed from the irksome and potentially damaging influence of the uninitiated and technologically unwashed. This closed-source development has been most closely associated with those wanting to exploit the economic opportunities offered by innovation protected by securely defined titles to intellectual property. From an economic perspective, it is only the prospect of monetary reward realized through revenues associated with development that will encourage programmers to work and innovate. No protection, no product. Most infamously associated with Microsoft, this overtly made order requires heavy investment in creating and selling products whose source code remains a closely guarded secret and whose development is the responsibility of a well-organized hierarchy of paid developers. The business model requires these closed-source systems to become embedded on computing hardware in such a way that it becomes onerous to decouple and tinker with either. This necessitates the product exhibiting a level of functionality that is sufficient to forestall the urge to try and improve it; that is resistant to manipulation and unauthorized appropriation by other applications; and that becomes as widespread as is possible, thereby eliminating alternatives. Aimed at consumers with little inclination to develop the technological nous necessary to make functional changes, closed-source systems have until very recently preserved a dense, privileged and lucrative made order as they have become the embedded norm on PCs and office systems.

In contrast to and running *sui generis* from this made order of the cathedral has been the bazaar architecture of open-source development. Raymond – the self-styled 'observer-participant anthropologist' for, and unofficial historian of, this open-source movement – has suggested that its beginnings and growth were entirely unplanned:

> The roots of today's open-source culture go back to the late 1960s and the first steps towards the Internet's predecessor, ARPAnet. From 1969 to 1983 the open-source culture evolved its practice completely without a theory or ideology. I personally became involved exactly halfway through that period, in 1976, and remember those early days well. We exchanged source code to solve problems. We learned how to manage distributed open-source collaborations over the infant Internet without labelling the practice or reflecting much on what we were doing. We (not I, personally, but the culture I was part of) were the hackers who *built* the Internet – and, later, the World Wide Web.[36]

According to Raymond's history, it was not until 1983 that the movement became something conscious and seen, when a programming guru of the movement called Richard Stallman issued a call to arms to develop freely available software based on Unix operating systems.

These were open source and offered programmers the opportunity to challenge the cathedrals being run by the likes of Microsoft. Raymond describes how this injection of egalitarian and democratic value galvanized and ennobled the community with a sense of mission as it steadily began to create products that eroded basic business tenets of rent-seeking, preserving intellectual property, creating rare and non-imitable assets, and so on. He also suggests, though, that the overtly political nature of Stallman's leadership began to alienate the less politicized members of the open-source community, for whom quasi-Marxist rhetoric was a disturbing distraction. These feelings of disturbance also stemmed from the technology itself, because the basic Unix operating system that everyone was using had itself remained undeveloped, leaving many applications limited in their scope.

Linus Torvalds, a new-generation hacker, began creating an alternative system to Unix – Linux – into whose development the entire hacker community might devote their energies. For Raymond, the success of Linux lay with its technical, problem-solving focus. It freed the open-source movement from the label 'subversive', allowing huge swathes of them to collaborate on creating better open technology without the political agitprop. This was further enabled by developments in the wider technological field affording programmers easier communication channels (e-mail lists, for example) and storage (CD-ROMs) for sharing their work. The problem with closed-source software had always been 'bugs', and the denser and more complex the code became the less insight the closed coterie of expert programmers had into the nuanced system relationships by which these bugs arose. The sharing of open source was premised on a reverse logic: 'Given a sufficiently large number of eyeballs, all bugs are shallow.' Rather than a protected made order of experts ordered around hierarchical procedures, good software development came from open-ended, collective collaboration enlivened by a culture of what Raymond calls 'gift-giving'. Programmers devoted themselves to make the Linux source code and its application better in return for repute that stemmed from continuing involvement and that was marked on the code using credit files on each released version; theirs was a public display of personal reason by which others might be inspired in offering yet more insight.[37]

The rise of open-source systems and applications in opposition to the closed-systems offered by the likes of Microsoft has been growing rapidly, not just because of growing organizational acceptance of Linux (for example, IBM now uses Linux in its systems integration business, as does Google in its search engine) but because other closed-system developers have been persuaded of the redundancy of their hermetically sealed made-order model. At the turn of the millennium Netscape managers explained the reasoning behind releasing their own products' source code as a strategic volte-face; they recognized that robust software was not a product of planned design but an evolving structural system of adaptive, mutual endeavour. Recall Herbert Simon's suggestion, however, that human systems develop and survive through competition and anticipation. The emergence of open-source was not entirely spontaneous and unorganized. The better-performing products coming from open-source development are the upshot of competitive programmers (each of whom is searching for better alternative strategies to preserve and enhance his/her peer repute) held in a common, open-ended endeavour. These programmers only ever have a partial awareness of the evolving structure, there is no conscious design or designer, and the knowledge sustaining this organized endeavour can never become anyone's property because it resides implicitly in the evolving, relational system itself. Some programmers enjoy greater repute and visibility, however, and with this success become increasingly aligned with the movement's inner circle.

Linux survives and flourishes not because of raw spontaneity but because it displays the characteristics of what Charles Leadbeater calls 'we-think'. It has a strong core; its founder provided an offering that was worth becoming involved with because it is robust; it is based on established programming routines with which others are familiar; it provokes others from a range of backgrounds, each of whom felt excited by the prospect of contribution and each of whose diverse viewpoints could be brought into play on one aspect or module of the whole; and, finally, it is organized in such an intense way that multiple and diverse activities do not spin out of control. Similarly, Ragu Garud and his colleagues describe the evolution of Linux as an ever open process of *guided* renewal that allowed for continued inventiveness (an open product invites involvement and innovation in ways that a finalized, tested product does not) in the nuances of the code itself, as well as in finding new areas in which the code might be used.[38] Meritocratic divisions of labour, conversational manners (largely virtual) and agreed protocols relating to development, testing and sequenced product release were creating a well-governed rather than a random design. Linux is not a completely open or spontaneous bazaar but an ongoing and systematically organized incision by an identifiable core of knowledgeable programmers aware of how their own survival is linked in to the collaborative endeavour of a host of wider systems. Torvalds and a small coterie of programmers still look after the kernel of the programme. They are plugged into and filter suggestions coming from user groups, each linked with the centre and one another through websites, open-source application firms, blogs and journals, and meetings.[39] This is no free-for-all but in some ways a highly ordered system, with its own high priests, nested in other systems yet retaining a keen sense of modular dissolution as its members constantly anticipate and strive for technological betterment.

Complexity, emergence and self-organization

The recognition of organized forms characterized by an apparently contradictory organized spontaneity is increasingly shared across academic disciplines; it is a characteristic of all life and of all knowledge of that life, no matter how abstract. Mathematicians such as Henri Poincaré, Giuseppe Peano and Benoît Mandelbrot have long since set in train pure speculation on the inherent instability of apparently stable functional relationships between values, yielding arresting but uncontainable self-similar orders such as fractals. Equally, for many biologists it is a defining feature of all life forms that self-organizing entities, through their actions and reactions to the local demands of the environment, unwittingly help to create an emergent order. The concept of self-organization appeared around 1960, when Heinz von Foerster discovered that organisms engage and deal with the chaotic perturbations that threaten their existence by modifying their internal structures and producing new and more complex forms in response to such threats. This idea of self-organization is also found in the Chilean socio-biologists Humberto Maturana and Francisco Varela's use of the term 'autopoiesis' as a self-referential and self-constituting feature of an organism's response to its surrounding environment. In both these cases the emphasis is on order emerging spontaneously, so much so that chaos itself is now viewed more positively as a deep source of order and ordering rather than a negative condition to be overcome.[40]

The science of complexity thus brings a new and radical challenge to the traditional reductionist view that a system can be understood by breaking it down (hence *analysis*) and studying each component part in isolation from the rest of the system. Instead, it is now well appreciated that 'the interaction of components on one scale can lead to complex global behaviour on a large scale that in general cannot be deduced from knowledge of the individual components'.[41] Indeed, attributing any cause and effect relationship becomes difficult, because there is no way of isolating events and entities in such a way as to trace a cause and effect connection: the events and conditions by which movement scatters and reconfigures are inseparable; order emerges. It appears therefore as if there is some kind of an immanent, self-generated intelligence produced through the ongoing interactions of elements in both natural and social phenomena that can account for the emergence of order without any prior reliance on the notion of a pre-established plan or design. This is the central, radical insight of complexity theory. Contrary to some of our most deep-seated beliefs, which presuppose order to be the basic starting point for understanding the material and social worlds, it now appears that order can actually emerge out of chaos.[42] *Kaos*, the primordial 'soup', it seems, contains within itself the potential for life, creativity and order.

One of the more prescient expressions of this emerging sensibility is found in the work of the meteorologist Edward Lorenz, who was trying to use the work of Poincaré to improve weather forecasts. It was Lorenz who coined the term 'butterfly effect', to describe how a butterfly flapping its wings in the East could affect the conditions for hurricane formation in North America; huge storms could brew darkly from the palest of beginnings. Lorenz described what he was observing using the term 'non-linear feedback'. Climatic conditions arise from a complex array of mutually influencing entities and events, none of which lends itself to being identified in terms of stable characteristics or effects, nor in isolation from the others. Cloud patterns and types, sea temperatures, lunar cycles, sunspots, algae blooms, deforestation and a myriad other things contribute to the experience we call weather, without any determined direction or outcome. There is an absence of predictable patterns because the interaction of cloud cover with rising sea levels, say, can as easily amplify a rise in air temperature as dampen it depending upon the wider system conditions.

Lorenz accepted that there were limits to weather patterns; there is a tendency of weather systems towards equilibrium, a settling down of events into some kind of predictable order that we call the seasons, or a regional confinement of weather types distinguished by terms such as 'temperate' and 'tropical'. Here there is a broad balance achieved by corrective influences in an interacting system of events and entities. This is the negative feedback that Maruyama identified as deviation-reducing, a progressive compensating movement by which instances deviating from a norm are gradually eliminated. In summer the proximity of the sun determines, by and large, that temperatures will be higher than when the sun is further away, and any shocks to the system – such as the temperature falls in medieval Europe created by the ash cloud from the eruption of Vesuvius blocking the sun – would represent a deviation from which the system would gradually recover. These constraints are basic orders produced by the non-linear interaction of elements in the system itself, however; they are not imposed upon it. Moreover, within these basic orders weather is also subject to positive feedback, typically within these broader background patterns, in which disturbances are spread and intensified to points of unpredictable instability, as in the case of storms, or heatwaves. These are Maruyama's deviation-amplifying influences.

The interaction of negative and positive feedback loops mixes the stable and unstable, meaning that there is system structure, but events are not confined to predictable patterns. In rare moments the increasing volume and messiness of positive feedback threatens basic structural patterns. The recent discovery of a drop in salinity in the Atlantic Ocean may be a case in point. Gradual warming of the air and sea temperature is melting landlocked ice, which spills into the ocean and dilutes the salt in sea water. Salt, it is believed, is integral to the circulation of the Gulf Stream current, part of the Atlantic Meridional Overturning Circulation, whose vast circulatory rhythm carries warmer waters northward, which then cool and begin to sink before being carried southward. If the water doesn't cool as quickly it doesn't sink as quickly, and so it is not carried back along the sea floor as quickly. This slowdown is being amplified by the steady dilution of the heavier salt water in the north by melting ice sheets, because the fresher the water the more it pulls towards the surface. Though the risk of a complete shutdown is minimal, a slowdown in the pace of the circulation has been noted, with some climate change models suggesting that the climate along the northwestern European seaboard might alter rapidly, becoming more akin to its latitudinal kin in Canada.[43] There is, however, no real predicting what will occur, as other studies suggest rising salinity levels in more central parts of the Atlantic, linked to higher temperatures and subsequent water evaporation. All that is really known is that the hydrologic cycles of the earth are profoundly effected by salinity levels, and that changes in these might bring about exponential changes in climate.[44]

From the early 1990s onwards a number of theorists have begun to speculate on the links between chaos theory, economic systems and organizations, and the management of those systems.[45] David Parker and Ralph Stacey, for example, suggest that, contrary to the abstracting, equilibrium-hunting neoclassical economists, the preferences, expectations and decisions of buyers and sellers are insufficiently regular to warrant the assumption that the system is characterized by tendencies to the norm. As well as external shocks upsetting market balances, turbulence is something endemic to what is an inherently fragile and unknowable dynamic. Of course, natural disasters or terrorism will inject uncertainty into market behaviours and forecasts, but it is a mistake to assume that the market will respond with compensating negative feedback in order to restore the previously disturbed steady state. Indeed, what characterizes markets is their inherent inventiveness, their restless adaptability and flexibility, in the wake of which the ways of the past often seem anachronistic, uninventive, even backward. Here Parker and Stacey are pushing a view of markets that takes them beyond the confines of chaos theory. Whereas the weather systems observed by Lorenz do display determinate behaviour (there are negative feedback loops and basic behaviour patterns) but are so complex as to make comprehensive knowledge of the effects of these basic tendencies impossible, economic systems are qualitatively different, insofar as there is a complete absence of determinate behaviour.

This, at least, is the view of Hayek and the other Austrian economists, for whom markets are understood as spontaneously integrating and disintegrating activities of individuals without any overt governing laws. Here the market is always on the move; it resonates with activity – a restlessness fostered by inherent uncertainty. It is the very lack of perfect information and perfectly coordinated activity that characterizes markets, because it is only with the resultant indeterminacy that over-looked possibilities and inchoate opportunities present themselves. If there was no uncertainty there would be no incentive to innovate; if all variables could be determined and the effects of all actions foreseen there would be no market, because there would be no chance of securing economic rents by investing in ideas that others had not recognized. The kind of order demonstrated by markets, then, is not fully explained by interrelating positive and negative feedback loops. Chaos theory is valuable in suggesting how it is that markets and other more structured modes of organizing can persist at far from equilibrium states, disturbed as they are by apparently small events, but maintaining their identity on the edge of chaos, so to speak. It is a bounded instability in which, because of the inherent complexity and sensitivity of the environment of relations within which entities such as made orders exist, the experience of change is an irreversible one. There is no possibility of going back, nor is the future conceivable in any terms other than an array of next steps informed by immediate happenings.

Within such a system the future is unknowable and cannot be controlled, or directed by prefigured designs. What emerges as order is in fact self-organized; it emerges from the self-adjusting actions of individuals. Stacey uses the flocking bird analogy. The rapid and almost magical ink-black flash of flocking starlings against a yellowing evening sky is performed without any conductor or plan. A few basic rules (maintain a minimum distance from one another; match the speed of others; move towards a perceived centre) suffice to create a rapidly moving adaptive system. In markets and the organizational forms that occupy markets, which Stacey suggests are *complex* adaptive systems, such basic structural conditions are neither comprehensive nor perfectly adhered to. Human agents in a market might acknowledge dominant criteria and behave in regular fashion. They might keep broadly to contractual terms, for example, or adhere to timetables. These patterns are always negotiable, however. Moreover, running alongside these dominant criteria are recessive criteria that are also being adhered to, albeit playfully, even subversively, and these can rapidly subsume the dominant order without notice, fundamentally changing the self-organizing order of things. It is the *presence of absence*, so to speak, that affords markets their dynamism, because it is only by experiencing disorder that economic agents have any incentive to innovate, to work at new ways of doing things, to develop the taste for the entrepreneurial spirit by which improvements are wrought.[46]

Stacey is quite explicit about the implications for strategy here. If we are to take complexity theory seriously we have to accept that any talk about occupying the edge of chaos in order to better position oneself for the future, or to have greater insight into what is likely to occur, is bunkum. Complexity goes right the way through – period. There is no possibility of grasping complexity, of realizing pre-designed aims, of planning how to absorb shocks, because any future arises from internally governed dynamics whose intricacy is structured as events occur. This is what 'emergence' means. Emergence, as Stacey puts it, means that 'there is no blueprint, plan or programme for the whole system... In other words, the whole cannot be designed by any of the agents comprising it because they collectively produce it as participants in it.'[47] Like Mandeville's individual acting and interacting according to his/her own preferences, a complex adaptive social system comprises a large population of individual agents who, using simple local rules, interact with and constantly adapt to other agents, and in the course of their ongoing engagement unintentionally create a patterned order that can be viewed as an emergent feature of the population itself.

'Dynamic' does not refer to a complex relational exchange of complex entities but an inherently contradictory system of irresolvable forces. Here strategic management becomes a radically different practice. Attempts to define and impose order consciously and to control future events ignore the non-equilibrium world of trade. Rather than isolate states and structures, the job of strategic management is to recognize processes of evolution into which temporary structured activities can be productively inserted. These organized structures are necessarily devoid of hope, because to hope is to pressurize what we know and care about within the confines of expected outcomes. Thomas Hobbes called hope a whetstone human desire: it sharpens our sense of what might be achieved and in doing so gives us delusions of an external systemic environment that can be controlled. The leviathan is a fictional expression of such a system, and it is the dark genius of Hobbes' creation that reveals just how tenuous and dubious such a system might become. Rather than risk the architecture going wrong and having systems that are wayward, ineffectual or even both, the alternative is to eschew authoring hoped-for systemic outcomes. Instead, good strategy is about letting alone, about creating the conditions of innovative adaptation and entrepreneurial insight at market level without presuming any distance from them. The best strategy for coping with chaotic economic systems is to encourage acts of enterprise, letting individual agents choose their next actions based upon their immediate experience and own sense of purpose.[48]

2 Economic agency and steps to ecological awareness

[T]he resolution of contraries reveals a world in which personal identity merges into all the processes of relationship in some vast ecology.

Gregory Bateson, Steps to an Ecology of Mind, *p.306*

In chapter 1 we showed how the idea of spontaneous order can account for the emergence of coherent patterns of behaviour as well as centralized planning and design. We traced this idea of spontaneous emergence to the thoughts of ancient philosophers and discussed how subsequent important writers from a variety of backgrounds and disciplines have taken up this argument and elaborated upon it. This eschewal of the necessity for deliberate intention and pre-planning to account for the emergence of social and strategic orders opens up a new and difficult conceptual territory, however, for those looking to explain how it is that we as human beings can come to know about and influence our world under such conditions of uncertainty. If strategy amounts to anything, it is predicated upon a sense of being able to do something, of intervening deliberately to change the course of events in one's favour. If the conditions in which agents act are themselves inherently unstable, however, then there seems little to distinguish between strategic activity and chance and serendipity. This chapter is devoted to the further exploration of this question.

We consider the strategic dangers in deferring to a view of the world in which the individual is construed as an isolate, detached entity who engages with and seeks to control the world around him-/herself – an epistemological stance of methodological individualism. We discuss this stance in relation to the already discussed work of economists associated with the Austrian school. We then introduce the work of the anthropologist Gregory Bateson, for whom human beings are better understood as systems set among other systems rather than isolated and autonomous units. For Bateson, any strategic concern with developing one's potential requires the maintenance of a balance between systems. A shift in epistemological sensibility is proposed, whereby life is apprehended not as a problem of realizing ever more refined individual purposes in inherently complex and uncertain contexts but as a shifting array of potential value, of which we humans are but one expression. Bateson calls this apprehension 'systemic wisdom':[1] a persistent submission to the open-ended interconnectedness of things brought about by relationships of self-correcting balance. We discuss Bateson's views in the light of the 2007–9 global credit crisis.

At the end of the last chapter we were left with an image of isolated strategic actors working in an inherently chaotic and complex world. The recommendation was that, as designers of our own futures, we humans would do best to abandon any ambition of economic oversight. We ought to stop interfering with the world at a general or macro level and, instead, concentrate upon our immediate, individual and practical purposes, looking to respond to what life throws at us with a kind of flexible and knowing humility. One reading of this individualism is that it casts human individuals in a somewhat limited vein; in the words of Hayek, 'All man's mind can effectively comprehend are the facts of the narrow circle of which he is the centre that whether he is completely selfish or the most perfect altruist, the human needs for which he *can* effectively care are an almost negligible fraction of the needs of all members of society.'[2]

This reliance on localized, individual response, however, carries its own problems. The warnings proffered about the sheer hubris of attempting to perfect deliberate strategic design should not be taken as an invitation, or even an excuse, to abandon a sense of collective endeavour, collective experiment or collective belonging. The work of people such as Smith, Bastiat, Hayek and Simon, along with the case of open source, suggests that, whilst it might not be predictable, certain or controllable, human life is not entirely without systemic influence. Like the phenomenon of a flock of birds, what is distinct is that it retains its order in spite of an apparent lack of deliberate coordination; the orchestration is silent and all the more remarkable for it. Indeed, successful lives are often ones lived by those intuitively capable of understanding not just themselves and their own systemic requirements, but how they affect the requirements of other systems they encounter, whether these systems are other humans, other organic systems or social and economic systems.

The challenge posed by complexity theorists for strategy, therefore, is how we might generate awareness of and knowledge of ourselves and our wider environment if, as Hayek said, no human individual can possibly know about the wider set of systems of which he or she is a part without using the very kind of language and theoretical baggage that obscures and even denies the potential of those wider systems. To investigate this question, we begin by considering not so much the nature of the world we confront but the epistemological tendency to regard the world as something that can be confronted and ourselves as entities that can confront. If, as we suggest, there is little sense in understanding ourselves as quite distinct from the world we inhabit, then the problem of how we comprehend this world (whatever its uncertain nature) becomes a very different one from considering how we can impose order *upon* it. In other words, instead of relying on a controlling epistemology to guide our actions, we would begin to embrace a more relational one.

The observer and the observed

The identification of a human individual separated from and observing the world perhaps receives its most notorious and resonant expression in René Descartes' phrase *Cogito, ergo sum*. Amidst the turbid and often disorienting phenomena we encounter during our uncertain lives, what remains fast – indeed, the only thing that remains fast – is our persistent ability to doubt the existence of things. The entire edifice of human knowledge rests on foundations of a deeply felt awareness that the triadic godhead of the true, the good and the beautiful can, ultimately, never be got at. All we can know for sure is our own thought, our own mind, and it is this nebulous mental part of us that takes precedence and defines our individuality, exercising some form of conscious, unilateral control over us. What distinguishes human agency is not bodily action but the prior capacity to notice, choose, opt, judge, and so on. Just as we understand ourselves, so we understand what is beyond ourselves in relation to what we remain sure of. We are sure of who we are, and so we, as individuals, are distanced from other individuals, as well as from our natural and social environments.

One far-reaching consequence of this epistemological attitude is that the distinction surreptitiously creates a gap between an observer domain and the observed, with the claims of the former epistemologically elevated over those of the latter. It is now possible to construe the observer as having the ability to stand outside his/her situation and to say what a state of affairs is or is not without implicating him-/herself in these affairs. An apparent degree of objectivity ensues. For instance, when we make an observation 'This table is brown', it seems to express a state of affairs from which we are removed. Such statements refer only to the object of observation and not to the observers themselves. The twentieth-century Japanese philosopher Nishida Kitaro points out that to neutralize the role of the observer in this way is to implicitly say that his/her role can be ignored in this assertion. This is actually an arbitrary judgement to make, because what is really being asserted is 'I see a brown table and, since what I see is real and external to myself, I can ignore reference to myself'. It is this arbitrary denial of a subjective presence that allows a seemingly objective statement to be made – a denial that creates an unresolved tension in knowledge claims, for the objective is that which 'objects' to being construed as an object of investigation. All claims of objectivity of knowledge are essentially contested.[3]

To say with Descartes, then, 'Myself who thinks, I think, I am, I am a thinking being' is to claim something by doing it, thinking it and seeing it; the identity being claimed is inseparable from the originating activities, by whose underlying style we are able to establish an identity that is certain enough to be communicable to, and recognized by, others.[4] The influence of such an underlying observer style and influence is strikingly set out by John Berger in his discussion of the portrayal of nudes in Western art. The subject – typically a woman – is treated not as she actually is but as an abstraction of femininity as understood by the painter.[5] This is the reason why the artist Albrecht Dürer, for example, argued that the ideal nude would incorporate the head of one woman, the shoulders of a second, the legs of a third, and so on. What Berger is alluding to is the inevitable influence of 'observers' on what is 'observed'. The painters, and the owners of the paintings – typically men – occupied a certain prejudicial background. The nude, whilst ostensibly an image of 'external' reality, is, rather, a creation of the painter and spectator. To follow Kitaro, the influence of these observers was typically underplayed and even ignored. The resulting representation remained an expression of a desire to take possession of and control over objects, especially those considered beautiful, rather than a neutral rendition of the world as it was. Berger argues that it was only with Edouard Manet that this presumed neutrality was brought into questioning relief. Manet's stark and defiant nudes challenged the idealizing tradition and its implications for how people conceived of themselves and others. Manet's sitters are portrayed with a sense of self-awareness; their mien is active, arresting; their gaze pierces the divide between observer and observed; they interrupt the presumed objectivity of the representation. Manet's response to the patriarchy of portraiture was almost necessarily theatrical; a counter-blast to the lazy and exploitative disposition to impose an idealized view of beauty under the pretext of objective representation. It is this problematic attempt to separate the observer from the observed that underpins the form of individualism widely embraced in the social sciences.

Agency and methodological individualism

Agency is a central notion in theorizing human action in general and strategic action in particular. Broadly conceived, an agent may be a person or an impersonal force that produces an external effect or observable change. In the case of human agency, this frequently implies a driving force or a generative mechanism behind human interventions into the ongoing process of events-in-the-world. Within mainstream social theory, agency typically conveys a view of human action as intentional, volitional and purposeful in character. This implies a degree of autonomy and conscious awareness of actions taken. Rational choice and a 'consequentialist' mode of thinking that relies on a means–ends logic of action are frequently viewed as inextricable from the notion of human agency. In this regard, patterns of social and economic orders are deemed to be a consequence of actors intentionally organizing and giving meaning to their activities, and in so doing helping to create and recreate the conditions for social life. Borrowing a metaphor from Willard Quine, the social anthropologist Clifford Geertz observed that man 'is an animal suspended in webs of significance he himself has spun'.[6] These 'webs of significance' comprise networks of cultural symbols, schemata and programmes that have evolved through civilizing processes. The idea that humans, unlike animals, collectively construct for themselves cultural symbols and material edifices and self-consciously modify their environment in order to suit their needs in terms of food, shelter and protection has, therefore, been a pervasive one. Thus, unlike the beaver's lodge or the bird's migratory flight patterns, which emerge entirely instinctually, human beings deliberately construct the world they live in.

This argument for the distinctiveness of human individuals hinges upon a presumed autonomy and detachment from their environment that allows them to survey their circumstance and then to determine appropriate modes of engagement *before* acting. Its founding assumption is that people come to know what is 'out there' only by representing what is out there 'in here' in the form of symbols and mental models that are produced from processing the information initially received by the senses. According to this perspective, acts of cognition and representation precede acts of doing. We author designs and plans and then execute them, whereas the beaver's construction of its lodge is a programmed instinct incorporated into the development of the beaver's body. In the latter case, it is merely what Tim Ingold calls the '*executor* of a design that has evolved…through a process of variation under natural selection'.[7] Humans, on the other hand, are the authors of their own design. As Joseph Rykwert puts it: 'Unlike even the most elaborate animal construction, human building involves decision and choice, always and inevitably; it therefore involves a project.'[8] Thus, when trying to understand phenomena such as strategy, the presumption is of individuals collectively making judgements about their choice sets as to which course of organizational action to undertake and how it is to be accomplished; it is assumed that agents engaging in strategic action have deliberate intentions, clear end goals and act purposefully to achieve those ends. This assumption of autonomous individuals planning and acting purposefully to achieve predetermined outcomes remains one of the key presuppositions in much of the social sciences.

Within the study of socio-economic phenomena and society in general, there has been an ongoing debate between those who see society and socio-economic institutions as an aggregate effect of complex individuals and those who view them as coherent unities or ordered wholes in their own right. These debates about the nature and scope of human agency – what has often been called the agency/structure debate – appear to revolve around the questions of *individualism* or *collectivism* and that of the *voluntarism* or *determinism* of human action. Advocates of the primacy of macro-entities such as society and social institutions insist that such 'social phenomena can be adequately analysed and explained only by reference to facts about and features of *collections* of people...as opposed to individuals'.[9] The term *methodological collectivism* has been used to describe this holist position. Its exponents, such as the sociologist Emile Durkheim, argue that many features of social collectives are distinct enough to warrant analysis in their own right, and as such should not be reduced to the characteristics and attributes of individual members: 'Social facts must be studied as things, that is, as realities external to the individual.'[10] Since the individual is an inherently social being through and through, he or she is, as such, born into social institutions and structures not of his/her own making. These social orders exist *prior* to autonomous individuals and have a significant influence on their perceptions, choices, attitudes and dispositions. The individual is, for the most part, unconscious or unaware of the influence of these deep social structures shaping his/her preferred 'choices', intentions and actions. The painters of nudes need not have known of the bias that Berger finds so striking in their paintings. Indeed, so engrained can these structures become that they generate their own momentum independent even of collections of humans. Thus, for structuralists such as Claude Lévi-Strauss, our social existence and mode of thought is largely predetermined by the overall structures and transmitted myths of society – so much so that the individual's capacity for transcending and transforming society itself is largely restricted. This means that the driving force behind societal transformations derives from the emergent properties of the social structures themselves and not from the actions of individual human agents. On this reading, the painters of nudes were simply skilled but largely unwitting conduits of collective prejudice; they were working under the impress of an external and unconscious structural determinism.

For advocates of individualism such as Karl Popper, explanations of social phenomena, 'especially the functioning of all social institutions, should always be understood as resulting from decisions, actions, attitudes, etc., of human individuals and...we should never be satisfied by an explanation in terms of so-called "collectives" '.[11] Removing the agent from explanations of social phenomena somehow removed the point of explaining things. The ultimate unit of social analysis, for advocates of this individualist view, therefore, is the sovereign individual unencumbered by a 'sociality of inertia' in which there is no presumption of a past or an exteriority constraining action and who is thus essentially 'free-floating'.[12] Social theorists of this persuasion view the individual agent as central to the construction and reconstruction of his/her social world. Conscious cognition, meaning, intention and deliberate choice are presupposed in this explanatory schema. As such, the 'proper' unit of reference for an analysis of action has to be the *person*, or what Anthony Giddens calls the 'acting self'.[13] *Methodological individualism*, in its strongest form, therefore, upholds the primacy of deliberate intention and conscious, purposeful action in its mode of explanation. It denies the existence of social structures and institutions, and maintains that these must be necessarily reduced to individual endowments, desires, intentions, expectations and aspirations.

Despite its widespread use in social science, the term 'methodological individualism' has no single widely accepted definition. It has its origins in the writings of Max Weber, who argued in contrast to Durkheim that only individuals are real, and that they and their interactions exhaust the social world and its systems without any structural residue. Moreover, for Weber, what defines 'action' as opposed to 'mere' behaviour is that it is motivated by a mental state with a propositional content. Action presupposes meaning and intention and self-conscious awareness whereas behaviour implies unthinking, instinctive and absorbed engagement. To subscribe to methodological individualism is, therefore, to privilege the assumption that actions are the product of conscious deliberation and are necessarily motivated by prior intentional states relying on mental representations. The three key features of methodological individualism are thus: (1) individual autonomy; (2) a rejection of the primacy of social structures; and (3) the central role ascribed to cognition and conscious choice. Where collectivist or structuralist approaches to understanding social life attempt to look beyond the humans composing that life, those espousing a methodological individualist world view regard talking about 'individuals' as unproblematic (because their existence is incontestable). Indeed, as the sociologist Margaret Archer notes of methodological individualism, it is only by confining serious intellectual conversation (concepts, theories and laws) to this bedrock that we can avoid the pompous hyperbole of those social theorists always looking for meaning behind or beyond that assigned by ordinary individuals; social structures as such are not taken to be 'autonomous, pre-existent or causally efficacious'.[14] A methodological individualist perspective therefore maintains that collective social structures and institutions such as firms are largely artefacts of individual action and are thus only secondary considerations in the study of the kinds of social order and transformation exhibited by strategy.

The actual term 'methodological individualism' was first employed in an article published in English by Joseph Schumpeter (a student of Weber), who used it to express the view that the analysis of economic relationships should always start 'from the individual'. Schumpeter was not always consistent in his use of the term, however, and it is particularly unclear whether he meant to suggest that explanations of social phenomena should be constructed in terms of individuals *and* their social relations or in terms of individuals only. This suggests that there are at least two possible interpretations of what methodological individualism might mean. Lars Udéhn points out that the perspectives of individualism 'range from versions requiring that social phenomena be fully explained in terms of individuals, to versions requiring only that they be partly explained in terms of individuals'.[15] At its extreme, methodological individualism posits a discrete, isolated and atomistic individual existing and making deliberate choices prior to any interaction with others. Weaker versions of individualism, on the other hand, admit of the influence of social structures and interactions affecting individual behaviours and dispositions without losing the priority of individual choice over social circumstances. This weaker version of methodological individualism, with appropriate qualifications, begins to approach the kinds of concerns expressed in this book. To create an epistemological space for a weakened version of methodological individualism, however, we first need to examine critically its root premises of individualism.

Entitative thinking and the 'fallacy of misplaced concreteness'

Methodological individualism is, first, a theoretical approach to the understanding of society and social phenomena. Although it is often contrasted with methodological collectivism, what underpins both is a shared belief in the materiality and bounded character of the phenomenon being investigated. Both view their objects of analysis as entities, one micro, the other macro. Such an approach to social analysis reflects a way of thinking about the social world that is theoretically consistent with what is known as a *general systems perspective*.[16] Systems thinking assumes that systems are discrete entities separable from each other by definable boundaries and that they are essentially disposed towards maintaining stability, equilibrium and hence self-identity. In the course of their existence, they engage externally in interactions with other systems to form a supra-whole, so that what defines systems explanations are 'wholes, boundaries and levels'.[17] In all this, however, their basic internal constitution remains relatively unchanged. In this way, it is possible for both methodological individualists and methodological collectivists to accord primacy to their own unit of analysis and to view the other as epiphenomena of the basic entities central to their approach.

This insistence on the primacy of individuals or collectives leads to giving one or the other ontological priority and so to the elevation and stratification of things. Thus, instead of thinking about both individuals and collectives as secondary emergent effects of social actions and interactions, they are now construed as primary concrete entities in their own right. As a number of commentators have pointed out, both methodological individualism and methodological collectivism share similar presuppositions, in that they both construe the fundamental unit of analysis in essentially static and entitative terms; so much so, in fact, that collectivism is what the social philosopher Ted Schatzki recognizes as 'just a more capacious form of individualism'.[18] Similarly, Margaret Archer insists that the very 'terms of the confrontation between Individualist and Collectivists have to be queried before we can appreciate their growing rejection'.[19] Both methodological individualism and methodological collectivism block an appreciation of the essential interplay between 'structure' and 'agency', because each considers the other a dependent variable leading to either an 'upward' conflation of 'structure' or a 'downward' conflation of 'agency'.

This entitative way of thinking about social phenomena, whether as macro- and/or micro-entities, has been roundly criticized by a number of social theorists in recent times. For the much-travelled sociologist Norbert Elias, methodological individualism construes individuals, institutions and society as inert 'stationary objects', making them appear as if they were 'pieces of matter – objects of the same kind as rocks, trees, or houses'. Such 'reifying ways of...thinking about groupings of people...greatly hampers and may even prevent one from understanding the nature of sociological problems'.[20] According to Elias, the common-sense model that dominates the individual's relationship to society is a naively egocentric one, whereby a structure of invisible walls is deemed to exist, which, at one and the same time, both separates the individual from society and yet includes him/her in it. The assumption of the existence of these invisible barriers seduces us into thinking of social phenomena in fixed, bounded and hence isolatable terms, rather than in terms of action and interactions. In view of this distorting tendency, Elias proposes a 'figurational' sociology, in which social entities are conceived of in terms of 'webs of interdependences' rather than as isolated, circumscribed entities. Robert Cooper and John Law note how Elias's alternative notion of *figurations* is a way of getting us to reverse the common-sense view of social systems, including individuals as 'thing-like' entities with definable boundaries, and instead to recognize that social practices and processes are themselves the real 'stuff' of social life.[21]

The seemingly irresistible presumption that all phenomena, including social phenomena, are to be understood in entitative terms may be traced further back to an analytical impulse identified by Whitehead in his critique of the dominant modernist world view. For Whitehead, the influence of Isaac Newton's laws on our ways of thinking remains deeply pervasive, entrenched and hence unchallenged. Newton's first law states: 'Every body continues in its state of rest, or of uniform motion in a straight line, except so far as it may be compelled by force to change that state.' This formulation contains a fundamental assumption, namely the concept of an *ideally isolated system*.[22] By identifying the idea of an isolated system as a crucial analytical impulse, Whitehead shows convincingly that we have developed an instinctive tendency to view phenomena, including social phenomena, as possessing the property of *simple location*. 'By simple location, I mean that...material can be said to be here in space and here in time, or here in space-time, in a perfectly definite sense... The answer, therefore, which the seventeenth century gave to the ancient question of the Ionian thinkers, "What is the world made of?", was that the world is a succession of instantaneous configurations of matter.'[23] Rather than an intricate, fluxing and ever-changing web of interconnections as the basic fabric of the material and social worlds, we still think of the world in terms of discrete and isolatable entities that can be linguistically captured, classified and conceptually represented unproblematically in the mind.

Furthermore, the notion of causality can now be introduced to show how change is brought about. An epistemology of representation and control that views the world as 'instant configurations of matter', and hence amenable to classified packaging, thus ensues. Through this conceptual innovation, the world had got hold of a method of dealing with phenomena that it could 'neither live with nor live without'.[24] It is this presumption, however, that distorts our experience of reality and that leads us to mistake the abstract for the concrete: what Whitehead has famously termed the 'fallacy of misplaced concreteness'.

This tendency to mistake our theoretical representations for actual reality has had dramatic consequences for our modern understanding of economics and the social sciences in particular. As Whitehead writes: 'The science of political economy, as studied in the first period after the death of Adam Smith..., did more harm than good. It destroyed many economic fallacies... But it riveted on men a certain set of abstractions which were disastrous in their influence on the modern mentality. It de-humanised industry.'[25] By fixing our attention solely on such abstractions and neglecting everything else, it has led us to regularly 'mistake the wood for the trees'. As Whitehead puts it powerfully, '[W]hen you understand all about the sun and all about the atmosphere and all about the rotation of the earth, *you may still miss the radiance of the sunset.*'[26] Here we recall the shock and subsequent disillusionment with the neat answers provided by economic theory that befell Muhammad Yunus in the Grameen story. What Yunus experienced at first hand was the effect of this fallacy of misplaced concreteness (or what Taleb, as we saw in the introductory chapter, calls 'Platonicity').

In terms of our study of human agency, we can then see how this form of entitative thinking has influenced the choice of methodological individualism as the basis of social analysis. As a theoretical construct, methodological individualism has largely prevailed over its structuralist opposition, because the propensity to locate agency within a self-contained unit that is co-terminal with our physical and biological actualities is overwhelmingly attractive. In short, the overall tendency to construe either individuals and/or collectivities (e.g. groups, social institutions and society) as solid social entities – ideally, isolated systems with the property of simple location – is a result of subscribing to the kind of entitative thinking that Whitehead is at pains to criticize. As we try to show, however, there is a 'weaker' version of methodological individualism that, rather than moving slightly towards structuralism, is distinct because of its beginning to question this entitative view of the social world. It is one that appears to be more consistent with what has come to be called the 'practice turn' in social theory and philosophy. This revised understanding, we argue, offers a genuine 'third way' for theorizing agency, purposiveness and self-interested action such that it enables us to show subsequently how strategy may emerge spontaneously from the complex milieu of social actions and interactions without anyone deliberately willing it to be so. We begin, however, by discussing the strong version's dominance in economics and business.

Economic agency

Within the field of economics, Ludwig von Mises, a contemporary of Schumpeter, has been a major exponent of a strong methodological individualism in explaining human action. The bedrock conviction on which Mises developed his approach to economic enquiry was the belief that the science of human action differs qualitatively from the science of nature. This is because '[w]e approach the subject matter of the natural sciences from without... In the sciences of human action, on the other hand, we comprehend phenomena from within. Because we are human beings, we are in a position to grasp the meaning of human action, that is, the *meaning that the actor has attached to his action*.'[27] Mises took his point of departure from the positivists, who had begun to grow into prominence after World War I, by insisting that the subjective insights of agents were vital and legitimate aspects of any understanding of human action. As such, the focus of economic enquiry ought to be on the logic and reason underlying all our actions: 'Being an acting being, himself, man has in his mind and consciousness a knowledge of the essence and logic of action...this insight...does not require him to observe external facts.'[28] A 'principle of choice' in the course of action taken is implicated a priori and this underlying logic can be rigorously captured in the study of human action. Mises therefore insisted on 'both subjectivism and science'.[29] Accessing the subjective insights behind individual action in a rigorous and scientific way provides the basis for social enquiry.

Clearly, this singular emphasis on the internal mental state of the individual led Mises to champion a more definitive version of methodological individualism than Schumpeter – one that has come to serve as the primary basis of much of classical economic thought. Thus, in a crucial section of his *Treatise on Human Action* entitled 'The principle of methodological individualism', Mises writes: 'The hangman, not the state, executes a criminal...' for a social collective has no existence and reality outside of the individual members' actions. The life of a collective is lived in the actions of individuals constituting its body... There is no substratum of society other than the actions of individuals.'[30] Portrayed as such, the impression Mises leaves is of an autonomous individual devoid of social context and influences as well as history, to such an extent that only an a priori internal logic of rational action is capable of revealing the underlying reasons why people act. A reifying form of *social atomism* is implied.

Mises' elaboration on methodological individualism and how it could be used to explain economic activities associated with trade (and, by implication, most other forms of organizational activity) has come to be a dominant influence in economic theory. Mises was a friend and colleague of Weber (whilst Weber was a guest professor), and, for a time, Hayek's teacher, at the University of Vienna. Mises never held a tenured academic post, and did most of his work on economics whilst working for the Austrian Chamber of Commerce, advising government figures on monetary and banking matters. He had begun his career as a doctoral student researching the effects of structural reforms aimed at alleviating the lives of domestic servants and agricultural workers working in the Austro-Hungarian Empire. Convinced of the ineptitude of such planned interventions, he advocated a loosening of social regulation in order that individuals were able to act more freely. It was through unfettered human endeavour that sustained social and economic improvements would come about. His policy work drifted into work on taxation regimes, money supply and ultimately economic theory, but, throughout, his emphasis was always to focus on the real actions of individuals rather than on the non-existing aggregates commonly used by economists.

In this fixation on individually located meaning, Mises was inspired in part by his familiarity (but not wholehearted agreement) with a group of philosophers, scientists and mathematicians that came to prominence during the 1920s as the Vienna Circle. One of Mises' students, Felix Kaufman, was affiliated, and his brother, Richard von Mises, was a leading member of the circle's Berlin offshoot, known as the Society for Empirical/Scientific Philosophy. The Vienna Circle, headed by Moritz Schlick, championed a thoroughly scientific understanding of the world, along with what one of the circle's main luminaries, Rudolph Carnap, described as the 'elimination of metaphysics'. Theirs was an overtly Enlightenment project: an urge to restore science and faith in science by providing a rigorous language of logic, in which knowledge could reside free from the obscuring and emotionally loose language of the everyday. The distinction between the unifying language of science and the disparate, ad hoc language of the street was attained and sustained by the method of experimental verification (*certification*) first sketched in the thirteenth century by the Franciscan 'Doctor Mirabilis', Roger Bacon.[31] Whereas Bacon continued to believe that the existence of God was demonstrable, members of the circle confined speculation on any possible afterlife, or any other emotive and imaginative concern, to the folk language of poesy, leaving knowledge an uncluttered terrain of *positively* defined positions established and defended by *logical* methods – hence the label 'logical positivism'. Verification can take place analytically (to verify that corporations have limited liability, for example, is to recognize the necessary grammatical or logical connexion between limited liability and the entity known as a corporation) or empirically (if prices rise, demand typically falls). Other than this logical and empirical knowledge there are simply the confusions wrought by incorrect or lazy – namely Hegelian – use of language. Knowledge is something precise, a distillation of the ordinary.

This emphasis on verification puts the individual in some kind of epistemological priority to what is being understood insofar as it is only through the auspices of experimental and grammatical judgement that we arrive at a knowledgeable state. It is our methods of approaching the world (our concepts, equipment and rules) that govern conditions of truth and falsity, and so ignorance is our condition to correct. Verification, then, is a grammatical concern: the logical impossibility of something existing is a conventional rather than an ontological issue; a lack of meaning stems from rents in the weave of our theories, our observations and our language rather than in the fabric of the universe. As well as placing the individual observer at the helm of knowledgeable enquiry, therefore, logical positivism encourages the observer to adopt a critical mien towards the cosiness of convention. If the status of knowledge claims – whether scientific or common-sense – are a function of their propinquity to common and communicable empirical experience, and the evidence from the experience is always subject to change, then knowing observers should always be prepared to look for surprise encounters with counter-factuals as arguments are brought to bear from rival theories based on new observations or new interpretations. These bouts of hoped-for confirmation create an implicit hierarchy of disciplines, because it is natural science, logic and mathematics that have recourse to the kind of linguistic structures in which testable exchanges can take place. Repeating laboratory conditions (hermetically sealed arenas of enquiry with standardized equipment, rules and scales) and isolating the same variables (holding other things equal) is harder when it comes to explaining human lives. The application of veiling conditions to human lives (assuming that we are all profit-maximizers, for example, or risk-averse) in order to make comparisons nullifies these lives, which are far more sensitive to such descriptions than, say, a marvellously indifferent star cluster or a speechless bacterium. The more language deals with the recalcitrant side of human nature – its emotional unpredictability, its imaginative lines of flight – the less the knowledge claims made in that language can be subject to verification. On one side we have the open-ended, emotionally charged statements of significance. On the other we have calm, cognitive representations of logical or factual meaning.[32]

To understand economies, then, one needs to cognitively apprehend and understand the actual and possible empirical experiences of those engaging in the practice of trade, and to avoid using obscuring, emotional and untested generalities. On these terms, members of the Vienna Circle were typically sceptical about the so-called positivist science of economics. They thought observations of production and trade would only ever yield temporary alignments and vague theories and generalities, and so would always be struggling to realize the kind of testable representations that explained how birds flew and water boiled. Social science bordered on nonsense. Mises, accepting the need to analyse experience and action as it occurred, was still committed to the possibility of discovering law-like regularities, however. Like the Vienna Circle, he accepted that any verification of the observation of human events is inevitably contested, because human history cannot be faceted and isolated in the way natural variables can be: the events cannot be replicated, they are complex and they are irreversible. He also argued, however, that the split between cognitive representation and emotional significance was harsh and unsophisticated, not least because it failed to acknowledge the qualitative distinction between a science of human action (such as economics) and a science of nature: the human condition cannot be verified without invoking what is to be verified (namely an independent observer), so it remains self-evident, it cannot be tested and forms the background for any knowledge claim, scientific or otherwise.

Given this Kantian turn, Mises maintained that it was itself nonsense to suggest that any knowledge claim concerning human activity was bordering on the nonsensical simply because it presupposed rather than verified an autonomous observer. Economic theory dealt with the fact that human beings exist, that they act upon the world and that this action has a logic of means and ends. Taken together, this theory offered scope for an accurate, non-metaphysical understanding of how humans experience the meanings and practices associated with material wealth production. If, self-evidently, each agent made things and bargained with another only on the prospect of self-benefit, and any attempt to interfere or control with this making and bargaining inevitably failed, then the appropriate institutions were the minimal structures associated with specialization, markets and private property. Mises believed economic theory capable of highlighting the reason underlying an individual's calculative actions. Accessing the subjective insights behind individual action in a rigorous and scientific way provides the basis for social enquiry into, and control over, phenomena such as money.

His enquiry begins with Menger's story of the organic emergence of money from basic systems of bartering. Mises recognized money as a medium that in itself was of no value (and so, fundamentally, a different kind of entity from a product or service with use value). Being devoid of value apart from its use within trading relationships (or the residue/prospect of such relationships), an increase in the supply of money will not increase social benefit. Money has no utility of its own, so to explain and control economic systems one cannot limit one's analysis to money – or any other abstract entity, come to that. One has to get at the conventional acts of use value. For Mises, it was the failure to acknowledge this that fundamentally undermined socialist planned economies. Without private ownership and the exchange of titles there is no price system for the means of production, and without prices planners would have no knowledge of the productivity and profitability of available resources. Even assuming that the planners' goals coincide with those they are planning for (that they could somehow echo the available innovatory potential and knowledge necessary to sustain economic activity), the denial of ownership means that the spontaneous, individual human act of judgement to prefer or set aside is neutered – an absence of individual valuation without which money value cannot exist, which in turn would eliminate the possibility of a price system and hence of any accuracy of information upon which planning depends.

Mises supposed that it was from these primitive beginnings that economic knowledge is built, and to which it can be reduced. The basis of any economy, it seems, are isolated evaluating agents loosely tied through weak market relations, who, with a growing familiarity with the imperfections and failures of these relations as well as with organized modes of contract and governance, become increasingly sophisticated in their orchestration of trading positions. They have a sense of what is efficient and can learn the effective means for realizing states of affairs governed by the dictates of such efficiency. Any economy can be investigated empirically, therefore, and its functioning reduced to elemental components, of which the rational chooser and optimizer gathered with like-minded others is the originating source.[33] Here what counts as knowledge is ultimately reducible to the primitive, immediate experiences of those struggling to cope with and make sense of their everyday lives. Any theory or concept that cannot be tied into the weave of individual action is, by that fact, nonsense.

On these points, Mises remains very much wedded to the Vienna Circle. Any legitimate knowledge claim about human society and human meaning is grounded in the empirics of human action, and those actions remain the actions of individuals (rather than institutions). Cultural norms and values, regulations, procedures, expectations, regimens and all the other assorted social clutter accumulating in institutional attics influence action, but they are always the upshot of actions, and hence reducible to them. Mises' logic of reduction stopped with the individual and his or her self-understanding. Whilst accepting the need for a common empirical foundation for social science, he remained committed to the idea of the human subject as an impermeable entity, and it was here that he diverged from members of the circle such as Rudolph Carnap. Carnap believed, at least early on, that, with the advance of scientific methods, explanations that linked human beliefs and intentions to observable and verifiable individual behaviours could eventually provide further rational reconstructions in which the shifting, troubling question of human identity could be nicely confined to the measured to and fro of physiological and neurological events. As Herbert Feigl points out, Carnap was engaged in conjecture here, pushing at the edges of our epistemological habits in order to ascertain whether the language of mind and agent self-identity was in fact nested within a more structured, scientific language of isolated behaviours.[34] The point was that, once stripped of any preconceived intuition or expectation of what it means to be an individual, we may very well find that, at root, it is simply physical events that constitute a human being. In this, Carnap was looking to extend our knowledge of what materially exists and could be verified into the realm of human action and intentionality. If laws governed the spatial movement of planetary entities then why not the economic movement of trading entities, provided these too were reduced to their elemental states?[35]

The dangers of decontextualized thinking

It was the disciplined and unwavering adoption of methodological individualism in the study of our material-wealth-creating behaviour that led Thorstein Veblen, an American political economist of Norwegian stock, to voice a stinging criticism:

The hedonistic conception of man is that of a lightning calculator of pleasures and pains, who oscillates like a homogeneous globule of desire or happiness under the impulse of stimuli that shift him about the area, but leave him intact. He has neither antecedent nor consequent. He is an isolated, definitive human datum.[36]

This is a telling comment. Methodological individualism meant that all explanation of how and why we trade the way we do was rooted in the actions, beliefs and judgement of isolated beings, and it was this reductive focus that, somewhat ironically, began to hollow out what it might mean actually to *be* an individual. Reduced to the kind of raw, physical stimulus response envisaged by Carnap, the very qualities that make the individual human begin to dissolve; there are no contrasts, no tragedies, no examined life. The only sure things, the only fixed things, are identified in the knowledgeable ascription of an internal, hedonistic logic of pain avoidance and the pursuit of pleasure to a rational, conscious observer of a world understood entirely under the rubric of more or less perfect choice sets.

It was in a kind of millenarian contemplation of the possible effects of this elevation of a decontextualized, supposedly neutral agent-observer that a fifteen-day-long Congress of the Dialectics of Liberation for the Demystification of Violence was held at the London Roundhouse in 1967. Prominent amongst the speakers was the anthropologist Gregory Bateson.[37] Bateson's extended oratory at the congress was later published as 'Conscious purpose versus nature', in which he elaborates on what he saw as three interrelated, self-organizing cybernetic systems: the human individual, human society and natural ecosystems. Modern life – our life – was dominated by one of these systems, the human individual. Indeed, so dominant was this system that the others were regarded as separate repositories, resources to be exploited for the hedonistic goals of human individuals. Natural ecosystems provided raw materials whilst social systems provided the institutional and technical procedures to ensure that the use of these materials was organized more rather than less efficiently. This is where our isolation placed us: so preoccupied with our own consciously articulated, studied and defined minds that we have become congenitally unaware of the other systems by which such a mind, body and lifespan are sustained.

What Bateson argues is that the systemic nature of all life has been serially ignored in favour of pursuing the specific conscious purposes of individual human systems. The result has been a meteoric rise in the relative status of the human species, but one bought at the expense of sustainability. Bateson, like James Scott in our earlier discussion, uses the example of woodland. Woodlands are ecosystems that have persisted for aeons in what he terms an alliance of competition and dependency, a community of entities held in some sort of structured balance: competing to survive by attempting to extend their imprint exponentially whilst being checked in such by similar tendencies in other entities. It is precisely this kind of dynamic balance that permits mutual survival. As we have seen with the example of the German forestry practices discussed by Scott, these balanced systems are precarious, and should the system slip at any point then exponential change can occur. The monoculture practised by the German foresters meant a slippage in the richness of the soil and in beetle life and in the types of ground cover plants, which in turn led to slippage in the kind of birds and types of prevalent disease, meaning a new balance had to be realized. In this disturbance there is danger that the system may slip further and start to skew radically because the compensating responses to exponential change may themselves be harmful, resulting in accelerated positive escalation, for example if the use of remedial pesticides contaminates groundwater to such a degree that the entire ecosystem begins to corrode.

Bateson's narrative applies quite obviously to the self-organizing system that is humanity. As individuals, human entities are physiologically predisposed to focus, to package certain phenomena systematically as images of conscious awareness from a larger array of unconscious scanning. This selection of unconsciously scanned life is edited by human purposes; our consciousness is a short cut to afford us efficient means to secure given aims. Bateson gives medicine as an example. The purpose of patient and doctors alike is to alleviate, cure or prevent certain debilitating occurrences in the human body. Conscious focus is on isolating signs or symptoms, then the search for causes by which these appear (called etiology), before finally the development of treatment. The symptoms are granted the status of a disease, sometimes ennobled by the name of those who discovered them, or who first suffered, but secured by virtue of the etiology by which treatments are found.[38] Bateson calls the upshot of this focus on purposes 'a very useful bag of tricks'. Cures are found, and lives are deemed healthier, and then new symptoms are isolated warranting a switch in purposeful endeavour. Smallpox is cured and we move onto cancer, continuing to investigate our surroundings in line with our own, very human concerns. In this practice, as in most human practice, our purpose (prolonging individual psychological and physiological well-being) dominates how we organize ourselves. What is lacking is any awareness of the wider self-organizing system, in which we are placed but to which we remain insensitive. In the past this might not have mattered, but as humans become ever more technically adroit their trickery preserves one species at the expense of others.[39] Human beings have fixated on their own purposes and in doing so ignored the context in which those purposes have life. Our technical abilities have resulted in a profound and pervasive success at meeting immediate needs. The etiological analysis and consequent plans have elevated us to unparalleled species status; we have more tricks up our sleeve then ever before.

Nonetheless, this very technical proficiency and the attendant controlling epistemology are, in Bateson's terms, simply hastening or amplifying our exposure to disorder. Only dimly have we been aware of this in our material-wealth-producing activities; blinkered by immediate purposefulness we bear down upon acquisition and control without deviation.

Any onset of systemic disequilibrium has escaped our notice, and the political, environmental and financial turmoil we experience we attribute to external disturbances to which we must adapt, or to failure in our planning, requiring better concentration and application. In both cases we are always looking to change our environment, to create ever more impressive single-species ecosystems, such as well-ordered, clean and predictable cities, and subservient single-species ecosystems, such as factory farms or laboratories. These ecosystems are further refined with self-maximizing subsystems, such as firms, political parties, professions, and the like, by which we better arrange our purposeful, organized pursuit of wealth. No matter how autonomous, the purposes generated by an individual system are never self-contained, but are continually influenced by the behaviour of other – largely unconscious – parts of its own the system, by its own history of previous behaviours and their effects and by its being woven into other human, social and natural systems.[40] What we know of a system and our place within it is immanent not to some part of a system, therefore but the systems in systems, the edges of which can never be closed. There are always contexts of contexts of contexts. Here, how we go about acting purposively is inherently relational; we educate our attention within an ongoing and irreversible history of environmental influence. In all this we remain unaware that the problems we experience in fulfilling our purposes, or designing the right purposes, are ones of persisting positive feedback (Maruyama's deviation-amplifying forces) over which we have very limited linear control. Awareness of this requires us to have a sense of how we fit in with other human systems, social systems and natural systems; to accept that this is never a static fit; and to refrain from reaching after knowledge of where such interactions might end up.

Herbert Marcuse, who shared the Roundhouse platform with Bateson, toyed with this ecological theme in a swingeing critique of the so-called affluent society produced by late modern capitalist strategies and their uncritical relationship with the colonizing tricks of technology and the rationality of productive efficiency.

The problem we are facing is the need for liberation not from a poor society, not from a disintegrating society, not even in most cases from a terroristic society, but from a society which develops to a great extent the material and even cultural needs of man – a society which, to use a slogan, delivers the goods to an ever larger part of the population.[41]

As more was produced more was being destroyed to serve that production; growth was accelerating under the impress of waste, obsolescence and destruction. Awareness of the ensuing damage to the wider ecosystems was ignored, necessarily so, as the individual managers and financiers took it upon themselves to think narrowly, to focus solely upon the purposes of the firm for which they were an agent, or even just themselves, no matter how many longer-term problems might ensure. Stubbornly holding onto this idea of self-interested action in this way inevitably brings its own tensions.

Though apparently secure in Mises' eyes, the idea of a sovereign self maximizing his or her life chances using rational calculation to occupy his or her environment is a taxing and even exhausting prospect if we consider it from the perspective of action. Each attempt to make our purposes more conscious and their realization more tractable brings with it an accompanying Cartesian strain. Our contextual condition is unknowable, the effects of our actions uncertain; the only security we have left is our awareness of ourselves as thinking, doubting beings, and it is here we fixate. It is here where we devote our strategic energy: our own immediate purposes and how we can become increasingly conscious of and successful in realizing these purposes.

In modern life, however, the range and character of these purposes, though conscious, is becoming ever more attenuated as stated options are superseded by 'better' alternatives. It is the prevalence and sheer rapidity with which individual purposes are crafted, expressed and die that is proving tiresome. The sociologist Zygmunt Bauman calls this condition 'liquid life'. He comments on how the irresistible attraction and spread of supersession means that anything with duration is treated with suspicion, as it hints of backwardness. There is no time for dalliance, for curiosity – the urge to linger is squeezed out from us by exhortations to limitless production and consumption. Here any made order is subject to the overriding concern of individual purpose, which is the purpose of constructing and reconstructing individuality.[42] For Bauman, such self-generating individuality is an ever-renewed, dialectical task of improvement. The notion of community in which made orders might persist has given way to self-expression and self-reliance; what was performed habitually through participation in tradition is now consciously held by each individual as a portfolio of relationship failure and success for which he or she alone is responsible. Simply put, this struggle for uniqueness is played out de facto by what Bauman introduces as the two prevailing concerns of such a precarious 'liquid life': disposing of waste and avoiding being consigned to waste. The task of Mises' individual is to disassociate the self from its previous associations as these seep into the wider, uncertain and ever-shifting environment.[43] The autonomous individual moves through wider social and natural systems without stopping to contemplate its effects or alternative trajectories:

> It struggles to embrace the things that 'one cannot be, nor be seen, *without*' today, while being fully aware that they are most likely to turn into things that 'one cannot be, nor be seen, *with*' tomorrow.[44]

Bauman argues that nothing more clearly demonstrates the complicity of human ideas with their ontologically biased, systemic contexts than this 'permanently impermanent self'. Despite the best Cartesian efforts to secure feelings of repose using intellectual structures, other organizing forces always interpose and jeopardize the independence of this hard-fought, sovereign enclave. These rivals even use the same concepts of autonomy, suggesting that it is our invigorating immersion in the ever renewed events of the life stream that signifies a free and human life rather than a clinging to an outmoded idea of human inviolability.

This warning of Bauman's brings to mind Italo Calvino's invisible city of Leonia, so successful at producing new and exotic objects that it rapidly and with great gusto began also to excel at expelling its waste. The more impressive and resistant Leonia's new products the more pressing and more persistent its waste. It is surrounded by its own leftovers, and other cities also press at its edges, until the neighbouring cities get so close that Leonia's street cleaners and refuse collectors are forced to pile up the city's waste in an ever more precipitous and dangerous arête:

> The greater its height grows, the more the danger of a landslide looms: a tin can, an old tire, an unraveled wine flask, if it rolls toward Leonia, is enough to bring with it an avalanche of unmated shoes, calendars of bygone years, withered flowers, submerging the city in its own past, which it had tried in vain to reject, mingling with the past of the neighboring cities, finally clean. A cataclysm will flatten the sordid mountain range, canceling every trace of the metropolis always dressed in new clothes. In nearby cities they are all ready, waiting with bulldozers to flatten the terrain, to push into the new territory, expand, and drive the new street cleaners still farther out.[45]

As with cities, so with strategically driven firms. The purposeful strategic impress is an abiding concern with the promotion of immunity. The more aggressive and powerful this independence from one's surroundings the more impressive your future as you control your environment, at least in the short term. In all this controlling there is no sense of what Friedrich Nietzsche calls dominion; strategy is the practice by which managers refuse to consider themselves as themselves, and instead continually look to place the firm in a favourable position vis-à-vis the observed environment, expelling waste whilst producing output to earn revenues. Externalities are strategically relevant only if they can be made internalities – if by absorbing them into the confines of firm activity they benefit the purposes of that firm in some way. This is how actions such as avoiding tax become an imperative, a duty to shareholders and customers to consciously produce more with less uncorrected by wider systems (the economy, wider society and natural ecosystems) whose influence is regarded as a restraint on the pursuit of purpose.

With increasing focus on explicit purposes comes a fixation on widening the technological capacity to govern one's own limited terrain coupled to an increasing aggressiveness in preserving and enhancing that control. 'Threaten us with tax reform,' say the managers of successful large firms, 'and we will relocate and take our jobs with us.' The threat is taken seriously. The 'regulating' external systems back off. With every improvement in productivity comes an erosion of opposition; the result is a positive feedback loop of purposeful myopia fed by the conscious acquisition of more and more information and animated by technological amplification. In the setting of ever tighter goals informed by ever more detailed data and ever more explicit specifications of and investment in the means (standards, specialization, technology) to realize these goals, the environment is foreshortened to a series of linear, simple and temporally brief causal chains whose management presents us with a potentially stable world and yet, following Bateson, results in something more precarious, as General Motors found out. For Marcuse, this preoccupation with fixed objectives and their ever more consciously managed pursuit resulted in an economic system ordering itself in increasingly stark opposition to other human, social and natural systems; there was no counterbalance, no room for unproductive imagination, curiosity, lingering; no room for social activity that could not be packed and sold; no room for environments that could not be subjugated under the calculus of cost–benefit analysis. The wasteland grows.

The credit crisis, 2008

Following the arguments of chaos and complexity theory, the wider context or territory into which such controlling calculus is thrown remains inherently uncertain and non-linear. The response to this uncertainty by those adopting what we might call a controlling epistemology is to concentrate upon what can be known and controlled, namely individual purposes, and it is in their unfettered pursuit that innovation and, so, productive activity are realized. People become ever more focused on satisfying immediate, individually authored ends and enlist ever more powerful technological 'tricks' in pursuing them. A controlling epistemology is inherently individualist; it inevitably narrows conscious focus to a limited and apparently tractable set of autonomously authored concerns of the kind envisaged by Mises and lamented by Bateson and Marcuse. In strategy terms, the classic form of such confinement would involve managers isolating and targeting resources that are valuable and organized. Performance is understood as a function of securing the maximum amount of these resources at minimum effort. In an inherently complex environment these resources may never be static, and they can be immaterial, such as requisite attitudes or reputation, as much as they are material.

Nevertheless, performance is a function of their continued and appropriate acquisition. The focus, then, is upon short, causally bound chains – or what Bateson calls the 'arcs of system circuits'. The firm's employees and associates become skilled or innovative in focused, purposeful activities, such as web searches, or project management or hydrocarbon extraction, and adept at enlisting ever more powerful technologies in the service of these. Strategic goals are realized when the firm's employees confine their wider environment to an articulated and codified regimen of specialized and standardized means for explicitly framed ends. Whilst this controlling epistemology yields a sense of homeostatic preservation, it is an energy-expending, short-term and hence fragile order of individually located conveniences bought at the expense of creating debilitating externalities. Bateson calls it potentially pathological, because of its being blind to forces other than, and bigger than, those of the individual or organization whose purposes are being pursued. There is no wider wisdom; understanding is confined to the purview of explicit knowledge, and what lies outside this is unclear or not rational and hence ignored. This blindness clears the field for clearly defined purposes and the array of accompanying technological force. The balance between individual, social and natural systems is upended as the autonomous (separated) system strives to dominate.

The 'credit crunch' that started in late 2007 and its subsequent escalation into a liquidity crisis describes an unfurling of events that nicely illustrate Bateson's and Marcuse's concerns. The finance and banking community had for more than a decade been growing fat on the expectation of arbitrage: opportunities to earn abnormal profits. For 'abnormal' read 'irresponsible', if by 'responsibility' is meant a preparedness to acknowledge the needs of other systems. Financiers were in the business of providing capital, and the more they could provide the greater the returns, the greater their firms' profits and, correspondingly, the greater the size of their earnings and bonuses; the financiers became increasingly technologically aggressive in fixating on this singular purpose. The growth in the uptake of loans – fuelled by aspirant advertising, confident lending, a burgeoning of customized financing packages, lax and/or weak national and international regulation and complex global credit lines – had multiple, interrelated effects. These included: increasing the pressure on the available liquidity in the wider financial system (insurers, issuers of bonds, and so on); increasing labour mobility, and even immigration, to sustain an aspirant economy; fuelling material expectations founded in a growing sense of wealth; and depressing biodiversity and eroding alternative land use as more and more resources were commanded by construction. These effects placed credit availability under stress; yet the financiers' response remained fixated on the singular purpose of earning cash, and so they eschewed actions that might restore a balance.

Calls for credit restrictions, for taking time out to reflect on why and how all this money was being made available, were understood as signs of weakness, of letting the symptoms of economic illness back in. The etiology had been set in place, the box of tricks was being used to good effect, the treatment would continue with more refined offerings. The response was to create more complex instruments to better realize arbitrage. In Bateson's language, this involved stretching the tolerance limits of the variables rather than looking to rebalance them. More money was made available through the complex bundling and sale of liabilities. This bundling took the form of sophisticated derivative contracts that were ranked and then badged under the moniker collateralized debt obligations (CDOs). These were used by banks and other lenders to release debt from their books and so provide access to yet more credit for new customers, which could then be repackaged and sold on. Buyers for CDOs were spread throughout the global financial system, assuring themselves that the debt they had purchased was sound by using ratings provided by reputable credit agencies. There was little awareness of the unsoundness of these debts, nor much willingness to investigate their provenance. The initial rewards were high, and this attracted more customers in: insurers, pension funds and the banks themselves. The financial system remained garlanded with confidence, unaware of the growing 'toxicity' of the sources upon which this confidence flowered. Even the issuers themselves lost sight of the flimsiness of these bundles (balanced as many of them were on loans made in the US sub-prime mortgage market), persuaded by their own risk models that because CDOs had always been easy to sell on they were of sufficiently low volatility to hang onto whilst weightier risks were absorbed. The more fixated on sustaining the provision of revenue-generating credit lines the system became the more data were collected by fee-generating ratings agencies 'proving' the soundness of the resulting debt bundles, and the more intricate the technologies being used to design and construct yet more novel financial architecture. For 'novel' read 'impenetrable', and then 'fictitious'. The lenders and purchasers of CDOs discovered that, once unravelled, the bundles of debt carried little promise of repayment. What was lost was any awareness of the context, and the context of the context. There had been no attempt to recognize the need to balance this eye-catching sale of securities with the demands of the wider financial system for balanced lending, or with the demands of other human systems, and as a result of these machinations many people were beginning to suffer economic and social hardship.

Salutary though this tale is to those smitten by the obligations consequent on holding CDOs, there were even more disturbing elements of accentuating positive feedback. A significant minority of players did have sufficient awareness to witness the hollowness of the CDO products being traded, and yet their entire world view was focused on keeping up the appearance of ignorance, whilst clandestinely taking positions that would pay out in the wake of financial collapse. So strategically predisposed to earning revenue was the financial system that the rewards from wider failure were also sought after. The traders created arbitrage opportunities from 'shorting': gambling on collapse by borrowing shares in a strategically identified firm for a fee, then selling the shares with a mind to buying them back at some future date for a lower price, returning them to their rightful owner whilst keeping the difference as profit.[46]

Extracting rent from misfortune is not a new skill. Shorting, however, is of a different quality. It revels in failure, incompetence and malfeasance, as well as in upsetting efforts being made to stabilize and recover situations from crisis. The guilty, greedy or ignorant managers who run firms into a strategically weakened position are exposed and pilloried for their failure by traders who have seen and got behind the fabrication. Arguably, this strictly Darwinian arrangement serves to clean the wider economic system of waste: those who consume the commons whilst contributing little are found out and traded out of existence. As the psychologist Oliver James points out, however, investing in another's demise is a surer bet the more others invest similarly; what may be short-term or nascent weaknesses are rent into life-ending wounds inflicted by a clever pack of financial marauders.[47] Shorting is not a cause of malaise but it is often a symptom, because it relies on the secrecy of engagement, whereby insight is never shared, and on the existence of system elements being predisposed to failure. The new tricks in the etiology of financial investment are devious; they risk amplifying the disturbance right to the edges of the system because that is where they thrive. This deviousness is not necessarily bad – indeed, it can help sustain systems insofar as new tricks are being learnt: quicker responses to changing circumstances are made possible. The problem comes in the very immediacy and singularity of the deviant response, in which there is little scope for acknowledging the potential in looking outside the well-defined purpose of earning money whatever the impact on other systems.

The case of UBS

What remains quite apparent throughout this period is that the strategies informing bank activity leading up to the credit crisis were in no way considered outlandish; indeed, strategists were behaving in accord with basic premises of planned expansion. Looking back over the financial press over the decade leading up to the credit crisis, it is striking just how many pieces have been written conveying a sense of growing urgency about pushing on the edges of the rapidly expanding tide of securitization. One of the heaviest European casualties, UBS, so emptied of resources that by the end of 2008 it had become part nationalized by the Swiss government, was until 2007 being fêted for aggressively pursuing an acquisition and then diversification strategy that took it into structured credit markets. UBS's investment banking strategy was originally set out in the early 1980s, when the Swiss bank, rich with capital from its extraordinarily profitable private banking business, decided to expand into investment banking. Note that the profitability and positioning of the private bank is, essentially, based on one unique competitive advantage: being based in Switzerland, with its deliberately secure regulations that protect client anonymity and provide tax advantages. UBS initially deployed a strategy that mixed organic growth with bolt-on acquisitions – buying UK investment management firms such as Phillips and Drew and Laing and Cruickshank and US businesses such as O'Connor. These were largely focused on money management; on the trading and equities side, UBS grew organically. It made multiple expensive hires, trying to buy in key personnel and expertise. Efforts to compete with long-standing US firms in these areas proved only partly successful, however. It is questionable whether UBS was able to hire the correct people and whether it had the management expertise to supervise its staff and manage risk. Evidence of this was forthcoming in 1998, when UBS suffered under the collapse of Long-Term Capital Management, an investment fund run using a dodgy bag of investment formulae that were once thought so sophisticated and insightful that the inventors were awarded what is popularly (but erroneously) understood as the Nobel Prize in economics. Substantial losses forced UBS into a 'reverse takeover' by SBC Warburg – another Swiss competitor, but one with a better record of managing risk.[48]

The new UBS found its significant trading and fixed-income/debt divisions run by ex-SBC personnel. Again, though, through the late 1990s and early parts of this century the business struggled to keep up with the growth and profitability of its American competitors. While UBS was fairly successful in mergers and acquisitions and equity capital markets (where balance sheet leverage and capital needs are lower), it was not able to match the Americans in fixed-income and debt markets. From 2004 onwards, unchastened by its experience with Long-Term Capital Management, UBS aggressively pursued a 'catch-up' strategy – the term 'catch-up' being used by UBS managers themselves. The aspiration was to create the world's largest wealth manager and a 'bulge-bracket' investment bank. Getting a slice of the increasingly lucrative credit and securities trading market in the United States was understood as a logical step in reaching this destination. Playing catch-up meant playing catch-all, as UBS swallowed large amounts of triple-'A'-rated positions, many of which, once unwound, were found to be contain exposures to sub-prime debt.

UBS's experience of the credit crisis is indicative of how quickly large financial institutions were caught out and how little senior management understood about the products that their employees were both designing and investing in. Even so-called experts in the field, brought in because of their market familiarity, were unable to structure the business effect-ively to compete in these products and had insufficient awareness of how their actions were exposing UBS to a massive hit (by the second-quarter results of 2008, the losses or write-downs attributed to the credit crunch amounted to US$42 billion). The entire senior management team of the investment bank were replaced, as was the chief executive officer (CEO) of the whole UBS group. The remaining managers were willing to admit *mea culpa* publicly on behalf of the bank, making rather humble state-ments about the nature of both the strategic and management errors made in recent years. Marcel Rohner, the then new CEO of the whole firm (UBS AG), was candid, attributing UBS's problems to three 'primary mistakes': (1) the bank could not 'see the forest for the trees'; (2) it cross-subsidized certain businesses; and (3) it tried to generate growth by copying the strategy and processes of the competition instead of relying on its own inner strengths and identity.

Each of these mistakes is an admission of system blindness, both internally, where fixation on the health of specific institutional subsystems (notably the investment side) meant the sacrifice of other subsystems upon whose integrity the entire bank relied, and externally, where the bank's managers were transfixed on the potential earnings from a single arena. Rohner's speech to shareholders at the April 2008 annual meeting is worth examining in detail. With regard to his view that UBS's investment banking strategy failed to 'see the forest for the trees', he reports:

Most of our colleagues reviewed transactions, hedged risks, refined models and performed analyses with the best intentions. We use laborious, comprehensive control processes to review and analyze new transactions. We have had and continue to have armies of highly trained traders and controllers who evaluate transactions on an ongoing basis and model them in numerous dimensions. I believe that we relied both consciously and implicitly on all these processes and capabilities and that we therefore no longer asked the basic questions. As painful – if not embarrassing – as this realization may be, the conclusion it suggests is all the more important. The problem was not a failure to appreciate complexity, but rather the opposite – it was a lack of simplicity and critical perspective which prevented the right questions from being asked while there was still time.[49]

Here Rohner equates complexity with 'taxonomic', as opposed to 'dynamic', complexity.[50] Taxonomic complexity follows the principle of 'algorithmic compressibility', whereby a large mass of observational statements may or may not be compressed 'into a few clearly stated propositional statements thereby enabling economy of effort, transferability, and remote control.'[51] Dynamic complexity, on the other hand, is a consequence of the essential fluidity and temporality of event-happenings in the world. In the case of UBS, Rohner seems to imply that the inability to compress all the information available into a few simple key principles or propositions was the root cause of missing 'the forest for the trees'. Rohner does not consider the inherent uncertainty associated with 'dynamic complexity', however; complexity created not so much by a lack of capacity for distilling the masses of information available and making appropriate decisions but by the perpetually shifting nature of financial investment realities, which are constantly throwing out 'unexpected forms' at random because of the essentially interactive and 'reflexive' character of the financial world. It is this widespread underestimation that has led George Soros to call for a 'new paradigm' for understanding and dealing with the financial markets[52] – one that moves us away from the still prevailing belief that financial markets tend towards equilibrium and that deviations from it are therefore essentially random, and one that openly acknowledges the essential fallibility and reflexivity of human actions.

On the subject of capital allocation, Rohner states that UBS made the mistake of 'cross-subsidizing certain businesses'. According to Rohner:

[B]ased on our organizational structure of first four and then three business units, we often said that we were not a holding company but rather a single integrated bank. Yet it was this very focus on unity which created another problem. The whole can only function when all of its parts function. And the parts can only function if they are able to flourish on their own, without any outside help, under the same conditions as the competition. In essence, one of the main causes of the problem seems paradoxical. We did not question the integrated model enough. We used the strength of our balance sheet and compelling financing options for activities which should have been more expensive to finance based on their risk. We used our surplus cash flow from the wealth management business to promote organic growth in the Investment Bank. That was where we went wrong. Logically speaking, expensive cash and scarce capital should enforce the discipline needed when engaging in high-risk activities and deciding which activities scarce resources will be allocated to. Scarcity forces us to select only those transactions which have the best risk-return profile. And this scarcity of resources is critical to successful investment banking.[53]

UBS, in the view of Rohner, was providing capital at a minimal cost to its investment banking arm – an extraordinary admission, given the higher risk involved, and one that has resulted in the bank now splitting the investment banking, asset management and private banking roles into three separate divisions. Instead of recognizing the value of the revenue earned by the private wealth management activities in particular, UBS managers called upon it as a cheap source of funds for the more conscious and strategically explicit aims set by the investment banking activities. This desire to achieve the strategy of faster growth and a higher profile in investment banking led it to an uncritical and almost wanton exploitation of the revenues generated by its more secure and established financial activities. Rohner's identification of scarcity proves telling here. UBS was characterized by a lack of wider systemic awareness, whereby the demands and concerns of one system (the investment arm) were fixed in shortened causal chains that subsumed the needs and achievements of other UBS systems in such a way as to obscure the scarcity of the resources being consumed whilst delivering only short-term, unsustainable growth.

Finally, Rohner states that 'we tried to generate growth by copying the strategy and processes of the competition instead of relying on our own inner strengths and identity'.[54] Comparison with the competition is an example of systemic awareness, yet in this case the comparison was neither critical nor reflexive. Indeed, it proceeded on the assumption that a correct etiology had been found – structured credit markets were an effective source of rent – and that the problem for UBS was in demonstrating sufficient managerial nous to deliver. From a wider systems perspective, this herd mentality is perhaps the most worrying of all the mistakes and the one that mostly closely echoes Bateson's and Scott's examples of decaying woodland resulting from one system's fixation on its own immediate needs. The supply of revenue from structured credit seemed plentiful, and any failure to join in with this financial feeding opportunity seemed almost a dereliction of strategic duty. The emergence of this opportunity, however, had reflected a wilful lack of attention to the robustness of other systems upon which the strength of credit lines relied. There was a singular, systemic myopia to the fragility of the fixed-income and debt products upon which banks such as UBS had begun increasingly to rely. The bounty was short-lived, and, once exhausted, alternative sources of revenue were themselves severely depleted as the various subsystems within the financial world increasingly found it hard to maintain homeostatic balance.

In the immediate aftermath, UBS's strategy under the chastened Rohner became one of retreat and retrenchment. The system blindness remains, however. There is an expressed need for new knowledge. Rohner laments the lack of expertise amongst senior managers, unaware of the complexity and exposure of the positions into which they were taking the bank. Undergoing this chaotic situation, the instinctive tendency was to reduce the messiness quickly to neat and recognizable pre-established categories so that new choices could be made and positive actions taken. Rohner looks for simple questions and responses, to recover the core capabilities of the bank, to try and see the forest as well as the trees and to better instil a sense of UBS identity. This strategy is characterized by a continuing impatience of and intolerance for vagueness and ambiguity.[55] Rohner's immediate response to the crisis was to reduce, hive off and contain uncertain fixed-income activities, simplify decision-making processes and clarify responsibilities. In the medium to long term, Rohner's stated strategy was to restore the dominance and pre-eminence of UBS's 'Swiss business foundation', the private wealth management that was, is and will remain 'the backbone of our activities'.[56] This 'strategic positioning', in a less 'liquid' environment, looked towards more basic, inward-looking, nationally configured banking: better to lend your own money on your own terms to people you know and can control.

In Bateson's terms, though, this retrenchment of banks such as UBS to the steadying Victorian patterns of promissory notes and sober wealth generation based on a tradition of long-standing expertise may not stop the financial system becoming something very different from what it currently is, because it is doing little to acknowledge the wider system dynamics. Initial compensating moves by other systems have had little effect. Using rights issues, existing investors were called upon to bail out banks such as UBS, and then sovereign wealth funds were tapped. These investments proved difficult and costly, thereby exposing these 'other' systems to future potential losses as their existing holdings become diluted, or as once apparently cheap and politically expedient investments in strategic commercial assets turn sour. Governments and the central banks were then called in and asked to pump-prime the lending system with secure credit facilities whilst lowering interest rates to inject more spending power into the economy. Interbank lending rates remained stubbornly high for a long period, lessening the ability of wider economic and political systems to control the fallout. Eventually governments were forced to take stakes in banks, UBS itself calling for a significant loan of capital from the public coffers to try and replace the funds that had been haemorrhaging from its private wealth division as cautious savers took their once 'safe' cash elsewhere. The financial system began to look more and more like the decaying woodland, too far gone to survive in its current guise.

Perhaps most telling for UBS strategy has been the replacement of Rohner himself, caught out as he has been (along with the bank) by allegations of abetting tax evasion in the United States. Rohner's post-crisis strategy of returning to what was presumed to be the stable core business of private wealth management has itself suffered in a wave of positive feedback. The US authorities, stung by criticism of their own regulatory prowess, have moved to shut down the lucrative sources of income that Swiss banks in particular enjoyed when advising wealthy clients how to avoid tax liability. Rohner's strategy consisted of assuming that one subsystem really was separable from any other, when in fact the nested condition of finance has become patently apparent as the feedback from localized, sub-prime lending has amplified to such an extent that the age-old system of anonymity in Swiss wealth management is under threat.[57]

Towards 'system wisdom'

What was being lost in the case of firms such as UBS during the credit crisis was what Bateson has called 'the universe of relevance'. The methodological individualists might be able to get at core structures and influences of human agency, but only by abstracting from the human sentiments, styles and traditions by which human action was enlivened. It was only by accounting for these wider systems that any statement about the world was made sensible.[58] Similarly, the bankers were able to earn money by abstracting from the face-to-face relationships of crude barter, and so, privately and singularly, pursue a strategy of short-term revenue generation, but only at the expense of others' pain – and, of course, eventually some of their own. What is lost in both cases is a sense of how claims about the world make sense only against a background of other things that remain taken for granted. Economic agents can make rational choices only against a collective and unspoken background of values whereby things are deemed good or bad. Likewise, selling debt liabilities contracts is a money earner only if it can be taken for granted that there is collateral to sustain the ensuing level of lending. This ever-expanding universe of contexts is only ever implied – we could not go about consciously referring to the context of sense without engaging in endless qualification. Then what typically happens, however, is that we become preoccupied by our clever tricks, and forget our reliance on wider contexts. No matter how independent, the purposes generated by an individual system are never self-contained but are continually influenced by the behaviour of other – largely unconscious – parts of its own system, by its own history of previous behaviours and their effects, and by its being woven into other human, social and natural systems.[59] What is known of a system and our place within it, therefore, is immanent not to some part of a system but to systems in systems, the edges of which can never be closed. For Bateson, it was our human tendency to forestall this immanence by constantly looking for final end points, for definitive assessments, for neat theories, for well-conceived and easily explicable earning opportunities that, somewhat ironically, actually created a lack of awareness.

As we have seen in our discussion of methodological individualism, this distortion is not simply one of striving to make all things conscious as such (as the logical positivists were trying to do with explanations of economic agency) but is a consequence of what Bateson calls the code, in which this knowledge creation takes place: a conceptual pinning down and classification of fixed orders.[60] The ability to articulate the resulting knowledge claims is predicated upon the premise of fixity: that only what is *fixed* within the *flow* of lived experience is given a valid ontological status. Attention is hence directed towards the stable, the present and the permanent. What flows, or are unseen, or are not apparent or do not occur are presumed the less real epiphenomena accompanying real things. This epistemological stance lends credence to the widespread belief in the idea of knowledge as an accurate and conscious representation of reality authored by a knowing individual, and that the only really secure, solid and known thing we can envisage is our self – more specifically, the thinking part of our self. We end up, therefore, with Descartes's knowledge problem of how we, sure of who we are, can be equally sure of what we observe 'outside' ourselves. This dualism feeds into a sense of our social and natural environments being mute, and somehow entirely open to our own conscious design, for it is only us, ourselves, that we can be sure of. It is from this mindset that we are then able to treat wider systems as apart from (and not a part of) our self and hence available as 'resources' to be manipulated and utilized at will for our own ends.

An alternative response, and one suggested by Bateson's work, is to recognize our wider system reliance. Only by first acknowledging that our immediate sensible life is this ambiguous, fluxing reality of contexts set in contexts – of which we are an inextricably bound and technologically savvy part – can we begin to appreciate fully that what appears formed, structured and clearly defined are nothing more than islands of conceptually stabilized economic order in a churning sea of chaos. We might call this an ecologically informed or 'relational' epistemology, in which the world is experienced not as discrete, isolatable elements but as an 'open field' of balanced systems containing the 'uncommitted potentiality for change'.[61] Bateson wants us to shift our epistemological sensibility, to apprehend life not as a problem of realizing ever more refined human purposes in inherently complex and uncertain contexts but as a shifting array of potential value of which we humans are but one expression. He calls this apprehension 'systemic wisdom': a persistent submission to the open-ended interconnectedness of things brought about by relationships of self-correcting balance with this open field. In this exposure to contexts, and the context of contexts, we embrace rather than sidetrack troublesome disturbances. This persistent submission to the open-ended interconnectedness of things brings about a self-correcting balance between Bateson's three basic elements of human systems (human beings, social institutions and the environment). Adaptive changes in one of these *relata* uncorrected by changes in the others upsets and jeopardizes the system.[62] A relational epistemology exposes individual consciousness to variables encroaching from other systems; it encourages curiosity about potential relations with these different variables; and it eschews the temptation to look to define, isolate and fix these variables, including the variable known as the human individual. The question that remains, however, is to what extent we are capable of disturbing our epistemological habits with a sufficient level of agitation to enable us to begin to recognize our immanent, relational and inherently open-ended condition; of being a system set within wider systems without end. How can we nurture such systemic wisdom?

3 Reconceptualizing agency, self-interest and purposive action

Poor fool! in whose petty estimation all things are little.
Johann von Goethe, The Sorrows of Young Werther, *Book II, 18 August*[1]

In the previous chapter we showed how methodological individualism can create paradoxical and contradictory situations because of a lack of system wisdom. From the perspective of system wisdom, agents are construed not as isolated or isolatable entities but as unique accumulations of interactions; here the agent is assumed to be a thoroughly socialized being, able to demonstrate awareness not just of his or her own conscious purpose but of wider system influences, by which his or her life might be enriched and enhanced as well as threatened. This chapter, therefore, continues with this discussion of how the dominant view of human agency becomes complicated by the inevitable presence and persistence of organized and organizing systems, into which an agent is born, lives and dies and which are not of her own making. This redirecting of attention away from individual agency towards an awareness of the relational complicity implied in everyday social practice enables us to see how the complexities of our social world may be made more explainable through recourse to the practice of everyday coping actions and interactions. As advocates of this system wisdom, we argue for what might be called a weak methodological individualism: an interactively constituted 'self' that is associated with phronesis *(practical wisdom) and with* praxis *as a self-cultivating rather than a productive activity.*

This more modest view of human agency eschews the idea of the egoistic individual acting instrumentally to achieve his or her own selfish ends. It openly acknowledges the limits of human capacities and the realization of the ideas discussed in chapter 1: that, in an inherently chaotic and complex world, the idea of controlling and managing happenings in the world through some grand pre-designed strategy and oversight is patently unworkable. Instead of interfering with the world at a general or macro level we should, rather, concentrate upon the immediate, practical situations we encounter and recognize these as the originating source of our strategic adaptability: responding to what life throws at us with a kind of flexible and knowing humility. Two consequences ensue from adopting this revised 'weak' methodological individualist stance. First, it enables us to reconsider the current widely accepted but distorted understanding of the meaning of 'self-interested' action in the capitalist enterprise: a presumed selfish and egoistically driven mode of social engagement widely regarded as the essence of social and economic exchange. Second, it enables us to posit a subtle difference between purposeful *and* purposive *actions and the forms of knowledge and understanding associated with each of these. Purposive action is action taken to alleviate ourselves from a negative situation we find ourselves in. In everyday engagements, we might act to distance ourselves from an undesirable situation we face, but this does not imply having a pre-established end goal in mind. It is a moving away from rather than a moving towards that constitutes purposive actions. Purposeful actions, on the other hand, presuppose having a desired and clearly articulated end goal that we aspire towards. It is a product of deliberate intention. Since to act strategically is to act knowledgeably, we then go on to discuss how these different ways of understanding strategic action influence the kind of knowledge animating that activity.*

In an influential and lucid article aimed squarely at embedding academic influence within strategic decision-making, Donald Hambrick and James Fredrickson suggest that too often the concept strategy is bandied about without much forethought, its meaning being whatever one wants it to mean.[2] They note a tendency amongst managers, planners and academics alike to call everything 'strategy'; a marketing strategy, a growth strategy, and so on. This lack of clear distinction in how we use the word creates confusion, because in talking of specific divisions, or activities, people lose sight of what strategy really is: intentional (conscious, deliberate), informed (internal and external scanning) and integrated (concerning the whole business) judgement on how a firm (and, interestingly, their discussion focuses upon firms rather than the more general entity of an organization) engages with its environment. They take the reader back to the Greek root, *strategos*, or 'the art of the general', suggesting that what remains distinctive about strategy is its being the art of bringing elements into a comprehensive and coherent whole. The cohering elements they identify as: arenas ("Where will the firm be active?"); vehicles ("How will the firm get there?"); differentiators ("How will customers be attracted?"); staging ("What will the speed and sequence of initiatives and moves involve?"); and, finally, economic logic ("How will profits be generated?"). Strategy describes a practice whose exponents consider and align all five elements, purposefully and with a mind for conscious investment in their pursuit and for how other firm elements (organizational structures, mission statements, operations, etc.) are sustained by and sustain them. Hambrick and

Fredrickson's conceptual identification of strategic arenas of concern creates a formalized account of what might otherwise be the disparate, complex and open-ended approach characterizing the creation and growth of a firm.

In suggesting that business strategists should recover this art of the general, Hambrick and Fredrickson are firmly within the tradition so eloquently extolled by the military strategist Carl von Clausewitz, for whom this art was a general's continual struggle to become and remain aware of all relevant influences on the battlefield. Pillowed by aristocratic trappings, Clausewitz's insights on strategy come along like large cumuli set against a clear blue sky: slowly cultivated, densely packed epigrams that appear well defined, but emerge complex. Strategy, he says, is 'the use of engagements for the object of the war'. In terms of immediate effect, 'war' underlines this definition. The Greek root is *stratēgoi,* an individual who is a mix of military commander and chief magistrate elected from the Athenian tribes to organize a consistency of manoeuvre, context and expectation in order to protect and enhance the survival of the city state. The entire character of Clausewitz, a member of the eighteenth-century Prussian elite, was marbled by military practice; war and strategy were bedfellows and trade was war by other means. Read carefully, though, and his definition becomes replete with concerns well beyond those associated with the battlefield. It begins with a verb, an upfront reference to 'use'. Though Clausewitz remains at pains to separate the daily use of force (operations and tactics) from the consideration of the possible effects of such, strategy remains itself a practice, a thoughtful one of planning. The tools, entities or materials being used are 'engagements'. These can be understood most obviously and minimally as things such as military units, terrain and weaponry held in various and changing relations; but also, more generously, to include populations, symbols, propinquity, climates and even traditions.

This widening of the possible kinds and character of engagement bleeds into the purposeful element of Clausewitz's definition, the end not being war itself but the objects of war. These objects are defined by political policies, which are in turn influenced by values, histories and economic strength, and, though often stated, these restatements carry with them the inevitability of change to which good strategy is always alive. If strategy is the handmaiden of policy, then policy remains bound by the limits of the tactical engagements being directed by strategy; there is no obvious hierarchy. The policy, for example, may be one of the containment and protection of the oil supply and the strategy one of invasion, but as the forces being used grope across the battlefields the resolve of the adversaries is discovered and the wisdom of the policy comes into question. The daily operational life slowly and imperfectly traces a line of political possibility to which strategy is inevitably beholden. Colin Gray, borrowing a phrase from T. E. Lawrence, calls this shifting, expansive view the 'whole house of strategy', in which strategists become sensitive to the many dimensions that have to be identified and managed without recourse to rigidly theorized hierarchies of influence.[3] For Gray, as for Hambrick and Fredrickson, the good strategist is he or she who has a sense of the whole, down to the potential impact of daily tactical manoeuvres. These actions might appear more prosaic than the considered deliberation of a leader, but, as we have seen in chapter 1, they can have massive effects, the collapse of Barings Bank and the pictures of tortured Iraqi prisoners from Abu Ghraib being two further cases in point.[4] Moreover, this awareness of the whole is not limited to an awareness of human influence. The geography or demography of a region can emasculate any technical advantage in asset strength, as the Soviet and now Anglo-US military forces in Afghanistan will testify, and as will managers of large oil companies facing down protests from indigenous peoples and NGOs. These dimensions can never be discounted, nor can their particular nature ever become fixed knowledge, meaning that there is no surety of strategic performance that comes about from excelling in one or other territory. Strategy, as Clausewitz understood, is always and only ever an enduring assessment and reassessment of the whole.[5]

As discussed in the last chapter, however, questions of relevance still abound because of the inevitable limits to any conceptual scheme of measurement, planning and execution that by definition tries to outline a 'whole house' of arenas, vehicles, logics, measurements and the like. So, for example, in financial arenas in which the credit liabilities are becoming too great, managers of a bank might invest in financial instruments that restore more appropriate leverage ratios. The link between these immobile entities remains logical, but presumes that managers experience reality as though it consisted of isolated entities held in changing series and viewed from a distance. This links to another aspect of the etymology of strategy: the art of projecting and directing organized movements from a stretched-out or generalized position in order for resources to be deployed most effectively. This knowledge is static and inevitably individualizing if this is all that is being considered. The managers remain observers wanting to attain a sense of homeostatic preservation. Creating derivative contracts that mimic the risky debts and then selling them on appears a sensible strategic vehicle given the assessment of the arena of credit provision, and so should enhance one's position in that arena. Selling debt frees up the loan book to attract more debt. The stretched-out position begins to get very messy, very quickly however. The contracts are imitated by others, who then bundle them into CDOs, hiding each liability in a complex package that itself might form part of a complex position with a large number of parties, none of whom actually know one another. The manager's general knowledge begins to look a little simplistic. What began life as a focused financial technology to better manage the spread of risk at one investment bank (J P Morgan) rapidly became something very different. Through slight rearrangement and repositioning they spread into the wider system as known and attractive entities the like of which banks such as UBS could not afford to ignore. In being reused, however, their form and resonance shifted; the severance of debt and obligation made possible by increasingly widespread knowledge of this package opened up apparently vast seams of interconnected credit finance.

For Bateson, to 'know' something is always to know something *as* something. The phenomenon knowledge itself, for example, can be a skill, or a mental capacity, or a sensory experience; and, used as a word, it can convey facts, a sense of certainty, an unspoken expectation, or a stubbornness of attitude; and, in all such, the action of a human system *set amidst other systems* is involved. As we discussed in the last chapter, there are always contexts of contexts of contexts. Here, how we go about knowledgeable action is inherently relational; we educate our attention within an ongoing and irreversible history of environmental influence. The bankers at J P Morgan knew the contracts imitating debt risks as a way of reducing the bank's exposure, but when the technology was copied this originating knowledge was quickly forgotten; the whole was only ever a relational, almost personal whole that could not be replicated elsewhere. The attempts to remove the technology from its context and use it more generally, in other general contexts, warped the logic, exposing its users to all manner of persistent positive feedback over which there was very limited linear control. Rather than attempt to occupy a general oversight, therefore, cases such as the credit crisis suggest that it might be more efficacious to refrain from reaching after knowledge that consciously articulates and fixes elements of a general picture. In persisting with such generalized pictures and striving to constantly fix and maintain an observed sense of identity and direction, there is always a lack as well as a presence of knowledge. The more a strategist knows about and fixes upon a theatre of operations, a box of tools or a raft of legitimating principles the less he or she is aware of the wider system effects that will inevitably upset this knowledge. The kind of knowledge that Clausewitz alludes to as being necessary for good strategy is, somewhat curiously, the kind of knowledge that reduces what Bateson calls the flexibility – 'uncommitted potentiality for change' – in the system; the result is potential pathology.[6]

Human agency revisited

The need to recognize and preserve the potential of things was also an abiding concern of Hayek's, whose work on spontaneous, emergent orders we believe takes the discipline of economics back into a tentative, murky and non-analytic world from which Mises' theory of rational choosers had tried to towel it down. Hayek understood well enough that, to follow the positivist and empiricist logic of the Vienna circle, the thorny issue of human agency had to be addressed. Like Mises and Carnap, he too speculated on the reductive reach of verifiable explanation: just what could we know with any certainty about the way human beings do and should behave when organizing their trading activity? His answer was 'Not a lot'. Unlike Mises, he was unwilling simply to assert the primacy and irreducibility of the rationally choosing human agent. The existence of such an agent had to be shown empirically, tested and mulled over. There was no excuse for not finding out whether the assumptions about human judgement were sensible ones. In this he was like Carnap, believing that empirical analysis could indeed get at the more basic phenomena in which individual agency was nested. Unlike Carnap, however, he believed that our knowledge of human agents, and the intentional conditions of these agents, was not so readily confined to an *individual's* neurophysiological condition, and that the conditioning phenomena were, in fact, deeply engrained biological, psychological and social patterns.

Unlike many economists, Hayek was schooled in biology and later undertook a foray into psychology, during which period he actually sliced and fingered our grey matter in experiments on human brains. In his book *The Sensory Order*, written mid-career when he had become professor of social and moral sciences at the University of Chicago, he suggests that the data of perception and feeling upon which the verificationists of the logical positivist school relied to substantiate knowledge claims are inherently organized phenomena.[7] At its most basic, what we see and touch establishes a neurophysiological pattern in which brain cells and outlier transmitter cells establish connections, which are then re-enforced in the wake of repeated external events. The sensory order deals with direct experience of the world, happenings that affect life chances yielding problems of control and adaptation. The criteria for what becomes useful knowledge are entirely functional, or pragmatic. As human experience progresses, and adaptive skills become more refined, Hayek observes that satisfactory accounts of the world (legitimate knowledge claims) are presented in terms of observed relationships between objects rather than simply as the objects as they appear in themselves; empirical verification is inextricably bound up with the pattern recognition structures established in our neurophysiological make-up (the personal history of connections between brain cells) and the biological, physical and social structures in which these individuals find themselves through their ongoing sensory experience.

For Hayek, therefore, human knowledge was not reducible to isolated neurophysiological events linked to isolated empirical experiences. With the increasing habituation and sophistication of the relationship between human agents and the world, the possibility of knowledge became something in addition to the functional fit of the sensory order. In recognizing things as being significant (counting things or events as of interest), human agents were not guided simply by an immediate stimulus response but by a concern with the possible relationships between things. So, whilst a table, for example, appears solid and stable in its structure (and our sensory relationship is one of functional adaptation to this directly felt quality, along with others, such as its colour), its existence can also be explained in terms of molecular attraction, a patterned condition it shares with other physical objects. Likewise, whilst a manager behaves in an analytic and responsible fashion by suggesting that his knowledge of a general situation affords access to an opportunity to earn revenue from the purchase of CDOs, we might also relate to this knowledge claim as an attempt to claim status amongst his or her peers. Here Hayek was pursuing the kind of analysis that intrigued Carnap, yet the conclusions that Hayek was reaching were distinct from the loose behaviourism that Carnap envisaged as flowing inevitably from the increasingly sophisticated sciences of human agency. The difference lay with the presence of these internal and external structures and patterned interactions, which meant that apparently similar mental structures could undergo very different experiences depending upon the history of previous connections, and that apparently similar environmental stimuli could yield different behaviours. Where some managers recognize exposure, others see only opportunity. There was no way of reducing human agency to the interaction of basic (non-reducible), generalized elements, nor was there any way of assuming that a similar logic of interaction would pertain when different people adopted similar strategies, or the same people used the same strategies in different contexts.[8]

In a recent article, Brian Loasby suggests an interesting connection between Hayek and Adam Smith.[9] Like Hayek, Smith recognized the inevitability of human influence on organized, and the organizing of, human knowledge. Smith too suggested that the impulse behind the practice of verification that so entranced the logical positivists was that human agents were beings who enjoy order, and who, when confronted with disconcerting phenomena, look to restore order, if necessary by the generation of new forms by which a sense of repose (and satisfaction in the prospect of such) might be achieved. The assumptions being made by Hayek and Smith here are not about rational choice but a far more basic, almost ineffable, hankering after patterns. Because we are pattern-searching and pattern-recognizing beings, when orthodox orders become twisted and opaque because of some upsetting experience we hunt after some kind of annulment, or even new order. This presupposes, however, that we have first secured a basic, functional existence; that our sensory order is sufficiently stable (we are able to operate in the world to meet basic requirements) to provide the cognitive space for such speculation. Both Smith and Hayek are alive to how the ideas of conjecture that we use to realize and sustain a sense of order, those reifications criticized by Whitehead, have a palliative function, and so can quickly become sedatives if they are accepted as descriptions of the world rather than as arbitrary insertions into that world. The general knowledge claims associated with strategy are one such insertion. They invoke theories about phenomena that convey a sense of calm because they act as unassailable beginnings from which a series of isolated events reach out in causally connected chains of influence. As Loasby comments, what for Smith was of interest here was the sense of convenience and utility in coming to assume habitually the veracity of the theory or the perspicuity of an overview, along with the dangers associated with this uncritical acceptance.

Much in the way of economics is based on this predilection for the identification and management of fixed identities in confined territories. The basis of any economy, it seems, is isolated traders loosely tied through weak market relations, and the fact that, with a growing familiarity with the imperfections and failures of these relations, organized modes of contract and governance are used as compensating structures to better fix and predict subsequent relations. Strategy is a mature, insightful expression of this familiarity. Economic agents such as managers understand the rationale behind this orchestration of positions because they are rational choosers set amidst other rational choosers; they have a sense of what is efficient and can learn the effective means for realizing states of affairs governed by the dictates of such efficiency. This is the idea that Mises bought into. An economy, a firm's place within an economy and a manager's place within a firm can all be investigated empirically and their functioning reduced to ever more general, elemental components, of which the rational chooser and optimizer gathered with like-minded others is the originating source. As a theory it is plausible, but as a theory it carries limits. As our reading of Bateson and the example of the current credit crisis have suggested, the uncertainties and complexities of life are not containable in the way that the theory or the overview suppose, even with *ceteris paribus* conditions in place; the choice sets, judgements, outlined positions, technology and potential outcomes presented as being logical are riven with so many empirical exceptions that theorists have to repress, discount or ignore the open-ended nature of them in order to sustain or restore a sense of order.

We have suggested that, for Bateson and Hayek (casting us back to Smith and Bastiat), recognition of this open-ended contextual environment means that it is what is unsaid and unseen that is of interest. If everything was known or knowable (if strategy really did map out the aims and actions by which we can realize a determined condition and if economic science really did predict the behaviours of trading agents) then human life would be entirely mechanical, our actions simply faint and distant reverberations of an originating cause. The general knowledge and the theory cannot reach into what is as yet unseen and unsaid, and so any conception of how the world is has to be aware of its limits, content to recognize that the utility of outcomes realized in any given situation is really understood only by those nested in it, and that being so nested these understandings are never so uniform as to be entirely predictable, or even similar over time. Hayek argues that even at our most obviously individual, at the level of our own brain, the way it is ordered is inextricably bound of with the manner in which our relations with other systems are ordered, meaning that when we encounter puzzles, upsets, problems and the like in our lives we can resort to patterned responses that we have learnt through familiarity, imitation, trial and error, experiment, and so on. Knowledge is not determined in advance of our experience; things of strategic and economic relevance are not waiting to be discovered, but are invented as we go. Hence, what counts as knowledge is governed by the systems of enquiry in use: the manner in which we affirm phenomena through a sense of expectancy, rather than a sense of having revealed something that existed anterior to our claim.

True and false individualism

Here we begin to approach a view of the human agent as inextricably embedded amidst a plethora of social practices and conventions, all of which are gathering and divesting themselves of organized and organizing structures, as well as organized and organizing knowledge of such structures. The agent as such becomes less a clearly circumscribed entity capable of overseeing a general condition than an evolving locus of relationships. This is what prompted Hayek to identify a crucial difference between the 'false' individualism associated with the Cartesian school of thought and a 'true' individualism associated with the Scottish Enlightenment thinkers. In the latter case, there is an acute awareness of the 'limitations of the individual mind which induces an attitude of humility toward the impersonal and anonymous social processes by which individuals help to create things greater than they know', such things being greater than individual minds in that they induce an internalized readiness to submit to social processes 'which nobody has designed and the reasons for which nobody may understand'.[10] False individualism, on the other hand, is a product of an 'exaggerated belief in the powers of individual reason and of a consequent contempt for anything which has not been consciously designed by it'.[11] Hayek identifies the source of this exaggerated form of individualism, which is associated with many French thinkers, to Descartes' *Discourse on Method*, in which he proposed the deliberate design of social institutions by 'some wise legislator' as the superior founding basis for the progress and development of society.[12]

In making this stark contrast between two forms of individualism, Hayek intends us to understand that the form of 'strong' individualism associated with the Cartesian school is not what thinkers such as Adam Smith and himself have in mind when developing theories of social and economic action.

What, then, are the essential characteristics of true individualism? ... it is primarily a *theory* of society, an attempt to understand the forces which determine the social life of man... This fact should by itself be sufficient to refute the silliest of the common misunderstanding: the belief that individualism postulates...the existence of isolated or self-contained individuals, instead of starting from men whose nature and character is determined by their existence in society. ....there is no other way toward an understanding of social phenomena but through our understanding of individual actions directed toward other people and guided by their expectation... It is the contention that, by tracing the combined effects of individual actions, we discover that many of the institutions on which human achievements rest have arisen and are functioning without a designing and directing mind, that as Adam Ferguson expressed it, "nations stumble upon establishment, which are indeed the result of human action but not the result of human design" and that the spontaneous collaboration ... often creates things which are greater than their individual minds can comprehend.[13]

In such an environment, the capacity to gain perspective upon, know about and try and restore order is one of resilience and flexibility, as multiple conjectures are posed, worked at, supplemented, rejected and used in a spirit of cooperative discovery that is always operating with dispersed and incomplete knowledge.

What we find with Hayek is a richer and more nuanced form of methodological individualism; a 'weaker' version that ennobles human agents by recognizing how their identity is established through relational connections rather than rationally located perspectives and isolation. Hayek's individual agent is not an isolated entity to which things happen but the continually produced upshot of submission to sensory, physical and social orders with which he or she is complicit, but over which there is little of the kind of generalizing control envisaged by strategy thinkers. In such a condition, the agent is necessarily immersed and 'in amongst' kin in order to gain identity and to function effectively. A sense of self is constituted through social engagements and practices and his or her 'interests' are thus uncompromisingly socially shaped.

Hayek goes on to argue that it is the rationalistic 'pseudo-individualism' associated with the Cartesian school that has been instrumental in propagating the widely held idea of selfish self-interest as the founding basis for capitalism and economic exchange. He writes:

As the belief that individualism approves and encourages human selfishness is one of the reasons why so many people dislike it, and as the confusion which exists in this respect is caused by a real intellectual difficulty, we must carefully examine the meaning of the assumptions it makes.[14]

To be sure, the great Scottish Enlightenment thinkers did use terms such as 'self-love' or even 'selfish interests' in their treatises, but by these terms they were referring more to a moral attitude that was thought to be widely prevalent during that period. As we hinted at in chapter 1, they did not mean 'egotism in the narrow sense of concern with only the immediate needs of one's proper person. The "self" for which alone people were supposed to care, did as a matter of fact include their family and friends.'[15] Furthermore, by saying that people are 'guided by *their* interests and desires, this will at once be misunderstood or distorted into the false contention that they are...exclusively guided by their personal needs or selfish interests', while what is really meant is that 'they ought to be allowed to strive for whatever *they* think desirable', because the only way we can find out what is best for each individual is 'through a social process in which everybody is allowed to try and see what he can do'.[16]

If Hayek is right, the Scottish Enlightenment thinkers such as Adam Smith, David Hume and Adam Ferguson had a very different idea of what self-interest involved. To begin to resurrect this more nuanced appreciation of 'self-interest' and reappraise its consequences for our understanding of wealth-creating activity, we might begin by noting the etymological origins of the word 'interest'. In *What Is Called Thinking?*, the German philosopher Martin Heidegger makes an 'interesting' comment on how the meaning of the word 'interest' has been dramatically transformed over the centuries. Heidegger observes that nowadays the term 'interest' is used to denote what is distinctive, separate and worthy of special attention. Self-interest is the extension of this preoccupation with what is singular to the needs of one's own person; it is my need, my goal, my will that is of interest to me. For Heidegger, this use has been twisted out of the word's etymological roots: 'Interest, *interesse*, means to be among and in the midst of things, or to be at the centre of a thing and to stay with it.'[17] Here any individual distinctiveness and significance is illuminated by a covey of influences from whose often hidden circulation our sense of who and what we are emerges. This sense of self and self-interest, then, is not entirely within our grasp. We do not live our lives as more or less successful subjugators of a subjected, external environment. There is no sense in our understanding ourselves as originators or initiators if by these actions we mean mental start points configured by terms such as 'our individual will', or 'intention'. To act with originality and creativity is to excite the multiplicity of forces we encounter in such a way that what was once a random intersection of lives and influences achieves a sense of mutual recognition and balance in which opposites come into some kind of accord, but still as opposites. *Self-interest is not the competitive assertion of interests at the inevitable expense of others but an opening up of oneself to things and events that are different, and that therefore resonate with unrealized potential.*

Writing in an early edition of the *Harvard Business Review*, Alfred North Whitehead laments the growing tendency of the modern age to ignore this view of individuality and instead to equate individuality with the ability to sate one's desire for change. Whitehead finds that, in the past, the United States in particular was organized individualistically in ways that resonate with Heidegger's idea of *interesse*. Politically there were independent states, economically there was a market economy and religiously there were any number of sects. Whitehead nonetheless identifies these as collective expressions of self-selection, a conscious striving of settlers to rid themselves of old European habits through the mutual expression of belonging amid divergent and multiple values. With the rise of commercialization and mechanization, and accompanying changes in scales of control, however, modern conceptions of individuality have been confined by economic grand theories, in which, paradoxically, there is no room for difference:

The divergent urges of different individual temperaments can no longer find their various satisfactions in serious activities. There only remain ironbound conditions of employment and trivial amusements for leisure.[18]

The individual is no longer an opening up within life but something taken from the world and judged in isolation. As such, interests are severed from what gives them life; they are isolated. What Whitehead calls 'the vagrancy and delight of personal idiosyncrasy' is codified and typified by the force-feeding of isolating theories of what an individual is and can amount to, and in such isolation it can only wither.

It is perhaps an indication of such withering that we find ourselves mired in pathological situations such as the credit crisis. This, we suggest, has arisen at least in part because of a presumption that we can take a knowledgeable, generalized overview of the world and assume the represented state of affairs to be accurate and remain relevant. Strategists had a picture of fertile arenas of revenue-earning activity and understood the vehicles in which one could operate in that activity as well as the acquisitive financial logic by which that activity was judged to be valuable by self-interested individuals. The ensuing generalized image proved so enticing that others uncritically bought in, without even attempting a strategic analysis of their own. The result was rapid short-term gain and just as rapid widespread loss. Reading Hayek, Whitehead and Heidegger suggests that we restore to self-interest a sense of an individual being 'in the midst of' things and having his or her involvement, concern and awareness thereby 'awakened', rather than being resolved into a particular (structured) or universal (mental or physiological) condition. *Interest therefore reflects an empathetic urge to be in sympathy with and in the midst of significant others in one's social and economic relationships.* This seems to be more in keeping with the original sense of the term 'self-interest' understood by the Scottish Enlightenment thinkers, as Hayek notes. It does not mean, as commonly understood, to be selfishly and egoistically driven by one's own observed representation of organized engagement and the prospects for personal gain, but is one that reflects a concerned awareness of one's responsible complicity with the furtherance of prevailing social systems.

It is perhaps not a coincidence, therefore, that Adam Smith chose the metaphor of the hand rather than the brain, or mind, or will, to describe the collective emergence of self-sustaining patterns of social and economic activity through 'self-interested' activities. In chapter 1 we spoke of the metaphor of 'invisibility' being used to convey how the common mutual sympathy for the interests pursued by each other's trading projects typically went unseen. Here we pick up on the other half of the metaphor. We realize it is 'just' a metaphor, as used by Smith to describe the activities of a specific class of traders – merchants – in a particular kind of activity – investing capital. We remain struck, however, by its potential, its own reality, grown out of Smith's original usage. The hand is something that reaches out to touch other things, or to declare publicly and materially the presence of something, including oneself. Smith talked of our basic, pre-commercial sense of bargaining as one of mutual acknowledgement; self-love works only in its appeal to the self-love of others; in *The Wealth of Nations* Smith talked of us addressing ourselves *to* the self-love of the butcher, brewer and baker, rather than simply articulating our own selfish wants. To imagine ourselves outside this basic reciprocity, to really believe we are isolated, selfish 'islands', is something that Deirdre McCloskey calls 'an absurd mental experiment' designed by academics to explain how society is ordered, but in fact explaining nothing.[19] In everyday, basic life we find ourselves thrown into a cooperative state, and it is *out of* this rough condition that the kind of game-theory abstractions found in Hobbes' state of nature and repeated by modern economists try to remove us. We become imprisoned by abstractions of isolated individuals bargaining as pre-social reasoners, forgetting all the while the dense weave of accepted tradition that affords this activity its status as meaningful activity. We are only ever isolated in the company of others.

If this abstraction remained the concern of a few absurdist experimenters then little harm would come of it, but its arresting simplicity and logic has left a residue on much of what we now identify as legitimate trading activity. As the business academic Sumantra Ghoshal laments, these gloomy theories of self-interested 'man' are the ones that are accepted unquestioningly in many business schools and taught to students, who are then encouraged to regard the world of business as a kind of well-mannered dogfight, and business success as being, or being associated with, top dog.[20] Who, asked Adam Smith, ever saw a dog make a fair and deliberate exchange of one bone for another? This is a question that has fallen soundlessly as the shrill bleat of *evaluating maximizers* shout down any lingering expressions of mutual sympathy.

Smith had no truck with such fanciful and socially deleterious abstraction. His use of the hand metaphor takes us back into our natural state of reciprocity, in which we are disposed to acknowledge the existence of otherness and act accordingly. An outreaching hand can point at things, ostensively defining what exists outside the pointing body. It can also acknowledge others directly through handshakes, waves, salutes and the like, bidding them closer, or farewell, or in signalling disgust or merely frustration. More basically still, it affords us direct, unmediated awareness of the world through the unbounded sensation of touch, it is what affords us a grip upon our world and it is also our means of letting go, of relinquishing touch and control over other things. The hand carries with it a visceral, physiological quality; its presence is direct, feeling, grasping, foraying, reaching out into the world before we actually know or analyse our relationship with it. The hand extends our bodily contact with the world and allows us to 'feel' our way through the world. Through the hand the world becomes something we immerse ourselves in, rather than something we detach ourselves from and cognitively represent. It becomes something close, intimate and familiar that we work with through repeated experimentation. Richard Sennett talks of the hand as forming the basis for attaining a refined state of awareness of events and happenings in the world.[21] Such acute awareness and knowing is predicated not on generalized representations of static states but on a tacit sensitivity to how things are, and how our own expectations are woven into this everyday state with such refinement that when we engage with the world we do so from expectation. Our actions are oriented to an expected future of how things are; we take the next step knowing that we will find a sure footing rather than be engulfed by blackness.

What we now proceed to examine is how this kind of knowledge may be conceptualized and contrasted with the more formal, representational form of knowledge associated with strategy. This will enable us to appreciate and reconceptualize the knowing/acting agent as a relationally constituted, dispositionally inclined social being equipped with a *purposiveness* of action, rather than as a *purposefulness*-goal-oriented individual engaging in affairs of the world.

Forms of knowledge: *episteme*, *technē* and *phronesis*

In both the *Nicomachean Ethics*[22] (NE) and *Eudemian Ethics* (EE), Aristotle goes to great lengths to differentiate between three different forms of knowledge, which he calls *episteme*, *technē* and *phronesis*. *Technē* and *phronesis* are two different modes of what might be called practical, as distinct from theoretical, knowledge (*episteme*). *Episteme* refers to abstract, generalizable knowledge; it is scientific, explicit, universal knowledge that can be 'written, recorded, validated and protected'.[23] *Technē*, on the other hand, alludes to technical expertise; precise, codified technical instruction often expressed through quantitative measures and rigid procedures.[24] *Episteme* came to be construed as theoretical knowledge that, by definition, did not have to have any practical import. Theoretical knowledge is self-sufficient, 'loved for its own sake; for nothing arises from it apart from the contemplating' (NE, 1177b1–4). Through theoretical understanding we are made receptive to ultimate being and hence to an eternal order and harmony that is beyond our own powers of construction. In several other works Aristotle clearly elevates theoretical over practical knowledge, and in teasing out this almost moral severance a further distinction emerges between 'productive' knowledge and 'practical' knowledge/wisdom. This is where the difference between techne and phronesis becomes important for our consideration.

This difference is discussed at length in Joseph Dunne's Back to the Rough Ground,[25] in which he takes as his central concern Aristotle's distinction between making something and action. For Aristotle, 'making and acting are different' (NE, 1140b1–4). While 'making has an end other than itself, action cannot for good action itself is its end' (NE, 1139b1–3). In aiming for an end other than itself, making conforms to a purposeful and instrumental means–ends framework in which tools and materials are viewed as simply means and resources employed by the maker to bring about a predefined end. Moreover, the knowledge associated with this making (poiētikē), or orientation to fabrication, Aristotle calls techne. Techne is a hexis meta logou poiétiké: a 'reasoned state of capacity to make' that is so inextricably linked to the act of fabricating objects and situations that the source of these outcomes lies in the producer and not in the product itself. In other words, techne is a form of productive knowledge (poiēsis) that produces outcomes that, once produced, have a life of their own and are separable and identifiable from the producer himself. It is purposeful activity that is designed 'to bring about, and which terminates in, a product or outcome that is separable from it and provides it with an end or telos'.[26] Techne is the kind of knowledge an expert, competent individual, a craftsman or an appointed strategist possesses. It is the source of purposeful change, involving deliberate and purposeful intervention into the flux and flow of the natural world, shaping it and making it conform to human desires.

Action, in contrast, is its own end. It produces no tangible external outcomes other than helping to crystallize the actor's own individuality, identity and aspirations. The absence of disposable materials and substantial outcomes makes such non-productive action, or praxis, more conceptually elusive than poiesis. Whereas, in the latter activity of making, the producer can ultimately stand outside his materials and survey it from a detached viewpoint, in praxis the agent is constituted by the very actions that disclose him both to himself and to others as the person he is. He can never

possess an idea of himself in the way that the craftsman possesses the form of his product; rather than his having any definite "what" as the blueprint for his actions or his life, he becomes and discovers "who" he is through these actions. And the medium for this becoming through action is not one over which he is ever sovereign master; it is, rather, a network of other people who are also agents and with whom he is bound up in relationships of interdependency.[27]

This kind of acting as a disclosing activity rather than purposeful production is what Dunne argues Aristotle associates with *phronesis*. *Phronesis* 'characterizes a person who knows how to live well. It is acquired and deployed not in the making of any product separated from oneself but rather in one's actions with one's fellows.' *Phronesis* is associated not with *poeisis* but with *praxis*. By *praxis* we mean the 'conduct of one's life and affairs primarily as a citizen of the *polis*; it is activity which may leave no separately identifiable outcome behind it and whose end, therefore, is realized in the very doing of the activity itself'.[28] *Phronesis* arises from within the whole striving that a person *is*. It comes into its own in situations that draw the self into action, to the extent that genuine *praxis* involves 'absorbed action – action as an ineluctable movement that a person can never step out of. . . Each new act arises within the terrestrial magnetism of our past acts, which lie sedimented in our habits. . . Whatever issues from it, by way of action, already has the full weight of ourselves behind it.'[29] Whilst *poiēsis* produces results or outcomes that are clearly separable from the producer, *praxis* is inseparable from the kind of person the actor has become: it is a manner or style of conducting him-/herself. Translated into the terms of our exploration into strategy, this would mean that designed strategy is associated with *technē* and *poiēsis*: it is the visible end product of deliberate and productive action. On the other hand, *phronesis* and *praxis* are non-instrumental forms of action: action that unwittingly produces a coherent strategy through merely striving to cultivate oneself without any regard for a tangible output.

It turns out, therefore, that *phronesis* is not so much a form of knowledge as a 'resourcefulness of mind that is called into play in, and responds uniquely to, the situation'.[30] In *praxis*, one has no separating power, so to speak. Instead, one is 'fully engaged and whatever mistakes one makes must be put down to oneself; they cannot be ascribed to a lack of skill'.[31] *Phronesis* is not a consciously acquired ability; it arises in situations in which the self is drawn into action to realize itself.[32] We can therefore conclude from Dunne's careful examination that the activity of making (*poiēsis*) is to be importantly distinguished from *praxis* as the act of self-cultivation through sustained and immersed action. Furthermore, it is the purposeful and deliberate activity of producing outcomes that draws upon the form of instrumentally engaged knowledge that is called *technē*. *Praxis*, on the other hand, describes a form of personal engagement in which the self is totally immersed in the activity, of which it forms a part. Such action is not linked to the deliberate seeking of any intended outcome. This does not imply, however, that no great good can come from such *phronetic* actions. Indeed, it is precisely this non-deliberate form of acting that indirectly and unintentionally produces progressive and lasting outcomes.[33]

In summary, two main characteristics distinguish *phronesis* (and *praxis*) from *technē* (and *poiēsis*): first, its inseparability from self-cultivation and its non-instrumental character; and, second, 'its mediation of the universal and the particular in a way that puts a premium on experience and perceptiveness rather than on formulated knowledge'.[34]

From purposeful to purposive action

We can now begin to see that, associated with a 'weakened' understanding of methodological individualism, the 'self' can no longer be construed as a bounded, autonomous and detached entity acting selfishly, and relying on a deliberate, purposeful and productive form of action to attain her desired ends. In acting in 'self-interest', it is not meant that little consideration is given to the needs of significant others, but, as Hayek has shown, it is to acknowledge the inevitable influence of anonymous social processes upon choices, judgements and expectations, meaning that the agent is in fact *indivisible* from his or her social context. Nor can we presume that he or she has always the capacity to stand outside circumstances to survey, mentally represent and design purposeful actions prior to actually intervening with these circumstances. To be sure, there are moments when such detached apprehension and deliberate evaluation may appear possible. By and large, however, agents act from within their own absorbed circumstances without necessarily knowing all the eventual ramifications and consequences that will ensue from such actions.

Nevertheless, this lack of predetermination does not lead to chaos and disorder. On the contrary, such spontaneous actions may still display a degree of coherence and consistency despite this lack of a consciously coordinated plan of action, because of a largely unconscious cultural conditioning and the resultant habitus it perpetuates. It is the endless questioning and analysis of these habits, this Western tendency always to want to make the unknown known, that can lead to disorder.[35] As the pragmatist William James has remarked, we are all cast under the softening pall of habits, some of which are broader than others, and these habits can be very useful. Pity the man, says James,

> in whom nothing is habitual but indecision, and for whom the lighting of every cigar, the drinking of every cup, the time of rising and going to bed every day, and the beginning of every bit of work, are subjects of express volitional deliberation.[36]

Indeed, it is by nurturing such habitual, thoughtless activity in our daily lives that we afford ourselves opportunities to take an interest in how we lead our lives in relation to orthodox ideas, and how such lives might be led differently. The dauntless John Ruskin calls it overcoming the 'constancy of small emotions'[37] – someone who refuses to subject his or her life to constant analysis and instead concentrate on the exercise of the imagination in relation to the ideas that govern our conduct and identity. Concern with whether one's appearance follows the minutiae of the latest fashion, or whether transport systems operate strictly to schedule or that foodstuffs are sufficiently fresh are concerns that detract from the recognition of the hold that orthodox ideas have over us and that we typically invoke without thought. As a consequence of this habitual overcoming, there may be a detectable *purposiveness* in our actions without there necessarily being a conscious, explicit and *purposeful* plan of action. This is a crucial distinction, which relates inextricably to our prior discussion of *phronesis/praxis* and *technē/poiēsis* and which constitutes a central claim in our argument that strategy may emerge unintentionally and without any prior design.

Purposive action is *phronetic* action emanating from the internalized tendencies and dispositions of an individual as a thoroughly engaged being; a modus operandi acquired through the process of socialization and maturation. In a very real sense, therefore, in acting purposively one cannot help doing what one does in the way one does it, since doing otherwise runs contrary to our cultivated tendencies and hence creates a dissonance that threatens the very fabric of our identity and selfhood. Purposive action constitutes the kind of *praxis* associated with *phronesis* that realizes itself 'only in situations that draw the self into action'.[38] In such purposive action there is no arbitrary discretion that can be exercised by some detached transcendent self. Instead, such *praxis* implies 'an ineluctable movement that a person can never step out of', meaning 'one is irretrievably implicated by one's actions and any mistakes one makes must be put down, not to a lack of skill, not to wrong choices or intentions, but to a flaw in oneself and one's individuality'.[39] In the case of *purposeful* action, however, it is possible to distinguish between one's real state and the behaviour that one shows such that the distinction between what one *is* and what one *does* can be clearly made. In evaluating one's achievements, therefore, one may separate the accomplishments from one's own individuality. No such distinction is possible in the case of purposive action, which is *praxis*-oriented and which relies on *phronesis* as the basis of action.

The philosopher Immanuel Kant took up this distinction between 'purposeful' and 'purposive' action in his *Critique of Pure Reason*. Purposive action, for him, expresses a nature and a quality with no purpose other than its own self-expression. It is 'purposiveness without purpose'.[40] Summarizing this Kantian distinction, Ernst Cassirer writes: 'A purposive creation has its centre of gravity in itself; one that is goal-oriented (i.e., purposeful) has its centre external to itself; the worth of one resides in being, that of the other in its results.'[41] It is not difficult to see that Kant and Cassirer are struggling with a similar distinction to the one that Aristotle makes between *phronesis/praxis* and *technē/poiēsis*. Each of these issues from two fundamentally separate orientations and dispositions, one inextricably linked to *purposiveness*, the other to *purposefulness*. Thus, in *purposeful* activities, there is conscious deliberation and planning involved and cognitive representation is presupposed. The outputs of such purposefulness are tangible products: an automobile fabricated, a mortgage approved, or even a strategic plan realized and articulated. In *purposive* acts, however, there is no predefined 'endpurpose' in mind. Action emanates spontaneously from the internalized disposition of the individual; it is an act of disclosure more than an act of production. As Dunne has phrased it so beautifully, each such *purposive* act 'arises within the terrestrial magnetism of our past acts, which lie sedimented in our habits... Whatever issues from it, by way of action, already has the full weight of ourselves behind it.'[42] Purposive acts issue from an internalized modus operandi – so much so that we do not have full and conscious control over what we do. Our acts of strategizing – our *praxis*, in this respect – exemplify the essence of who we are more than what we are deliberately intending them to do. In many ways we cannot help doing what we do, and doing otherwise is, effectively, almost unthinkable, because it would violate our own sense of self. Now, then, it becomes possible to see that there may indeed be a certain *purposiveness* in the individual actions taken in spontaneous ordering, but not necessarily an overall deliberate *purposefulness* or overarching explicit plan guiding and steering such actions.

This distinction, between what Hubert Dreyfus calls a more modest 'absorbed *purposive* intentionality' and the more deliberate, detached and *purposeful* intention generally assumed to explain human agency and behaviour, is central to the argument being made here, for it allows us to recognize the possibility of the emergence of social order, patterned regularity and hence predictability without necessarily having recourse to some foundational individual being programmed with an unchanging set of physiological and mental procedures.[43] In other words, local absorbed purposive actions may often give rise unexpectedly to more systemic outcomes that were never intended on the part of the actors themselves. A weakened methodological individualism that acknowledges the socially constituted nature of human agency, and that revises our understanding of self-interested action along the lines of an embedded concern for being 'amongst' significant others, begins to offer us an opportunity for seeing that, by being thoroughly immersed in the ongoing activity of self-cultivation through action, we unwittingly help to create successful strategic outcomes for ourselves and our wider community that are often beyond our own immediate concerns and preoccupations.

4   The 'practice turn' in strategy research

> The *habitus*, a product of history, produces individual and collective practices... It ensures the active presence of past experiences, which, deposited in each organism..., tend to guarantee the 'correctness' of practices and their constancy over time.
>
> *Pierre Bourdieu*, The Logic of Practice, *p. 54*

We argued in the last chapter that the uncertainties and complexities of life as are experienced by strategic actors are not containable in the way that economic theory and strategy design theory suppose. Even with ceteris paribus *conditions in place, the choice sets, judgements and outcomes presented as being logical for the individual rational human agent or collective are riven with empirical exceptions, unseen ecological influences and communally felt limitations. Any theoretical understanding entails recognition of how we repress, discount or ignore elements of experience in order to attain, sustain or restore a sense of coherence. The distinctions we made between strong and weak individualism, between* technē *and* phronesis, *and between purposeful and purposive action push us towards recognizing that acting strategically is as much an instinctual, habitual and unthought response to experience as it is a deliberate, planned effort. In understanding economic activities such as trade and entities such as markets and prices, therefore, we ought to recognize them as socially organized, complex and open-ended institutional facts. Within such an environment, strategic action is not about an observer gathering information concerning an external environment in order to manage resources so as to occupy an advantageous position (a niche market, a rare capability, a competitive opportunity) but about attaining and sustaining a set of organized relationships nested within wider systems in order to experience the possibility of doing things differently and, potentially, better.*

Thus, whilst economists such as Ludwig von Mises had provocative and useful ideas about human agency, prices and the like, they were predicated upon what could be said either analytically or observationally. Current research on strategy seems to us to be in a similar state to that which preoccupied Mises. Both are characterized by the Procrustean influence of the Vienna Circle, which always urged upon its exponents a desire to locate, fix and classify things and situations so as to distinguish verified fact from passing fancy. It is this tendency in strategy research that we begin to investigate in this chapter. We then move on to show how the practice turn in social theory offers an alternative way of understanding strategy-in-practice in terms that are more compatible with a weakened notion of human agency and with the kind of non-deliberate purposive action that we have claimed is associated with undesigned strategy.

Henri Bergson and intuition

In a lecture entitled 'The perception of change' given in May 1911 at the University of Oxford, the French philosopher Henri Bergson – a contemporary of Mises – set out what he thought the implications were of our accepting the historically laden, dispositionally enacted and socially comprised nature of the human world. He began by reflecting on how it was that we fell readily into the habit of thinking ourselves as detached from the world we occupy, of how we coach ourselves in our explaining and managing activities to move from purposive to purposeful framing. As we noted in the last chapter, as biological entities our sensations and perceptions are not all seeing and feeling; we cannot keep pace or proximity with all possible sense data, and yet we have the rational capacity to appreciate analytically this lack of empirical presence. In response to this sense of lack we reach out for an intelligible, supra-sensible world of ideas and develop associated methods of abstraction, generalization and reasoning. Bergson calls this – in suitably supra-sensible language – the 'percept' (what we experience) giving way to the 'concept' (how we represent what we experience). This giving way is what is undergone by Whitehead's unfortunate man, who has to analyse his actions constantly. For Bergson, it is overseen by what he calls our intellect: the human capacity to speculate and decide upon what needs to be done to realize a desired result, and, more generally, to notice, memorize and classify the conditions under which certain phenomena pertain. We arrange, separate and move things that come to us through our perception in order to reach after more general conditions. The role of the intellect is to link sensations and perceptions to create knowledge by analysing, reconstructing and so completing a reality that we only ever empirically experience incompletely. The problem is that, in using the intellect to order and unify our sense data, we use our own standards and preoccupations to emphasize what is common and universal in different things (including amongst ourselves) rather than examine their unique qualities and what they might become. The use of the intellect is itself a habit, one that Bergson reminds us tends to blinker our perception of things. Far from making things more apparent by converting the unseen into the seen, the intellect marginalizes a host of experiences that do not fit well into established categories; and, in bracketing off certain sense data unthinkingly, advocates of the intellect come to regard alternative modes of human understanding as somehow inadequate, or even as dangerous challenges.

Bergson, like Bateson and Whitehead, accepts that we need to discount much of what we do and might experience in order simply to get ahead with living in the present; that to walk from one place to another we must discount lines of flight that might lead anywhere else. It is entirely pragmatic that we use our intellect to focus on what is of use to us rather than just on what exists. We tend therefore not to look at objects other than having first classified them as objects of a certain type. We break up experience into states (conjunctions of the subject and object) so as to act upon things. What Bergson wants to do, however, is to make seen our unseen reliance on the intellect and so get us to recognize how our tendency always to break things down and analyse their parts hides from us the reality of life itself, which is very unlike the life of things or objects presented as facts.

Our intellectually trained perception separates our experience with relatively immobile figures, objects and meanings. Mises' intellect suggests an isolated economic chooser, Carnap's an economic evaluator himself composed of behavioural impulses. Recalling our earlier discussion of Hayek and Smith, Bergson is expressing an equivocal relationship with these theoretical ideas of the intellect. What is important about intellectual ideas is their ability to recover order; they help arrest our feelings of unrest and lack, but they are in no way true because of that, and, should we come to believe them as true above all other ways of thinking about the world, much mischief follows. In understanding activities such as trade and business, then, we ought first to recognize their inherently systemic nature of which ideas (such as rational calculation) are an integral structure. This goes back to Loasby's point about the entities we identify when doing business – such as markets, prices and consumers – already being highly organized, albeit in complex and open-ended ways. The same goes for the ideas that we often invoke to represent and explain these entities. Take the idea of rational evaluation. This is a tactically helpful way of organizing (identifying choice sets and ranking the options in terms of their desirability), but, as our brief discussion of Shackle in chapter 1 suggested, this tactic of using probabilistic reasoning is part of the activity of doing business; it does not explain it. Indeed, it is a subservient part, the use of intellectual methods to distinguish possibilities that are then evaluated according to judgements on their desirability. Moreover, in elevating such ideas to the status of explanation there is a tendency to have them govern the activity they explain. This singular logic then restricts the activity because it curtails what we recognize as significant, or of interest and value when acting. Hence Sumantra Ghoshal's comments about the bad effects of bad theories of 'man' on management practice. Our perception of economic trade is restricted to its being the selfish pursuit of measured value, most properly conducted free from emotion and best left unfettered by other conflicting activities. A neutral, algorithmic idea of trade is useful, but it is also held taut by a logic that discounts phenomena that cannot be confined by financially represented economizing logic. If it does not fit into the rubric of a cost – benefit analyser it might as well not exist.

This was Hayek's primary objection to his one-time teacher Mises. Whilst Mises' logically positive ideas about agency and prices and the like were provocative and useful, they were too confining. The resultant representations (pictures or models of separated entities held in patterns) are continually being put under strain by the constant succession of exceptions and alternative hypotheses, imagined or actual. Experience seems to be constantly upsetting our attempts at fixing reality, and we continually look to reapply our intellect against our adversary: reality. The fixation of strategy analysts on revenue maximization, for example, does little to afford us a sense of why and how the associated heuristics or motivations arise, manifest themselves, dissipate across contexts and, over time, change. In fact, many decisions by strategy practitioners actively defy the presumptions behind a rationalized theory of revenue-maximizing behaviour: entrepreneurs will continue to trade in spite of the knowledge that they can earn more by simply selling up; corporate management teams sanction expenditure in environmental and social projects irrespective of any cost–benefit analysis. The intellect alone is inadequate to penetrate such phenomena, because it operates on a flattened-out, apprehended territory governed by a habit of rational oversight that looks to identify similarities and differences between cases.

Duration, process and creativity

Bergson did not deny the validity of intellectual explanation; clearly, the conceptual reduction of experience into objects such as business events is useful for doing and researching strategy. Understanding entities such as firms as though they were made up of components, and were themselves components within wider territories, means that experiences such as running a firm during various cycles of growth or divestment can be planned for, and invested in, with a sense that one's judgemental involvement has practical effects. It helps us identify beginning points within the manifold of our experience. In research terms, though, this has become *the* way that we deal with the demands of understanding human experience: we reduce it to what Bergson calls an 'extensive manifold', in which the personal and direct quality of change (the percept) is concealed by an intellectual concern with the conceptual isolation of entities as variables set in some sort of closed-off, theatrical scene. We as researchers (as well as many strategists themselves, insofar as they are predisposed to generating an entirely intellectual understanding of things such as businesses) risk becoming prisoners of our own predisposition to think of the world only as an extensive manifold – namely, we are unable to think of the mind as overflowing intellect and of experience and matter as anything other than a collection of parts external to one another.[1]

In addition to using the intellect, argues Bergson, we need to understand reality as intensive, where change is understood not as the speed and trajectory (moving between points) of unchanging entities but as a direct, self-sustained modification of being itself; an evolutionary *becoming* involving change without external cause. There is more to life than either the teleological or mechanical realization of pre-existing possibilities; there is an equally important and more vital form of life, what Bergson calls the lived experience of duration.

Reality is global and undivided growth, progressive invention, duration: it resembles a gradually expanding rubber balloon assuming at each moment unexpected forms. But our intelligence imagines its origin and evolution as an arrangement and rearrangement of parts which supposedly merely shift from one place to another; in theory, therefore, it should be able to foresee any one state of the whole: by positing a definite number of stable elements one has, predetermined, all their possible combinations. That is not all. Reality, as immediately perceived, is fullness constantly swelling out, to which emptiness is unknown. It has extension just as it has duration; but this concrete extent is not the infinite and infinitely divisible space the intellect takes as a place in which to build. Concrete space has been extracted from things. They are not in it; it is space which is in them. Only as soon as our thought reasons about reality, it makes space a receptacle. As it has the habit of assembling parts in a relative vacuum, it imagines reality fills up some kind of absolute vacuum.[2]

Duration is human experience understood as something immediate, expansionary, irreversible and creative. As Bergson's metaphor of the irregularly expanding balloon suggests, duration is the growth of what he calls a 'single, irreversible history' that is always in a state of 'becoming', 'a stream against which we cannot go'.[3] Such a life had to be understood as a whole, as what Bergson calls an 'intensive manifold'. An intensive manifold remains, ultimately, unanalysable by the intellect, because it cannot be readily unfolded into a flat plain of constituent elements, positions and relations. Here the past and the present have a virtual existence as derivatives of an ever-unfurling future (there is no temporal hypothesis of the 'if...then...' mould). The past is real insofar as it is the personal memory of lived, empiric experiences, and the future is real as a potential, but only the future present is actual, an ever renewed moment of becoming in which past experiences are selected and arranged and future events anticipated (more or less habitually) within immanent fields of action. As beings of action and habit we understand experience as a unifying interaction of perception and memory in which memory is the force by which the habits of language, norms and expectations are projected into our social lives. Our encounters with things are coloured by memory images (which, from the perspective of action [as opposed to, say, dreaming] are records of the past coordinated with the adaptive needs of present practice). These enduring memories remain distinct from perceptions; they are virtual (rather than actual); they coexist with the present without being the same as the direct perceptions by which the present is apprehended; novelty arises from an interpenetration of memory and new empirical experiences.

To get at this distinction between extension and duration, think of how we can parse a sentence into its component parts. In lingering too long on a word, sense seems to evaporate, so we arrive at a structure of grammar and phonemes whose divisibility is brought under the microscope with questions of the kind 'How many parsings will this sentence bear before we lose any sense of meaning?'. This is a form of intellectual enquiry. Bergson argues, however, that we can also recognize the pure, indivisible motion inherent in issuing the sentence, in creating meaning as we speak without knowing what we are going to say. In the former case we're dealing with extension and quantity, whereas in the latter it is an intensive (continuous and non-spatial) expression of our duration as we elaborate forms into something new (not simply rearranging what already exists).[4] When we investigate the human world we have to rid ourselves of the intellectual temptation to reduce our perception of distinctiveness to the motion of unchanging entities (parts within a systemic, mechanical whole) and, in addition, recognize the pure inventiveness of being as something within an indivisible, expanding whole (partial accounts – systems in systems – of an enduring universe).[5] Without this distinction, argues Bergson, we are not able to understand the inventiveness of life manifest in what Bernard Bosenquet calls the 'psychic time of creativity' (lived time) rather than the repetitive, clock time of the intellect; if everything was reducible to extension and movement, the future could be read off the present without any room for the individuality and creativity by which we hold ourselves distinct as living beings.[6]

The intellect works by using concepts and theories to represent the world in models, images, hypotheses and propositions, which inevitably confines much of what we experience to the realm of the 'outside'. Defining an inside from an outside helps us orient ourselves to our experience; it enables us to rationalize what happens and to plan for what might happen. What irks Bergson is our tendency to see in these representations the truth of our condition, when in fact they are a useful abstraction from what, understood intensively, is an assemblage of emergent creativity and action from which things such as motives, resources and goals can be identified only by acts of severance. When we research economic activity therefore, we recur to intellectual representations such as utility maximization and self-interest in ways that can seduce us into thinking there is nothing outside the frame, when it is only because of what exists outside the frame that these representations have any meaning or significance. The intellect presents only fragments, and the trick of what Keith Ansell-Pearson and John Mullarkey call Bergson's kind of 'superior empiricism'[7] is to let what is outside back in. The intellectual representations have to be saturated with the flow of life on the outside. In isolation, intellectual representations fail to get at and therefore fail to evoke what is moving about the way we relate to others (in terms both of our being emotionally moved *and* of being moved to act practically). The premises concerning rational evaluation make sense, but they are not exhaustive and always need to be filled out by the contextual influence of the entire duration of the lives that are successively brought into being, animated, dampened or destroyed by economic activity. It is by appreciating duration that we might get at how our own being (and the being of other systems) always bursts through the intellectual representations being made of them. This is an acceptance of what Hayek recognizes as the spontaneous, creative force of uncertainty, without whose dynamic and uncontrollable presence all organizations would collapse into an ever more restricted and inhuman calculus of known or knowable operations and transactions.

Process and practice in strategy research

Perhaps out of a growing awareness that there is more to strategic activity than the stipulation of purposes and the construction of formalized spaces to organize the fulfilment of these purposes, strategy researchers have in recent years become interested in getting into the 'bowels' of strategy-making. These researchers accept that the plural conditions in which strategic activity occurs cannot be confined by the intellectual coda of universal reality-capturing concepts. There is an increasing interest in closely scrutinizing the microscale processes, practices and activities within organizations that have been surreptitiously overlooked in traditional strategy research. In contrast to the rationalized identification of internal and external strategic variables, therefore, a more interpretive and even intuitive approach emphasizing the internal processes of strategy-making is being recommended. Though there are many influential books in this respect, one of the more significant beginnings came with Andrew Pettigrew's *The Awakening Giant*, based on research carried out with a British chemical firm, ICI. In this work the aim is to latch on to the everyday reality of organizational life – the nuances and frayed edges – in order to better understand how the managerial edicts, organizational structures, and material, political and economic conditions that constitute the phenomenon of strategy-making emerge and dissolve in patterns of events with associated outcomes.[8] This involved giving rich descriptions of the procedures, values and aims associated with the firm's strategy and an interpretation of the manner or style in which these are 'lived out' over time. In so doing, the aim remains to distinguish effective from ineffective organizational experience.

Whilst refraining from the kind of acute generalization offered by overtly intellectual approaches that isolate variables from contexts and typically underplay how these variables and their relationships can change, Pettigrew's more interpretive approach still offers a logical and coherent explanation of why specific strategic initiatives did or did not work, in what ways, and what might be learnt from these. The aim is to convey the depth, variety and fluidity of strategic activities, judgements and consequences that refuse to be contained by a solitary cause or definitive end point. This puts the onus on research involvement – an immersion in the field whose open-ended, plural and even improvised manner means that it upsets the presumption of being fully transparent or visible. The intellect is used to compare between cases to find patterns of experience and to isolate the physical, cognitive and contextual mechanisms of which these patterns consist, yet it does not occlude what we might call attempts at intuitively grasping what it was like to undergo strategic experience. The upshot is a nuanced, open-ended and complex knowledge of a firm's strategy and identity as it emerges continually from the ongoing practical problems experienced by its employees.[9] The problem set is less that of the scientific observer in isolation than that of the observer in consultation with the observed, allowing the reality of the observed to speak back; but it is a product of the researcher's observation nevertheless.

More recently, some strategy researchers have suggested that Pettigrew's work hints at, but does not get at, the actual practices of doing strategy hidden amidst the hierarchically larger and more structured patterns and outcomes of organizational life upon which he remained focussed. Building on strategy process research, these researchers call for a greater emphasis on understanding the minutiae of the processes and practices of doing strategy, leading some to call this emerging approach the 'activity-based view of strategy'.[10] Inspired perhaps by the seminal work of Karl Weick on organizational sense-making and enactment, the emphasis of these researchers has been on gerunds not nouns; strategy understood not as a thing in itself but as what people do. It is an organizational activity rather than a possession – hence the sobriquet 'strategy-as-practice'.[11] Exponents of this perspective study who strategists are (managers, advisers, commentators); what these strategists do (planning, reviewing, hedging, talking and so on); and the manner in which strategic activities become socially accomplished (legitimacy, presence, authority).[12] This involvement with the everyday lives of organizational members takes the researcher into messy, frayed and open-ended daily actions and inter-actions, it illuminates the personal and partial, it looks at the phenomena from the inside. There remains, however, an aspiration to connect to wider patterns of behaviour and outcome; hence the range of concern extends from the minutiae of organizational life to broadly experienced social structures, not least of which are the discourses surrounding the practice of strategy that is associated with attaining and sustaining a flourishing organization through the acquisition and arrangement of resources. Conceptually filling this range of concern, one such strategy-as-practice researcher, Richard Whittington, suggests that when researchers study a practice such as strategy they look for three interrelated units of analysis: *praxis* (socially constituted flows of meaning and value arising from the interconnection of individuals undertaking strategic action, whether at macro or micro levels); practices (the cognitive, physiological, behavioural routines and forms, as well as material things and conditions, that provide the resources associated with the successful accomplishment of strategic action and inter-action); and practitioners (those who use strategy tools such as budgets and plans, and who identify with and shape the practice of strategy).[13]

This shift in attention has resulted in a steady stream of scholarly research addressing 'where and how is the work of strategizing and organizing actually done; who does this strategizing and organizing work; what are the skills required for this work and how are they acquired?'.[14] The strategist remains the unit of analysis, therefore, but it is a strategist understood as an exponent of a practice. This entails the researcher becoming sensitive to different types of strategist (not simply senior managers but all employees who play strategic roles, in terms of the design, execution and review of how a firm performs, as well as significant individuals acting outside the organization yet nevertheless influencing strategy) as well as to the differing socio-historical and material conditions influencing the practice (identities, cultural aspirations, technology, communication norms, and so on). This turn towards strategic actors, and their activities and practices, echoes recent calls for more research into the organizational practices and routines that characterize the internal life of processes.

The distinctiveness of the strategy-as-practice research agenda lies with the avowed aim of its exponents to humanize management and organization studies by embracing what has been called more broadly in social science the 'practice' or 'linguistic turn'. The accompanying change in aspiration, method and, in many cases, unit of analysis has also changed the discourse through which strategy research is explained and communicated. New terms and phrases, such as 'activity-based view', 'core micro-strategies', 'micro-activities', 'micro-behavioural', 'micro-contexts', 'micro-level processes', 'micro-practices', 'micro-perspective', 'micro-sociological', 'practice approach', 'strategic activities', 'strategic practices' and 'nitty-gritty', all direct attention away from macro-processes to varying aspects of the minutiae of strategizing. There is clearly a straining towards a revised vocabulary for theorizing strategy practice. There is also an awareness, however, that studying these minutiae should yield insights into larger, macro-patterns of more or less successful instances of organizational achievements. In this aspiration, the idea of strategy remains one of distinguishing good from bad organizational planning, albeit from within everyday events such as departmental meetings or patterns of communication. The aim is to begin with the sayings and doings of contextualized individual strategic actors and, from these, to work upwards to ponder the possible consequences for wider system entities such as the firm, or industry, as echoed in what we read as this recent illustrative summary: 'Our central research interest focuses on explaining who strategists are, what they do and why and how that is consequential in socially accomplishing strategic activity.'[15]

In its aspiration the strategy-as-practice agenda is really a recovery of earlier research agendas, particularly those of Chester Barnard, Herbert Simon and Edith Penrose, from whose work the phenomenon of strategy emerged as a business practice worthy of concern. For Barnard, Simon and Penrose, understanding the activities and judgements that influenced firm and industry direction involved studying what was inside the organizational 'black box', whether it was the managerial capacity to identify opportunities and translate them into goals, the possession of specific and valuable resources to make these goals significant ones, the adoption of administrative routines whereby organizational structures were designed in order to pursue such goals, or the nurturing of executive behaviours and knowledge requisite to the appreciation of the continued relevance of those goals. The distinctiveness of the strategy-as-practice agenda is in the detail and extent to which it is willing to go. The box is well and truly opened up. Whereas early strategy research identified the kinds of assets and knowledge that rendered firms distinct from one another, strategy-as-practice researchers examine the agents, activities and material things by which these assets and this knowledge are attained and sustained. The greater detail renders the studies richer in the nuances and stories by which goal-setting and the pursuit of such goals are realized. With this greater involvement comes an extension of the humanist project to better appreciate how any understanding of economic phenomena such as firms, money and trade cannot be confined to an analysis of impersonal, structural forces and unfeeling, technically confined, rational calculations. Understanding production, trade and consumption requires an understanding of the people by whose actions these phenomena arise and upon whom they have effects, meaning that any analysis of these people cannot be reduced to algorithmic coefficients. Emotions, blood ties, personal histories, cultural expectations and communication breakdowns are as figurative in the landscape of strategic practice as path dependencies and evolutionary market forces. Strategy-as-practice is insightful in this regard because of the willingness of its exponents to confront and absorb the research challenges associated with getting within the firm to identify the micro-phenomena that resist explicit description in order to get a better grip on emerging macro-phenomena, such as a firm's competitive position, an economy's structural weaknesses, and so on.

Weak individualism and the primacy of social practices

It seems that logical positivist tendencies are finally giving way to the kinds of concerns displayed by Smith, Hayek and Bergson. This is not really the case, however. There remains a lingering reluctance on the part of many of the strategy-as-practice researchers to understand practice as anything other than the doings of individual agents: the actual activities deliberately performed by individuals within structured macro-contexts. Such a reliance on the micro–macro distinction remains inextricably tied to the entitative view of social reality that we have previously discussed and to the stronger version of *methodological individualism* that we have already identified and discussed. What are being theorized are conceptually presented realities with little acknowledgement that, in accounting for and explaining the coherence of such practices, a certain 'intellectuallocentricism' pervades and hence distorts interpretations of practitioner actions.[16] Mahmoud Ezzamel and Hugh Willmott suggest something similar when they point out that the strategy-as-practice approach still requires adherents to believe in something called 'strategy' existing prior to and distinct from the research practices being used to get at it.[17] What is often overlooked, then, is how strategy may emerge inadvertently and unintentionally from socialized practices engaged in by people who do not identify themselves as strategists.

The distinctiveness of this, therefore, is that, whereas more traditional 'rationalist' approaches identify strategic variables as discrete and visible collections of fixed entities (people, firms, assets, tools, markets) and activities (positioning, pricing, reviewing), exponents of the strategy-as-practice approach regard these variables as less immediately accessible; hidden amidst the nooks and litter of the organizational jungle. Using an intellectual approach, the researcher of strategy adopts the Baconian stance of a child before nature: stripped bare of corrupting tribal bias, observing the world by breaking it into separate components, understanding the characteristics of each and recognizing how these influence interactions (past, present and possible future ones). Using the strategy-as-practice approach, this researcher has to go native; like some mad-keen botanist, he or she gets right up close with a magnifying gaze in order to concentrate on the small things. What do the top team do to communicate with others and how do their audience respond? How are the procedures designed to realize goals actually followed and do these actions differ in different locations? 'To the details' is the rallying cry. This micro-attentiveness brings them proximate with the 'real', but their status as observing researchers relying on a means–ends logic as a basis of explanation still, apparently, absolves them from considering any complicity with what spills out in the form of knowledge claims.

This strained position would not itself be a problem were it acknowledged as such, much as many social scientists acknowledge that the virtue of their approach lies in its producing knowledge of patterns and outcomes with the potential to afford limited and pragmatic control over the world. The organizational dirt is an interesting place to be. Strategy-as-practice researchers often suggest, however, that their approach improves upon others because it provides more compelling and direct descriptions of the phenomenon we call 'strategy'; in short, because it understands strategy as a practice. Sure enough, the influence of historically constituted local contexts is recognized, but there is little if any propensity to appreciate what Ezzamel and Willmott call the constitutive power of their own presence, their own language, manifest in the specific case of strategy research itself in securing and legitimizing the concepts intellectually formulated and used to 'do' strategy research. The upshot is a disguised and hence theoretically troubled realism that has emerged from an inadequate appreciation of agency and the practice turn in social theory and philosophy. The strategy-as-practice agenda retains an observational logic in accounting for and explaining the 'doings' of strategists; the accounts are *about* the doings of identified strategists. Taking Whittington's triadic breakdown of *praxis*, practice and practitioner as an example, we can recognize in each a tendency to isolate, fix and classify things and situations.

Whittington uses the term 'praxis' in a much more instrumental and purposeful way than our earlier discussion of Aristotle's distinctions between *praxis* and *poiēsis* allows. For Aristotle, *praxis* is intimately associated with *phronesis* and the idea of action as self-cultivation. As we have shown in the previous chapter, *praxis* entails absorbed action that leaves no identifiable outcome, in that its end is realized in the very doing of the activity. *Praxis* emanates instinctively from a cultivated habitus. On our reading of Aristotle, following Dunne's, it is in fact *poiēsis* and not *praxis* that is associated with the kind of deliberate micro-strategizing that preoccupies Whittington and other strategy-as-practice researchers. In contrast to Whittington's attempt to 'instrumentalize' the term *praxis* by associating it with purposeful strategic action, Ikvjiro Nonaka and Ryoko Toyama, in their recent study of Honda and Seven-Eleven, recognize that strategy-making involves a form of 'distributed *phronesis*' whereby the internalized abilities and dispositions of organizational members across the various levels of an organization are crucial to the successful implementation of strategy.[18] Distributed *phronesis* alludes to a form of collective practical wisdom and predisposition unconsciously shared by organizational actors absorbed in their own individual situations. It implies a shared practice. Even in this more nuanced account of strategy-in-practice, though, there remains an insufficient appreciation of the significance of the 'practice turn' in social theory and its implications for understanding the primacy of social practices over individual agency.

The term 'practice' in strategy-as-practice research is spoken of using verbs – the doing of strategy, strategizing, and so forth – yet the view of what is being researched remains the deliberate 'doings' of intentional agents rather than practices, which are constitutive of the agents themselves. Critical accounts reflecting on the influence of traditions, prejudices and the habitual naturalness of doing something we call 'strategy' are largely absent, not least because the orthodox method demands the identification of minutiae; the 'resolutive-compositive' method (the elemental breakdown of phenomena into the smallest possible parts, the analysis of those parts, and their subsequent reassembly) taken to extremes. This provides detail but no context, and, as we have tried to show in our discussions of Bateson and Hayek, practice without context is not a practice but a series of primitive actions devoid of the animating colour of deeply held, largely unconscious manners and expectations.

Finally, the term 'practitioners' refers largely to agents understood as operatives engaged in the more or less skilful application of strategic tools. Here, again, the agents retain a degree of technical distance from their strategically relevant accomplishments; they use equipment in the manner of Aristotle's *technē*. The personal biographies, feelings of frustration and exploitation, the wider sentiments associated with practices beyond the doing of strategy are all acknowledged, but then enlisted so as to make sense of the singular moment that is identified as the strategist doing strategy.

In our view, whilst the rise in interest in phenomenological-based approaches with their emphasis on ethnographic studies of strategic actors is an important step towards recognizing the lived experience of practitioners, there is one more important aspect that needs to be incorporated: the shift from a strong methodological individualism to a 'weakened' understanding of human agency as constituted and reconstituted through the practices themselves. This is what marks a weakened individualism and *phronetic* approach out from a purely intellectual one underpinned by *episteme and technē*. The residual tendency to recur to actor meanings and intentions, to look to identify pre-existing characters and procedures, places many of these ethnographic studies squarely within the domain of a strong methodological individualism, associated with the phenomenology of the philosopher Edmund Husserl, with its emphasis on the meaning-giving, knowing subject. In contrast, the weakened methodological individualism characterized by Bergson's advocacy of intuition follows the *immanent* phenomenology of Husserl's student and dark nemesis, Martin Heidegger, as it aims to get at the embodied, doing and *coping* of a being-in-the-world. There is more to explaining strategy-in-practice than, in Bergson's words, waving a conceptual net in front of a passing reality ready to analyse what lies caught in its mesh. The issue is not how close you stand when you wave the net, but whether in waving *your* research net at all you really 'get at' the lives of strategy practitioners or simply locate what your own technologically embroiled epistemology allows you to.

In Bergson's essay 'On the pragmatism of William James', he elaborates on his sympathy with James' argument that truth is far richer than merely being an accurate, representative fit between the kind of knowledge claims made by academics and the world of experience. Any such fit is always arrived at *ex post*, and as a rendition (or performance) of truth it is, argues Bergson, too limiting because it fails to account for what lies beyond the fixing. What excites Bergson about James is that his version of truth affirms the existence of phenomena in ways that afford us an idea of what might follow. Instead of being fed by a retrospective account of past spatial arrangements made up of identified entities, therefore, James' future-oriented pragmatic truth proceeds from past to new experiences by offering clues or tendencies (rather than definitive or even rigorous statements), through which we are afforded a grip as we move with the flow of experience. Hence:

The true, according to William James, does not copy something which has been or which is: it announces what will be, or rather it prepares our action upon what is going to be. Philosophy has a natural tendency to have truth look backward: for James it looks ahead.[19]

True affirmations are not determined in advance of our experience; they are not waiting to be discovered, they are invented. What counts as knowledge, therefore, is governed by the systems of enquiry in use; the manner in which we affirm phenomena through a sense of expectancy, rather than a sense of having revealed something that existed anterior to our claim. Humans do not simply pick up external truths existing in the world or make the truth only through retrospective reflection but create truths through an intentional engagement with the world. It is how we look for and establish truth that governs the necessary conditions and it is the rules governing such a search that assist us in determining the legitimacy of knowledge claims. Truth is not a representation of reality but the manner by which we go about inserting ourselves into reality; of creating pathways and finding our way around. Because our perception of experience is imbued with memory we filter experience according to the vestiges of those past hypotheses that have proved useful and harden them into tradition and habit. As a result, Bergson accepts that the paths we trace through reality can be more, or less, plastic. Some are very dependent on where we focus our attention or which mode of utility concerns us, whereas others follow closely a prevailing current in reality.

Knowledge is never fixed, therefore; enquiry is always ongoing and uncertainty is an integral aspect of such enquiry. Bergson's super-empiricism is realistic rather than realist; it acknowledges that problems of meaning (not fact) are never solved but wrestled with, temporarily allayed, dispersed and reconfigured. Meaning is the continually renewed product of enquiries into how new and potentially antagonistic experiences can be satisfactorily reintegrated with an established stock of tradition. In this it is both method and a theory of truth, in which truth emerges from successive, successful attempts at acting appropriately. It is from this approach, for example, that we 'get at' the post-credit-crunch strategies of banks such as UBS that we discussed earlier. Max Rohner's avowed aim was to strategically reposition the bank with its core activity of wealth management as the heart. The language used by Rohner is largely intellectual, peppered with terms such as 'positioning', 'risk reduction', 'identified areas', 'separate units', 'into line with', 'firm objectives and metrics for every business area', 'losing one's way'. There is also mention of 'inner strength', 'identity' and trust', however. Even the term 'value' – the lodestone of economic strategy insofar as it is the creation of value that is the sine qua non of any firm's existence – retains an amorphous quality in its being associated with 'sustainability' as well as the more easily confined 'revenue'. The intellectual terms suggest a future envisaged by Rohner and his ilk as something akin to an already lived golden past, a recovery of appropriately balanced wealth steward-ship. From Bergson's perspective of duration, however, this attempt at recovery is not really desirable or indeed possible. The bank and its personnel have undergone irreversible change; having experienced the credit crisis they are no longer the same entities, and neither are the customers, many of whom withdrew their wealth from the purview of the bank's management. The involvement of the Swiss government, for example, which would undoubtedly have been a source of shock and some shame to bank members a few years ago, now appears a useful intervention in shoring up confidence in the bank's capacity to meet its obligations. Rohner's statement, then, as well as being an identified document written in intellectual language and analysed as a strategic call for the repositioning of key resources, can also be read as a nascent expression of future potential and loss. The talk of trust opens up the possibility for events such as government involvement or the desertion of thousands of customers no longer enamoured with the bank's character and probity.

Investigating social phenomena in terms of future potential rather than just retrospectively ascribing truth values carries with it a vastly different research orientation and agenda. As well as attempting to gain perspective *on* the world, to reach after that upon which everything stands, the *sub stantia*, researchers and strategists alike (insofar as strategists themselves are engaging purposefully in a search after the meaning of organizational life) are required to reach into the being-amidst-things, the *interesse* that Martin Heidegger talks about, to investigate the ways in which all of us, as beings interested in leading a life, are thrown into and become absorbed by circumstances that we engage with in collectively agreed ways. To investigate a phenomenon such as the practice of strategy is to understand how it is that the lineament of actions, symbols, tools and agents conspire in stances of what Heidegger calls a 'coming toward' things. For Heidegger it is the future that is the generative condition of human life, because human actions carry meaning insofar as they demand something of us; they orient us towards an unfolding of who we are, our potential. This life history unfolds in the company of other life histories, the entire panoply of which is thrown into a backdrop of already existing practices. It is this future-oriented *dwelling* that precedes any subject–object distinction and hence any explicit reliance on mental content.[20] It is not the agent him- or herself that gives meaning to his or her activities but the fact of each agent always being under way, a duration expressed in projects enlivened by relational concerns with other things, other people, and the settling of these relations in ways that endure. So, for example, we will read a cookbook as part of our being under way in the project of being a cook, itself perhaps part of a wider project of becoming aware of and intimate with those things that we consume, whether it be food or the doctor's drugs. We might not be consciously aware of these projects; indeed, many such form unquestioned backgrounds against which it is possible for actions such as reading a cookbook to demand things of us, such as attending to the locality or seasonality of food.

Understanding actions and practices in this way casts the knowledge-in-practice of the *phronetic* kind that we have identified in Aristotle's works, and that is being researched by strategy-as-practice researchers, in a more primordial form of involved practical engagement than the phenomenal agent standpoints associated with mental cognition and linguistic articulation.[21] It is an interest in this absorbed condition of human life that has precipitated the 'practice turn' both in philosophy and in social theory. The practice turn is concerned with acknowledging a kind of non-thematic knowing-in-practice – in Bergson's terms, a willingness to let duration seep into intellectual representation. Dreyfus describes the ensuing reorientation of research thus: to ask 'What is our relation to practice?' is to pose the question the wrong way, 'since it suggests that there is us, and then there are practices'; rather, we are by-products of social practices: '[T]hey set up a...space of possibilities [that] is not something that we have a relation to but, something embodied in us.'[22] Practices are patterns of saying and doing that 'do not arise from beliefs, rules or principles' but are expressions of a shared know-how and generationally acquired discrimination that resists any attempt to fix and limit it completely.[23] Practices orient and educate our attention, and shape our dispositions and tendencies, thereby affecting the way we 'choose' to act. We understand what it means to be human and how to act or not act, not by having mental images or representations but through being socialized, often unconsciously, into certain ways of doing things. Practices are social skills that enable us to come to know 'what it is to be a person, an object, an institution'.[24] They are like water to a fish swimming in it, and practice-oriented research if it is undertaken in the true spirit of the practice turn must be intuitively sensitized to this transmission of background practices that engender the simultaneous materialization of both strategy and individual identity.

The practice turn and the documenting of strategy-in-practice

This way of understanding the emergence and evolution of social practices, including in particular the practice of strategizing, is based fundamentally on a practice-sensitive set of philosophical presuppositions, each of which shares one important characteristic that has implications for our understanding of strategy practices: that it is agents and institutional structures that are subordinate to, and constituted from, practices and practice complexes. Consequently, it is the unconsciously acquired practice complexes, and not so much conscious intentionality, that accounts for social order and the patterns of regularity that we call 'strategy'. There are three key features of this practice approach.

First, the efficacy of actions is attributed to historically and culturally shaped internalized propensities and dispositions rather than to an individual's deliberate intentions, meanings and choices. There is what Bourdieu calls 'an economy of practices, a reason immanent in practices, whose "origin" lies neither in the "decisions" of reason understood as rational calculation nor in the determinations of mechanisms external to and superior to the agents'.[25] Practices are constitutive of agency, identity and the strategy that emerge from human action; these practices are replete with habitus. Broadly put, the term 'habitus' describes a durable disposition or attitude toward the world that is common to a group of people. Bourdieu likens it to a *style of engagement*: a generic 'strategy' that expresses itself in the many different activities and thoughts that make up an agent's life. It is a style that is unintentionally learnt and expressed unconsciously through accumulated exposure to the stabilizing values, gestures and outlooks by which a group is held together. It is by acquiring *habitus* that we are able to get an intimate, unspoken feel for the variety of moves and thoughts that we might make as agents; it offers us a sense of the potential of life by exposing us to an unquestioned background set of dispositions from which to explore that life. There is an absence of the kind of prediction that purposeful strategy imposes through some imagined future-determining present actions:

> Even when they look like the realization of explicit ends, the strategies produced by habitus and enabling agents to cope with unforeseen and constantly changing situations are only apparently determined by the future. If they seem to be oriented by anticipation...this is because...they are determined by the past conditions of production...that is, by the already realized outcome of identical or interchangeable past practices.[26]

Bourdieu retains use of the term 'strategy', however, at least adverbially, describing our relationship with 'habitus' as strategic because in submitting ourselves to established ways of doing things (manners and mores) we imbibe a set of structured relationships from whose stability we might explore possibilities

Second, such human action must be understood in terms of a *sociality of inertia*: cultural transmission, socialization, institutionalization, disciplinary regimes, etc., ensure a regularity of behaviour that makes the latter more or less socially predictable; a modus operandi and hence 'strategy' is apparent even though the agent may be unaware of it. Practices are carry-overs from a cultural tradition and our physiological being and so infused into our very ways of thinking, acting and knowing that they often resist cognitive conceptualization. They form the background of skilled coping capabilities that enable us to act appropriately, but not necessarily consciously, in specific cultural contexts. Most human action takes place through this form of thoughtless practical coping, and it is only when a breakdown of coping occurs that we then become aware of the cognitive boundaries between the actor and the object of action.

Third, what Bourdieu calls 'the field' of practice is to be construed as the locus of engagement, not the interaction of individual actions or an amalgam of properties and characteristics of those individuals.[27] Even the seemingly enduring identities and characteristics of persons are explained as the effects of what the anthropologist Tim Ingold calls a 'condensation of histories of growth and maturation within fields of social relationships'.[28] Becoming skilled in a practice, therefore, is not simply a question of deliberately acquiring a set of generalized capabilities that can be transmitted from one individual to another. Rather, skills are 'regrown...incorporated into the modus operandi of the developing organism through training and experience in the performance of particular tasks'.[29] As a result, the study of practice demands a perspective that situates the agent, right from the start, in the context of an active engagement with the constituents of his or her surroundings.

Because of the necessarily embedded nature of an internalized skill, having expertise in a particular field of activity in no way presupposes the ability to articulate what it is that one is actually able to do. Indeed, pressing an expert for an explanation of his or her action or decision may actually be counterproductive, since it may force the expert to 'regress to the level of a beginner and state the rules learnt in school' – rules that 'he or she no longer uses'.[30] What this implies for strategy-as-practice is that neither interviewing strategy practitioners about the meaning and reasons for their actions nor asking them to reflect on their actions, as with the use of diaries,[31] can give us assurance of the actual character of strategy-in-practice. What is needed to truly reach what Whittington and his colleagues call 'the close understanding of the myriad, micro activities that make up strategy and strategizing in practice'[32] is a sympathetic grasping of the nuances of this practice, and this requires a different research orientation; one involving a heightened sensitivity and perceptual awareness of the essential incompleteness and open-endedness, as well as the embedded tensions and contradictions, contained in such social practices. The cultivation of this sensitivity and perceptiveness is well understood in the arts and humanities.

As a practice, art revels in the negotiated relationship between the depiction and the depicted. The adequacy, appropriateness and insight of the depiction are expressions of a wider sensitivity to the role of depictions in our lives. Consider here our earlier example of the Western nude discussed by John Berger, whether depicted as an object suffused by patriarchy or as a challenging antidote provided by painters such as Manet. Here the role of depiction is one of isolating the depicted as a framed and known entity; the poses are theatrical, staged outside the slew of life in order to be viewed. Berger's reading of Manet suggests that our understanding of art inevitably involves some suspension of disbelief. Viewers are an audience to whom the piece is displayed. The piece can confirm and embellish orthodox 'ways of seeing', and so reinforce accepted understandings of the world, or it can upset our conceit by showing us alternative 'ways of seeing': that is you, this is me. This veers towards the intellectual; the depicted is framed by the method of approach. Not all painting is done in this way; even the ostensibly representative portrait art is capable of another mode of performance, one that Michael Fried, in an echo of Heidegger's *interesse*, calls the absorptive. Provoked by the portraits of Pierre Chardin, Fried finds a mode of depiction and understanding that does not require us to suspend our disbelief in the same way. Chardin's subjects are utterly engrossed in their own experience, without any awareness of being seen; they are under way. In this absorptive mode the viewer is cast aside; what is conveyed is the elementary possession of a moment being lived – a girl reading; a child being taught in a schoolroom.

Of course this 'near-documentary' mode is never complete; the artist and even sometimes the subject remain aware of processes of artistic creativity, and a work of art, a representation for viewing, is still being produced, often with measured and intensely crafted manipulation. In portraying the practices of reading or teaching, however, the artist is not trying to get at details but, rather, a suggestion of how people are under way in such practices. The depiction is getting at the everyday by stilling and suspending it, allowing us to look askance at how things are in the world when they are not being looked at.[33] The subjects remain elusive, temporary, everyday, unadorned; they are prosaic. The artists remain observers; they are practising their own craft by rendering other practices visible in some way. They are not observers in the way that Berger suggests Dürer is, however. In rendering the ordinary as being something 'of interest', the artist – and by implication the viewer, appreciative of the near-documentary aesthetic intent – occupies a disinterested netherworld that is the shadow of the ordinary but that does not in turn shadow those worlds. This is the kind of superior empiricism being aimed for by Bergson. The images do not generalize, fix or define so much as articulate what Heidegger calls the 'ability-to-be' under way on projects. The artist's skill is in maintaining a 'technical coolness', whereby everyday absorbed life is made apparent to others without its being coloured by the generalizing values of those doing the painting or viewing the art. The practices are left as they are, so, whilst there is a distinction in perception or aspect (the artist and viewer are not there; they are observers), there is no distinction in ontology (they are not of a different world).[34]

Here we wish to suggest that a near-documentary stance of researchers investigating the practice of strategy involves the use of concepts and images in ways that are similar to the absorptive mode of Chardin. We want to get at a sense of strategy as an undertaking of disclosure in which the future and past are felt in the unfurling present rather than set out along linear extensions and measured entirely in clock time. As much as it is about planning and confining experience to realize goals, strategy is also about a field of significance being opened up, opportunities being discovered, and this potentiality is experienced on an intensive rather than just an extensive field.

5   Building and dwelling: two ways
of understanding strategy

> The ordinary practitioners. . .live 'down below'. . . [T]heir knowledge. . .
> is as blind as that of lovers in each other's arms.
> *Michel de Certeau,* The Practice of Everyday Life, *p. 93*

*In the previous chapter we showed how research on strategy, and in particular the recent strategy-as-practice movement, retains affiliations with a strong methodological individualism. We then moved on to show how the practice turn in social theory offers an alternative way of understanding strategy-in-practice in terms that are compatible with a weakened notion of human agency and with the kind of non-deliberate purposive action that we associate here with undesigned strategy. In this chapter, therefore, we draw from Martin Heidegger and the Heideggerian commentator Hubert Dreyfus, as well as sociologists and social anthropologists such as Pierre Bourdieu, Michel de Certeau and Tim Ingold, to identify two distinct modes of engaging with the world strategically that, following Heidegger, we term the 'building' and 'dwelling'. Although Heidegger conceives of these modes as being naturally sympathetic, he suggests that modern life, and notably the rise and spread of technological sophistication, has wrested them apart, making them almost antithetical. The building mode is exemplified by the agent-strategist consciously constructing mental representations and models of the world and only then acting upon them.[1] Therefore those studying strategy in this vein presume action to be deliberate, purposeful and goal-directed: agent intentions, meanings and interpretations feature prominently in explaining strategic behaviour. It presumes that actions taken are instrumentally motivated and outcome-oriented (*poiēsis); they are synonymous with making. What is attended to in the research process is what strategists see as descriptions and justifications for the corrective actions they take rather than what may actually have happened without their awareness.*

In the dwelling mode of engagement, on the other hand, it is local adaptations and ingenuity in everyday practical coping that are of particular interest: the world is deemed to emerge with all its attendant properties alongside the emergence of the perceiver; the two are so mutually constituting that the identity and individuality of the person is inextricable from the identifiable strategy associated with his or her actions. Phronetic *actions are as much situation-resolving as self-constituting (*praxis*), to the extent that the 'coming-into-being of the person is part and parcel of the process of coming-into-being of the world'.[2] It is not difficult to see that this dwelling mode of engagement presupposes an internalized, tacit and largely unconscious form of knowledge and capability of the kind exemplified by our discussion of* phronesis *and purposiveness of action. In what follows, therefore, we begin to unravel the roots of this dwelling approach to understanding the practice of strategizing from within 'the real activity as such...in which the world imposes its presence... its urgencies, its things to be done and said...which directly govern words and deeds without ever unfolding as a spectacle'[3] for the external observer.*

Building and dwelling

We ended the last chapter discussing how artists attempt to get at and understand the experience of human action as a kind of immersed, purposive engagement with an ever-expanding world; to absorb and document how life would be were it not the subject of purely intellectual research. To recover this kind of *phronetic* awareness, however, is difficult, because it runs counter to our prevailing occidental mindset in social science in which the human relationship with the world is typically understood in detached and linear causal rather than relational terms; it is instrumentally rather than ecologically expressed. We have already introduced Nonaka and Toyama's study in which they began to wrestle with the demands of adopting such an ecological approach in the study of strategy. For them, following Aristotle, an understanding of distributed *phronesis* comes from paying attention to the collective tacit knowledge enabling people to act appropriately and with prudence according to the dictates of the situations in which they find themselves, mindful of, but not slavishly acting in abeyance to, traditions of values and ethics.[4] Recurring to our earlier discussion of *phronesis* in chapter 3, it is the ability to apprehend why and in what circumstances something can be said to have equipmentality, to be behaving with sufficient reliability, to be good. As Nonaka and Toyama make plain, this is not technical awareness but a value-laden sensibility of what is right. To extrapolate from one of their examples concerning car production, *phronesis* is less the technical skill and know-how involved in building a car (*technē*) than knowing the subjective reasons why that car can be called a good machine; it is the car understood through its expressive use rather than its technical design. A strategy that is *phronetic* would similarly occupy a territory of judgement and use value rather than one of engineering facts and proofs; it would look to generate a common good in each situation, knowing that this idea of the good can change from one situation to the next as the strategist reads from particular events to general principles and ideals, and back again, in a way that is open, collective and inclusive. Nonaka and Toyama suggest that what characterizes such *phronetic* awareness in strategists (they are less concerned with how researchers of strategy might equally be called upon to act phronetically) are: an ability to understand what is in the common as opposed to the individual good in any one situation; the ability to empathize with and accept the legitimacy of other opinions and concerns by being able to read the differing demands of situations; to understand the essence of things and correctly interpret situations by attending to details; the ability to communicate in language that resonates with others; the accrual of organizational power and influence sufficient to be a difference that makes a difference; and the capacity to instil *phronesis* in others.

We have some sympathy with Nonaka and Toyama here, yet in our view there remains a lingering, albeit implicit, commitment to strong methodological individualism. The *phronetic* strategy suggested by Nonaka and Toyama is realized by 'leaders' who know what is good and apply this knowledge in specific situations. Arising from this application, their ideas of the good may be revised, or sustained, and other actors such as employees, peers, customers and suppliers can be brought into similarly so-called *phronetic* ambits of appropriate and hence good activity. As we suggested in chapter 3, however, in our view *phronesis* is neither so noticeable nor so pragmatic a characteristic; indeed, it is not a characteristic of an isolated individual at all. In part it is knowledge without discretion or discrimination; a mute, spontaneous and habitually acquired awareness of things (*pragmata*) encountered as being ready to hand or potentially so. The existence of things is disclosed pragmatically as we act upon the world from within our everyday worlds. Hence there is no possibility of an overview, or a sense of *common* good, nor a discernible boundary that can trace out a collective body or an inclusive act. Rather, *phronesis* is an expression of being a system-in-a-system of which any strategic actor remains a part. Moreover, we also want to suggest that *phronesis*, as distinct from *technē*, is not simply confined to a pragmatic relationship with things, unspoken or otherwise, but extends towards an awareness of things-in-themselves and our appropriate place amid them. Hence in part it is an attunement to our own possibility as belonging beings.

Bateson explains this distinction using an analogy. Imagine a man felling a tree with an axe. The scene can be considered as a set of isolated entities with the man at its centre, in control and with a conscious purpose.

For Bateson, however, it is better to understand it as a circulating, relational unity consisting of: tree-eyes-brain-muscles-axe-stroke-cut-tree. The elements are distinguishable, but only as parts of the system; their identity is bonded through successive transformations of difference. As the man cuts, the tree yields, the eye adjusts, the muscles tighten, the stroke angle alters, the tree yields again, but perhaps differently, and so on.[5] Here it is better to say that thinking and acting take place at a system level. It is an epistemological bias that sees the man as the figure of control, or as transcending the mute system within his grasp. Rather, the man is receiving information in the form of communicated transformations or differences, some less typical than others (say in a toughening of wood texture, a blunting of the axe edge, or muscle fatigue, and so on), and then transforms these differences in his action to cut at different angles, to swing with more rhythm, which in turn reveals yet more states of the tree, whose transformation in turn alters the state of the axe, and so on. There is no unilateral control over the entire system here. To describe the phenomenon as 'The man cut down the tree' presumes the man to be distinct from the system, and then by extension and implication reifying the mind of the man as the conscious, purposeful, controlling part of the man acting upon the muscles and hence the tree. The mind is understood as something distinct, like a billiard ball causally hitting and changing another ball, yet we are being confused by our grammar here. The 'self' is not like a ball, because there is no way of fixing the limits of selves, which are immanent to systems of the kind Bateson describes. What we know of a system and our place within it, therefore, is immanent not to some part of a system – the mind – or eye (window to the soul) but to the entire system, the edges of which can never be closed. The tree-felling man is as dependent on other systemic elements as they are on him; his felling is more a purposive act of relational and often unconscious engagement with other more or less familiar system elements (that wood is something you chop, for example) than it is a conscious design and control over a system.

The nature of such a systemic relationship is revealed only in moments of breakdown or unreliability; the equipment stops working, as when the eye loses sight or the axe blunts; or the equipment becomes absent or lost; or the equipment acts as a hindrance, when the woodsman encounters a knot in the tree and the axe gets stuck. The resulting disturbance requires that we consciously attempt to recover the once taken-for-granted availability of the axe, the eye or the tree. In this breakdown and attempted recovery we begin to experience what Heidegger calls a presentness-to-hand, in which the thing that was once ready to hand and intimately related to our immediate activity now appears as somehow apart from our own being. It has a sense of its own life in the system, of which we remain a part. Thus, whilst corrective inquiry might result in the axe being sharpened, the eyes being covered in protective goggles, or in straighter, less knotted trees being selected, a sense of the indifference of things, of their being outside our technical concerns, has been unconcealed. The things become present-at-hand in their own terms, and as they are let back in as equipment they continue to resonate with this self-sufficiency. Things such as axes and trees have their own authority, which we have to – and do, typically unthinkingly – accept in our use of them. It is how we acknowledge and accept this systemic relational unity that is a matter of our *phronetic* judgement. We can repress it by simply continuing to understand the world as something that will become fully compliant with our purposes eventually because of *technē*; we can confine it through the use of an objectifying science such as that used by logical positivists, whereby objects are understood as somehow distinct from us (even ourselves), but in a mute, material way, thus using *episteme* in maintaining an implicit hierarchy over them; or we can accept the occasional strangeness of things as being present on their own terms (rather than represented in theory) and so both a source of anxiety and attraction as we struggle to make them approachable within the systems we experience, without presuming them to be completely in our equipmental grasp.[6]

It was in furtherance of understanding this intimate form of purposive engagement that Heidegger delivered a lecture later published as 'Building, dwelling thinking', in which he poetically speculates on the question of our own being from the perspective of the systems we humans create and cultivate. He chose to conduct this enquiry using the terms 'building' and 'dwelling' as definitive modes of engaging with the world and being. In German these activities share a common root: *bauen*, to build, is rooted in dwelling. Conventionally, we might consider building to precede dwelling. We design and create a building using architecture and construction in order that we may then dwell in it. For Heidegger, though, this building, which relies on technique for its construction, takes place only because we are, potentially at least, entities that dwell on earth: '*Only if we are capable of dwelling, only then can we build.*'[7] In passages describing a bridge built over a river, his prose twists and turns with an expressive delight as he evokes what it might mean for us to understand how a bridge can dwell and ourselves with it, rather than just have us stipulate its structural condition. To dwell is to preserve and to make space for life itself. The bridge does not simply connect two banks, therefore, or punctuate an already existing sky or connect two routes already trodden. Rather, it gathers the earth, sky and mortal human activity into one location and gives them unique expression; the bridge brings a landscape into being around a stream, it anchors and gives relief to an endless sky and it affords travellers and traders the chance to meet. Heidegger calls such a construction, or building, a location, in which the bridge, the landscape, the sky, the tradition of human community and the human individual all meet, as a systemic unity, affording one another the chance to be, to live.

The problem in modern life is not simply that we often lose this sense of building as locating or gathering things but that we don't recognize this oversight as a problem. For us, with our clever trickery, we are able to assume control over the entire system, and the bridge becomes nothing more than a mute, disposable tool with height and weight limits. We might understand the bridge scientifically, its material composition, the mathematical formulae by which it remains strong, but we typically fail to appreciate it phronetically, as something whose rightness persists because of its locating us within a wider organic unity of things. Heidegger is pushing at what we mean by *phronesis* here. It is not just our unthought, equipmental use of things. We might use a bridge as a tool, a pragmatic means to an end, and the readiness to hand of the bridge casts it in a pall of invisibility. This is how we relate to things in the world, typically, and *technē* describes this condition of unhesitating, habitual and pragmatic use. Heidegger suggests that there is more, however. When a thing no longer works, or is absent, it becomes present, but typically it remains becomes present as *technē*; we attempt to restore its equipmentality, often invoking *episteme*, and for Heidegger it is our modern plight that we fail to recognize this tendency. The bridge, as with any other modern building, becomes nothing more than an expression of formally confined knowledge *of* the world; a confrontation with the world seen entirely as a repository of resources to be organized and manipulated for our own purposes. Any sense of being amongst things, of dwelling, has been hollowed out. We are left simply with a dimensional understanding of the space that the building creates: the span of the bridge, the weight tolerance, the longevity of its materials, its relative position to other land*marks*, and so on. We feel no anxiety about this – indeed, we often remain proud of such engineering achievement – and, were we to feel anxious, we would typically respond with more technology. The materials would last longer, the bridge's position be assessed more accurately, its span become more accommodating, its managed upkeep more regular and efficient. The boundaries of the bridge understood dimensionally are the fixed limits of where the thing stops and where other things start. What we miss in this assertive awareness of the proper limits of a construction such as a bridge are where in our relations with things they begin to unfold and disclose themselves to us as beings in the world of which we too are a significant part, as well as existing potentially outside our capacity to interpret or even understand them, as when they break down and we do not recur to the habit of our intellect and look for technical solutions. This is what we mean by building sometimes coming into opposition with dwelling.

Building without dwelling occurs when we presume what exists to be us and things understood separately and then wreathed in connexions of control – a purposeful individual confronting a world of mute, organized resources.[8] Dwelling is accepting one's place in a nested system, or context, and from within this location recognizing how things might exist in themselves, rather than just as things-in-relation-to-human-design. The manner of our dwelling suggests the unreflective, immediate and intimate familiarity that one has 'inhabiting a home'.[9] Like Nietzsche, Heidegger believes that it is through this dwelling activity that we achieve some form of everyday intelligibility and not through having ideas and mental images, as Descartes presupposed and Edmund Husserl upheld.[10] Nonetheless, it is this basic condition that we with our technological trickery ignore, not through choice but because we have become so inured with our ordering, controlling technology and the associated epistemology of a strong methodological individualism that we are habituated into understanding everything, including ourselves, dimensionally, within the confines of Bergson's extensive manifold. What Heidegger urges upon us in his lecture is a recovery of a sense of angst and resistance, a willingness to challenge our habitual reliance on technological ordering not so as to overcome it (we cannot rid ourselves of what is so deeply engrained) but to upset it sufficiently to recognize how we, as beings with an interest in leading a life, rely upon the world rather than control it.

Engaging with the world

To begin to appreciate fully how 'dwelling' differs from what Heidegger suggests is the modern, empty version of 'building', is helpful to recall an illuminating illustration provided by Humberto Maturana and Francisco Varela in their seminal book *Autopoiesis and Cognition*. Maturana and Varela describe two contrasting but equally successful approaches for explaining how activities may wittingly or unwittingly result in a house coming into existence. One is directed from what they call an 'observer domain' (which equates to what we call here a building mode of engagement) and the second from a more immersed form of engagement, which they call *autopoiesis*.[11] The second mode of engagement presupposes an immersed organism reaching out towards, interacting with and taking in its environment (what we deem here to be a dwelling mode).

Let us suppose that we want to build two houses. For such a purpose we have two groups of thirteen workers each. We name one of the workers of the first group as the group leader and give him a book which contains all the plans of the house showing, in the standard way the layout of walls, water-pipes, electric connections, windows, etc. . . [T]he workers study the plans and under guidance of the leader, construct the house approximating continuously the final stage prescribed by the description. In the second group, we do not name a leader; we only arrange the workers in a starting line in the field and give each of them. . . only neighbourhood instructions. These instructions do not contain words such as house, pipes or windows, nor do they contain drawings or plans of the house to be constructed; they only contain instructions of what a worker should do in different positions and in the different relationships in which he finds himself as the position changes. . . [T]he end result in both cases is the same, namely, a house.[12]

In the first case, the workers knew in advance through the design plans, linguistically coded instructions and representations what they were expected to construct and followed the plans accordingly, successfully producing the desired outcome. This reflects *purposeful* planned activity; the *technē* of the architecture was made apparent by a leader. In the second group, however, there was no end view representation of what was to be accomplished nor was it necessary to have such a priori knowledge. Rather, what was coded and internalized as a form of distributed intelligence was an equally effective process

that constitutes a path of changing relationships which if carried through. . . [invariably] results in a system with a domain of interaction which has no intrinsic relationship with the beholding observer. That the [external] observer should call this system a house is a feature of his cognitive domain, not that of the system itself.[13]

The point Maturana and Varela are making is that from this dwelling world view the practical ability to construct a house successfully, run a business or act strategically does not necessarily presuppose detached planning, distancing, linguistic justification or cognitive representation. The local *purposiveness* of individuals acting in relation to significant others may unwittingly give rise to a constructed house, a successful business or a winning strategy as a by-product of such interactions even though the individuals concerned may not intend that to be the case at all. Indeed, there is not even the necessity of knowing the language or conceptual category (e.g. 'house', 'profit', 'strategy', etc.) employed by the observer to describe the eventual outcome. Unlike a researcher/ observer, the practitioner is not disposed to standing outside his or her situation and to surveying it with a detached eye the way the intellect does. Rather, what preoccupies him or her is how to respond *in situ* to the changing relationships he or she encounters in a manner that ensures the smooth and productive functioning of his or her everyday world. This is what begins to characterize a dwelling mode of engagement, a mode that generates what Bourdieu calls an internal logic of practice that is effectively incompatible with a world of intellect intent on seeking neat, logically coherent and comprehensive explanations. Intellectual approaches common to strategy and academic research cannot grasp 'the principles of practical logic without forcibly changing their nature'.[14] This is because, within the dwelling mode, the logic of practice exists only to facilitate effective action, not explanation or justification. Purposive action emanates as a modus operandi from one's cultivated dispositions for dealing with familiar situations in a relatively predictable and socially acceptable manner. It results from habitus: a predisposed style or habit of engagement that is acquired through the process of socialization. As such, this habitus, or dispositional tendency, serves as the unthinking source of a 'series of moves which are. . . organized as strategies without being the product of a genuine strategic intention'.[15] Strategies can emerge without there being any deliberate strategic intent. For us to truly understand strategy practices, therefore, we need to 'return to practice, the site of the dialectic of the *opus operatum* and the *modus operandi*. . .the incorporated products of historical practice', which produce systems of durable transposable dispositions that unfold through our patterns of responses.[16] This is the kind of endeavour that John Shotter and Arlene Katz talk of as articulating practice from within practice itself, and that more recently Shotter has distinguished as 'withness thinking' rather than 'aboutness thinking'.[17]

The beginnings of this distinction between the building and dwelling modes of existence is vividly captured in Michel de Certeau's book *The Practice of Everyday life*. Here, de Certeau finds himself at the top of one of the ill-fated towers of the World Trade Center in New York, musing on the distinction between the view looking down on the city and enjoying the voyeuristic pleasures of seeing it all neatly laid out below as one would view a map of a city, and the perspective of the city as most ordinary people would experience it at street level.[18] Unlike the detached, transcendent observer looking from atop the building, the pedestrians on the streets down below do not have a map-like view of the city but instead experience a series of migrational outlooks, generating horizons of comprehension that are continuously evolving and changing as they actually walk the streets at 'ground zero'; unthinkingly and deftly avoiding traffic, sidestepping and negotiating their way around obstacles, ignoring the honking, but noticing the displays on the sidewalk, passing by, reaching towards and generally 'muddling through'.[19] This is the creative experience of weaving spaces, events and situations together in a subjective, self-referential manner. The richness of experiences involved in such pedestrian journeys cannot be captured and represented by static maps, tracing routes or locating positions, since maps, routes and positions are typically forms of fixing and pinning down the flux and flow of everyday life. The pedestrians 'down below', having no privileged 'bird's-eye' view, must act by 'reaching out' from wherever they find themselves, feeling their way towards a satisfactory resolution of their immediate circumstances.

De Certeau is making a vital distinction between the knowledge of a 'tourist' researcher/observer and that form of intimate knowing that results from being totally immersed in negotiating, overcoming and resolving material circumstances as they arise. On the one hand, it presupposes the ability to survey, abstract, fix and define. On the other, there is the kind of immersed knowing that is locally adaptive and inventive and that emerges from the immediate need to continuously revise, adjust and make do according to the changing needs of the situation. In other words, it presumes that individuals in the intimacy of their dwelling situations, like a fish in water, can operate only 'blow by blow. . . ([T]hey must) accept the chance offerings of the moment, and seize on the wing the possibilities that offer themselves at any given moment.'[20] Rather than relying on a pre-established plan of action or some grand 'strategic initiative', this kind of local practical knowing manifests itself in small, unheroic and seemingly inconsequential moves: 'tactics' involving ingenuity, wit, trickery, surprise and opportunistic poachings. Timeliness in intervention is a crucial weapon of such 'tactical strategists'. For de Certeau, such a 'tactical' approach to strategy characterizes the 'art of the weak'; it is a strategy employed by ordinary folk in their unspectacular day-to-day getting by. What differentiates this local strategy from centralized deliberate strategy is that it is characterized by an absence of a 'proper locus' of control – a legitimate place or position from which resources can be mobilized and purposeful action deployed as well as events monitored and controlled. A tactic 'boldly juxtaposes diverse elements in order suddenly to produce a flash shedding a different light... Cross-cuts, fragments, cracks and lucky hits...are the practical equivalent of wit.'[21] Tactics correspond to a decentred and distributed form of strategy in which the notion of an isolated, circumscribed agency is 'weakened' – one in which the 'simple location' of the source of initiation is rendered problematic.

Like the walkers de Certeau describes, many (retrospectively identified) successful business practitioners (especially those who have never been in business schools, and we must remember that there are still millions of successful businesspeople all over the world who have never heard of nor bothered about an MBA qualification and who do not know of strategy frameworks advocated by the likes of Michael Porter) do not generally rely on the kind of formalized planning, organizing and decision-making taught in the business school curriculum to guide their actions and decisions. Rather, they feel their way through the world, unconsciously acquiring social and managerial coping skills that are 'passed. . .through individuals without necessarily passing through consciousness'.[22] 'Decisions' and 'actions' arise from within the habitus of established social practices, occurring *sponte sua* in response to events *in situ*. Here, the efficacy of action in achieving successful outcomes does not depend upon some predesigned plan of action, nor does it even rely on the deliberate intention of a singular individual, but, rather, it results from her internalized *phronetic* capacity to continuously make timely and ongoing adjustments and adaptations to local circumstances. The involved strategy practitioner, like the pedestrian, is more like a skilled blind person attempting to negotiate her way around an unfamiliar room. He or she does not and need not have a 'bird's-eye' view of the room to cope with his or her predicament successfully. Instead, with the aid of a walking stick (a prosthetic device that extends and reaches out to feel the world around him or her), he or she is able to find a way around successfully, relying on the tacit knowledge and coping capabilities acquired through continuing immersion in his or her life world. Similarly, the strategy practitioner develops a local insider's 'feel' for the problem situation he or she finds him- or herself in and responds accordingly, relying on accumulated experiences, wisdom and wit and using all the means immediately available to effect a satisfactory resolution. This is where we might start to identify the strategy practitioner's dwelling view of the world: one that begins where detached seeing and contemplation give way to a locally sensitive, immersed, guileful and opportunistic form of doing; it recurs to the heightened sensibility, alertness and resourcefulness that Aristotle associated with *phronesis* and *praxis*.[23]

Dwelling and the Gothic sensibility

According to a revised social epistemology that is more consistent with the possibility of a dwelling world view, social reality does not come to us already patterned or 'ready-made'. Instead, what we fundamentally perceive prior to conscious conception is what William James likens to 'a big blooming buzzing confusion as free from contradiction in its "much-at-onceness" as it is alive and evidently there'; it is 'aboriginal', it 'means nothing and is but what it immediately is'.[24] Only by first acknowledging that the primary condition of human existence is this ambiguous, fluxing reality and not some pre-ordered condition can we begin to appreciate fully that what appear to be formed, structured and clearly defined are nothing more than islands of stabilized social order in a churning sea of chaos. Only then can we realize that these are precariously forged and hard-won achievements, sustained and embellished through ongoing actions and social interactions. Ordering affords control and hence the ability to exploit what we find. Following Bergson, our habitual use of this intellectual ordering to understand life has become so ingrained that when we apprehend any chaotic or problematic situation the instinctive tendency is quickly to reduce the messiness apprehended to recognizable pre-established categories, so that judgements can be made and positive actions taken. Such a tendency to view 'imperfection' in negative terms may lead us to overlook its hidden benefits.[25] This general attitude of impatience or intolerance for the messiness of imperfection is openly confronted in the world of art, literature and philosophy, where vagueness and ambiguity are constantly celebrated as positive and fecund conditions for communicating the richness of reality.

Take the one-time controversial paintings of the Victorian artist Joseph Mallord William Turner. In the early 1830s comments in *Blackwoods Magazine*, an influential journal on art at that time, criticized Turner's work as *amateurish* and completely out of touch with nature as we see it. Thanks in part to the spirited defence by the art critic John Ruskin in his book *Modern Painters*, however, Turner is hailed today as one of the greatest painters of all time. In six copious volumes Ruskin painstakingly shows how works such as Turner's were more true to our direct experience of nature. Unlike many paintings of his time, Turner's did not depict so much as exemplify nature as it is actually experienced by one immersed in it. He understood what it meant to dwell rather than to build. In one painting entitled *Snow Storm*, for instance, he painted the intimate experience of being on a ship called the *Ariel* in the stormy sea off Harwich, after strapping himself on the mast for four hours and experiencing for himself the chaos and turbulence of being out at sea in a storm.[26] This is just one example of how great painters explore the realm of perception and comprehension by struggling to depict the actual ambiguities and emotional involvement of real experience; the struggle for coherence, the fear, the hesitations and the sense of being overwhelmed by a larger force beyond human comprehension and pragmatic control. The effect of Turner's paintings is to show us that life is never orderly, unambiguous or clear-cut and that this starkness is characteristic of an unmediated ordinary life. What are presented to us directly in any real-life encounter are precarious, ill-defined and emergent situations with blurry boundaries and shadowy penumbras; and it is from this cacophony of competing stimuli that, through each minute and laborious ordering effort, form and orderliness are gradually and painstakingly won, both by the painter and by the viewer. These are images that are self-consciously images that have to be worked at, transforming the painter in the painting, the viewer in the viewing and the images themselves as they are found in new contexts, new periods, new lights. This is life understood from within a system. The price we pay when we forget or overlook the struggles, the small painstaking efforts of distinction and the agonizing that goes into producing the transforming effects subsequently experienced is a certain superficiality; an artificial 'tinniness' in our attitude and disposition towards the understanding of life and all the variability and richness that it offers.

The love for this richness and the inexplicable attractiveness of the vague, the unwieldy and the sublime – an appreciation of the detailed variety of life experiences, in contrast to the neat and well-ordered symmetries we ordinarily encounter – led Ruskin to coin a phrase, the 'noble picturesque', to describe the difference of sentiment that the former evokes in us. He expresses this subliminal sentiment on one of his many visits to Calais:

I cannot find words to express the intense pleasure I have always in first finding myself, after some prolonged stay in England, at the foot of the old tower of Calais church. The large neglect, the noble unsightliness of it; the record of its years written so visibly, yet without sign of weakness or decay; its stern wasteness and gloom, eaten away by the Channel winds; and overgrown with the bitter sea grass; its slates and tiles all shaken and rent, and yet not falling; its desert of brickwork, full of bolts, and holes, and ugly fissures, and yet strong like a bare brown rock; its carelessness of what anyone thinks or feels about it, putting forth no claim, having no beauty or desirableness, pride, nor grace; yet neither asking for pity; not as ruins are, useless and piteous, feebly or fondly garrulous of better days, but useful still, going through its own daily work, as some old fisherman beaten grey by the storm, yet drawing his daily nets: so it stands, with no complaint about its past youth, in blanched and meagre massiveness and serviceableness, gathering human souls together underneath it; the sound of its bells for prayer still rolling through its rents; and the grey peak of it seen far across the sea; principal of the three that rise above the waste of surfy sand and hillocked shore, – the lighthouse for life, and the belfry for labour, and this for patience and praise.[27]

In contrast, Ruskin finds in England 'the spirit of well-principled housemaids everywhere, exerting itself for perpetual propriety and renovation, so that nothing is old, only "old fashioned", and contemporary, as it were, in date and impressiveness'.[28] There is a constant effort to rub out the past, to confine it to order. We are back with Calvino's city of Leonia.

Nineteenth-century England is suffused in a 'spirit of trimness', without any 'confession of weakness', and it is this admission of demise, decay and calamity absorbed with a calm patience that encircles the picturesque, an expression 'of suffering, of poverty, or decay, nobly endured by unpretending strength of heart. Nor only unpretending, but unconscious.'[29] Somehow, the gnarled, the weathered and the decayed harbour a certain strange attractiveness that evokes and awakens in us an appreciation of the nobility of the impoverished and the 'unconscious suffering' testified in the unassuming display we apprehend. It is this possession of an aesthetic appreciation for the noble picturesque that enables us to view social practices in general, and the practice of strategy in particular, not as exemplifying that spirit of 'trimness, orderliness, spikiness and spruceness' associated with order and predictability but, rather, as ennobled with what Ruskin calls the 'Gothic sensibility'.

A most passionate and sustained evocation of this Gothic sensibility comes in Ruskin's intensely individual guidebook, *The Stones of Venice*. By way of instruction, Ruskin requires his readers to examine in detail the decoration on the angles of the Ducal Palace. Instead of the contrast between England and Calais, in the doge's Venice his readers are directed to the carvings from both the Gothic and later Renaissance periods, and encouraged, with imaginative effort, to recognize the distinct tenor in each 'spirit'. The Gothic sculptures describe the fall of man and the drunkenness of Noah; possessed of human frailties, the sculptors have given a frank and public confession of weakness, of imperfection and of a desire for change:

It is that great disquietude of the Gothic spirit that is its greatness; that restlessness of the dreaming mind, that wanders hither and thither between the niches, and flickers feverishly around the pinnacles, and frets and fades in labyrinthine knots and shadows along wall and roof, and yet is not satisfied, nor shall be satisfied.[30]

In contrast to the Gothic, and like the English, the Renaissance sculptors broached no such weakness and restlessness, preferring the subject of Solomon as a tidy exemplar of human wisdom and settled achievement. The interweaving foliage of the Gothic work is characterized by variation, whose detail and flow evoke a natural unity without appeal to abstracting symmetries. The rib and vein of each leaf is set in relief in the stone with humble energy and obstinacy. The foliage in the Renaissance work, in contrast, though more studiously varied, has 'none of its truth to nature', the edges of the leaves are blunt 'and their curves are not those of growing leaves, but of wrinkled drapery'.[31] Gothic sculpture carries an elemental energy and personal vigour that could be formed only by an artisan for whom the sculptured forms were honest disclosures of real-life experience; they exemplify the pursuit of a vocational expression.

The harmonies in the stonework to which Ruskin points his readers are ones that are wrought through belonging to the hurly-burly of life rather than their idealizing and representing, as was the wont in later Renaissance work. Venice's second or Gothic period was the apogee of this Gothic sense of belonging to a place; a city that brandished its resilience, liberty and honesty in its very fabric. The stony mass of mosaics, panelling, sculptures, windows, finials, canal walls and door-ways were the very mien of a citizenry constituted by an open and spirited self-belief. With Venice's trading success came a weight of wealth that encouraged indolence, luxuriousness and therefore the cor-ruption of Gothic simplicity with all manner of enervating architectural trickery. It was this 'degraded Gothic' that elicited Ruskin's purging attack of the Renaissance in its artistic demand for universal expression. In the place of elaborate, wandering adornment came perfect axes, golden rules and vanishing points. The Renaissance architects and sculptors became imprisoned in their own intellectual devices;

Imperatively requiring dexterity of touch, they gradually forgot to look for tenderness of feeling; imperatively requiring accuracy of knowledge, they gradually forgot to ask for originality of thought. The thought and feeling they despised departed from them, and they were left to felicitate themselves on their small science and their neat fingering.[32]

Renaissance buildings were defined by a series of imposed patterns. With this 'brute force' they became lifeless and smothered the life of their occupants; their sheen was all surface and their idealized propor-tions obliterated what for Ruskin sustained any building: its ability to act and to talk as a place of dwelling. In acting as a dwelling, a building defended people from the weather, using vernacular materials and local know-how; it housed their possessions and helped order their lives. In talking, a building expressed the history and sensibilities of those who built and used it. In acting and talking like this, a building embodied the useful and contemplative knowledge resident in its surrounds. Good buildings, as places of dwelling, were native expressions, a channelling of intuitive skill, practical awareness and tradition that amplified the human delight of those involved in its being; in Ruskin's words, it was the 'the life and accent of the hand' that mattered, not the elevation of the intellect. This Gothic understanding of what a building is for chal-lenges what, for Ruskin, were two dominating forces in modern, techno-logically governed architecture.

The first was a preoccupation with orderliness. This desire always to intervene to make things tidier and to restore what is considered imperfect results in a lack of substance that arises from such simplifying uniformity. Buildings lose their distinction for want of contrast. Each architect and worker is compelled by the imposed common purpose inherent in trying to reach a given point, and all that Gothic complexity becomes waste, a dilatory mess of symbol and line read as an imperfect almanac of medieval superstition. Neatness demands that the contrasts are ironed out, the focal destination of a perfectly functioning building becomes ever sharper, and yet, in direct proportion, the character of the building becomes ever more anodyne. To combat this urge to improve, Ruskin called for temperance: the use of chromatic scales and contrasting elevations to break up the solid, universal mass. It is only by such contrasts (of colour, of spatial form and of material) that the distinctiveness of things comes to life.[33] In Gothic the contrasts are changed, almost at whim, lest they become too uniform; squares are met with diamonds, verticals with curves and courses with alternatives. The whole is a local assemblage, making full use of available materials in their most unadorned form and free from the overweening strictures of an imposed end point or purpose, to which it is simply a noisy crescendo.

As well as a lack of contrast, Ruskin was also irked by a lack of humility in Renaissance buildings, a pride encapsulated in the dominating role assigned to the architect's scientific knowledge. To be sure, initially there were great Renaissance figures able 'to join science with invention, method with emotion and finish with fire', yet these were rare, uncorrupted figures, such as Lorenzo Ghiberti or Leonardo da Vinci, who were blazing their own path. What Ruskin bemoans is the requirement that all work be like theirs, an exhortation that, given the relative paucity of genius, meant an emphasis on imitation. Method and finish became dominant, and the architect the prime exponent of the principles by which this dominance was secured. There was no room for individual judgement; the common mason and carpenter were compelled to follow rather than create patterns, to accumulate technical and pragmatic knowledge of things (*technē*) rather than express personal insight amid things (*phronesis*): 'The Renaissance frosts came, and all perished.'[34]

For Ruskin, the lack of temperance and humility in these buildings embodied a wider and still present socialized desire (much evident in the business strategy literature) to avoid shocks; a fear of failure, of shame, of dissent, of exposure. The imagined unifying end point and the 'brute force' of Renaissance designs were attractive because they expressed hope for pure order and hence predictability. For Ruskin, such hope was overrated. Recalling Thomas Hobbes' view of hope as a 'whetstone for desire', Ruskin too found that it served to sharpen our focus on goals and in doing so absolved us from a philosophical acceptance of living a life in the everyday, with all its attendant unfinished edginess. The Gothic was a recovery and acceptance of this edginess; an experience that was both functional and spiritual. Our functional problems and the manner in which we attempted to solve them were ongoing and of varied trajectories, rather than stochastic and cumulative; each solution threw up new problems, and what was problematic for some was not for others. Our spiritual sensibility was, likewise, inevitably imperfect; we sensed meanings and had insight without at all grasping fully the inner mysteries of life. The Gothic was an honest admission of these functional and spiritual limits. The function of Gothic buildings was revealed in their structure; their indigenous, human scale carried fallibility, and what, asked Ruskin, is wrong with admitting such fallibility? Indeed, it is all to the good that we endure it; hence his elevation of suffering, poverty and decay as encapsulating an 'unpretending strength of heart'.

The Gothic sensibility encapsulates an attitude not of passivity but of enduring life as naturally as possible, to immerse oneself in the open-ended intricacies of nature without hankering after completion and essences. There was no need for adopting the pretence of idealized structures, of constantly looking to impose symmetry and to restore order according to the latest fashion. In this, the Gothic takes as a pattern nature itself; its tempering and massing of light and shade, of colours, of rock and foliage, of sky and earth, in ways that cannot be reduced to constituent elements or repeating symmetries. In their buildings, Gothic architects embraced contradiction and contrast in their designs *and* in their methods, not least by allowing those they typically instruct (builders, masons and even labourers) and those for whom they work (clients, users of public spaces) to become involved in the conception, and by themselves becoming involved in the construction.[35] As with the brotherly bringing together of unlike natures, so with the bringing together of activities that create a building. In allowing this breadth and variety of expression a more naturalistic, nuanced and organic form emerges and the building becomes well suited to endure the discontinuities and changes inherent in its being used. Ruskin's veneration of the great Gothic cathedrals of Europe was born of this recognition. The buildings hit you not because of their perfection and completeness but because of their animated endurance. They were built over generations in a spirit of belonging, penitence, humour and emergence, becoming collective expressions of lived tradition, but never being constrained by them.[36]

Ruskin's 'Gothic sensibility', in its elevation of the varied, the nuanced, the imperfect, the inherent frailties and the limits of human comprehension as well as its unconscious appreciation for the 'unpretending strength of heart', encapsulates what we have termed here the 'dwelling' as opposed to a technically ordered and often intellectualized 'building' world view. Against the spectacular, confident, well-ordered, aspirational niceness of Renaissance designs, with their idealized forms, neat and tidy models, and sharp focuses, the Gothic sensibility – with its open-endedness, transparent honesty and frank and public confession of weakness – reverberates much more with the lived experiences and vulnerability of everyday lives, including especially those of strategy practitioners. What we therefore find in Ruskin's insights on the aesthetic sensibility are the very qualities that make for a deep appreciation of what a dwelling world view implies in the practice of researching, understanding and doing strategy. Embracing a dwelling world view with its sense of the Gothic as a strategic orientation towards understanding strategy-in-practice implies looking at the overlooked; sifting through the fragments, cracks, variations and inconsistencies beneath the superficial gloss and appreciating how these surface appearances of coherence and unity belie a deeper, messier and at times logically incoherent strategic reality. It is only through this painstaking attention to the irregularities and non-conformity of the detailed and the mundane that we will be able to truly follow the actual goings-on in the world of business strategizing.

Heidegger revisited

We have dwelt on Ruskin's idea of the Gothic at some length because we feel that it resonates with Heidegger's notion of dwelling in a profound way. The sympathy with Heidegger is very apparent. Ruskin's Gothic comes across as an attempt to elaborate on dwelling, through its resistance to order (through near-symmetry rather than a brittle annihilation, or negation), its undermining of individual, human elevation (the sense of a building being something that expresses an organic unity of elements, a system in a system) and its acceptance of failure and anxiety (it is only by admitting our failures and the edginess from within our projects that we can experience how things might be otherwise; the potential that lies outside the deliberate purposes we articulate and aim for with well-groomed design). Where Heidegger takes us on, however, is in his thoughts about how such a condition of enduring, dwelling life manifests itself not just in constructed buildings generally but in the building of a human life, for which he coined the term *Dasein*. Ruskin uses the term 'noble picturesque' to describe and evoke a sense of how a building such as the church tower at Calais endures. Unlike a church tower, however, *Dasein* has a sense of its life as something *to be led*; it is a life in which each individual has an interest. Here dwelling takes on a peculiarly febrile tone, because to live as *Dasein* is constantly to disclose a life in open-ended encounter with other entities. These encounters can begin with entities as they are, used by us as equipment that either works (in which case the things are not readily noticed, as they remain tools or means to realize pragmatic purposes) or does not work. When things no longer work they are typically understood as broken, requiring the kind of fix Bateson speaks of. Here they become isolated, subject to theorizing; a pragmatic *technē* gives way to one informed by *episteme* in attempts to restore their use value (readiness to hand). As *Dasein*, though, we might also linger on these things as things awhile, try and see them apart either from their instrumental life, or from their intellectual representation, and it is the singular expression of such multiple encounters that Ruskin finds in the Gothic character. What are fixed by the constructions of Gothic sculptors and architects are not static objects, nor theoretically presented objects indicating the restoration of some human end point, but things that are simply animated by the endless experience of being-in-the-world. The flux and movement being conveyed is not physical motion but a disclosure of dwelling; what is exciting about the Gothic world is not what is produced but the collaborative, open-ended manner in which any production takes place.

In Heidegger, this Gothic sense of dwelling is most closely echoed by the activity of *thinking*. Far from being a Cartesian separation, thinking is the experience of being amid the things of life in their enigmatic and untouchable nearness, a placing and sustaining of our own lives in the flow of events and things that are both with us and yet constantly turning away, withdrawing, moving on. This is why we wrote earlier of dwelling and *phronesis* in terms of beginning with, but not ending with, habituated activity. In *What Is Called Thinking?*, Heidegger expands on this with the example of a cabinet maker, an artisan who continually forces herself to answer and respond to different kinds of wood, the different temperament, the differing latency of forms within the wood. Heidegger regards this relatedness as a willingness to be amid things on mutual rather than one-sided terms, an acceptance of meaning that is typically concealed under the impress of overt or implicit individual purposes. What defines an artisan such as a cabinet maker is not simply the skilled use of tools, nor having undergone instruction using manuals and correction, but a heedful regard for the often disorienting and surprising experience of being under way amongst the things and events of the world without requiring them to conform entirely to our own designs.[37] The artisan is aware of an intrinsic richness of things and of the relations and feelings we have with these things (including one another). The cabinet maker does not simply move towards or away from a certain kind of wood out of entirely selfish, instrumental concern, but is aware of the wood being something that ought to be treated in a certain way; the wood is transformed from being simply a material asset or thing-in-relation-to-human-design, part of a standing reserve for her own immediate ends, into a thing with possibilities that demand consideration, curiosity, sensitivity.

The artisan encounters things such as wood, tools, the equipmental demands of furniture without reducing these encounters to an entirely instrumental logic of pragmatic confinement; her identity is one of constant disclosure within this relational condition that she animates, but over which she has no distinct perspective or control; the world resists in some way. In Heidegger's terms, she is always under way without any real sense of starting or end points; she is creating meanings as she goes, and in experiencing being under way she herself is changing, learning, accepting irreversibly that in her expressive activity things are brought into life in ways that are not entirely within our grasp, nor faithfully echo our purposes. The cabinet maker thinks because she is intimately aware of her unthinking, equipmental relationship with her tools, her raw materials, the functional needs of those using their furniture, and so on. She also thinks, insofar as she is aware, of how this equipmental relationship demands of things that they are disclosed in certain ways; that the wood be disclosed in forms conforming to the physiological framing of human anatomy or the symbolic framing of an economic good. She is alive to the latency, or potential of things being otherwise outside the confines of human expression. Thinking is not just recognizing an equipmental relationship with things and events but, even more thoughtfully, being inquisitive about the limits of the demands that we humans can make upon the world; thinkers accept the authority of the world, and their role as stewards in it.[38]

In our view, the representation or character of the strategist being portrayed by many researchers and strategists themselves is, typically, not 'under way' in the Heideggerian sense. He does not think. The strategist is always looking at the world knowledgeably, on his terms; the task is to subject the world into a condition of pliant and communicable phenomena such that his reach, and the reach of his organization, remains assured, governed and purposeful. Equipment is acknowledged as such only when it conforms entirely to the strategist's avowed aim; there is little of the sensitivity of the cabinet maker, who uses things aware of these things having their own terms of reliability, their own 'summons', to which she makes fitting responses.[39] The strategist's form of use is degenerate because there is no sense of things having any identity other than that conferred by the dictates of human users; things are put on a notice of stand-by; no thing calls on him to think; everything stands still, devoid of life, awaiting his ordering manipulation by which these things are understood identically, as resources.[40] In this the strategist evokes an all-encompassing technology rather than uses tools; the strategist is himself part of a wider technology of identikit ordering; the perspective and choice sets configured by the strategist are technologically determined. All things and all tools exist only insofar as they are connected into ordering technology by which all phenomena are to be made available for analysis and exploitation: land reveals itself as geology replete with mineral resources, or otherwise; people are made available as character types, as variable costs or as sources of demand. In this encapsulation of the world into small, law-governed variables, the strategist ignores something of himself and the self of others and other things. The strategist demands that nature become a 'something'; hence Heidegger's constant recurrence to the poet Friedrich Hölderlin's lament for humanity: 'We are the sign that is not read/We feel no pain, we almost have/Lost our tongue in foreign lands.'[41]

The loss is palpable, perhaps no more so than in the world of business. Representations of business strategists have become the apotheosis of the strategist character. Business has become a theatrical affair: goals and the preoccupations of managers are understood as concerning themselves again and again with how best to configure and change the resources at their disposal across the entirety of an organization and its wider institutional environment in order to maximize and sustain revenue streams. In the service of this purposeful endeavour, all manner of reviews, plans, data-gathering, technological systems, procedures and instructions are ordered into representational sequences. Whereas the cabinet maker belongs to a 'gathering' of things in which each thing (the tools, the furniture, the artisan, the wood, and so on) is inextricably woven and yet distinct, the strategist occupies an ordering of arenas, vehicles, logics, milestones and tools that make up an overtly organized world of challenge. Things are made available as 'inventory'. The world is a world that is organized so as to – first – tackle it, take it on, and – second – make it available as a resource; the strategic aim is to get clear and comprehensive views of everything, which is realized by viewing everything from a distance, and in an identical way, as a standing reserve.[42]

The term 'standing reserve' is a potent one. There is no time to let things emerge, to dwell with things. The strategist's demands are too urgent, too specific; the bridge is not in communion with the river; rather, the river is brought into the road network, of which the bridge is an element. The strategist acts so as to work and move upon this institutional landscape; the organization goes from where it is to where strategy deems it should be; it grows, evolves, changes configuration under the aegis of planning and calculation in order that the challenge issued to nature as a stock of resources continues to be a successful one. Heidegger uses the term *Gestell* (frame) to describe the technological system in which the strategist acts and thinks. The *gestell* envelops us all; we are all complicit with its ordering, distancing, dividing modes of organizing that seep through to our very basic awareness of need and belonging. In contrast with the cabinet maker, the strategist lives in a deadening world: standing resources are simply moved from one place to another; there is no sense of what it is like to think with them, changing irreversibly with such unfolding experience, encountering resistance from things in themselves (rather than as resources that are desired and yet others possess) by simply letting those things be. There is little awareness of the world as inherently open, ongoing, latent; no willingness simply to let an almond tree blossom without having then to enquire after the disaggregated machinery and causal logic by which such an unfurling takes place or after the commercial potential of its pollinating bees. The world of the business strategist has withdrawn completely into a flat and familiar landscape of resources, goals, representations and expectations, all of which conspire to make the world smaller; a known world of known latitude and redundancies without sparkle or obscurity.

Expressing thought

What Ruskin found expressed in the Gothic and in Turner, Heidegger found in the works of Vincent Van Gogh. Van Gogh's images are alive with meanings inherently bound to the life world of the artist, to the lives of those viewing the painting and to those of the subjects being painted. An artistic insight is realized through letting oneself be drawn into the inevitable movement of life, immersed in the things that resonate with their own, unique history as well as anticipate their future. They are entirely latent and they resonate not with completeness but with an attractive ambiguity that invites the viewer to participate in their fuller expression.[43] It was the feeling of involvement and anticipation on seeing Van Gogh's portrait of a pair of peasant's clogs, for example, that prompted Heidegger to write 'The origin of the work of art'. Rather than represent a piece of practical footwear, Van Gogh discloses the being and becoming of a mundane thing, much as Ruskin tried to do in his description of the Calais church tower, and to an extent Chardin did with his 'near-documentary' style. Van Gogh's clogs hang there in examined close-up, without context; no wearer, no sign of mud, no background of a field and hovel. They hang there, apparently abstracted from the world, yet

[F]rom the dark opening of the worn insides of the shoes the toilsome tread of the worker stands forth. In the stiffly solid heaviness of the shoes there is the accumulated tenacity of her slow trudge through the far-spreading and ever-uniform furrows of the field, swept by a raw wind. On the leather there lies the dampness and saturation of the soil. Under the soles there slides the loneliness of the field-path as the evening declines... This equipment is pervaded by uncomplaining anxiety about the certainty of bread, the wordless joy of having once more withstood want, the trembling before the advent of birth, and shivering at the surrounding menace of death. This equipment belongs to the earth and it is protected in the world of the peasant woman. From out of this protected belonging the equipment itself rises to its resting in itself.[44]

From this rendition of the shoes the painter is conveying the existence not just of a thing, but a thing disclosed in a world: its equipmental being; its stoical reliability; its endurance and steadfastness under the impress of rotting weather and the denuding passage of time. The image disclosed what a pair of shoes is, the knowledge being knowledge not of a thing in matter and form but of a thing being used; the painting, as in the Gothic sculpture, discloses the being of what is in the actual work of art. As we encounter them, the shoes can be broken down through representations, parsed into constituent elements, subjected to rigorous testing for safety and functionality; but all this analysis will never reveal what the shoes really are. No explicit epistemology can do this; but what can be done is to make things more apparent by setting them forth in a context of being, a space of disclosure, in which the constant struggle between being and becoming can be witnessed as such by outsiders, viewers, and who can preserve and learn from the struggle in their viewing. The clogs are rendered in duration; the static image resonates with an entire history and prospect of use, and which, as an image, also resonates with viewers with their own constituting powers. The viewers themselves are not separated from the image but brought in by a sense of personal anticipation. Unlike the rigidly outlined foliage on the Doge's Palace, the image of the clogs is incomplete, suggestive, an absence that provokes the viewer and painter alike into a state of *interesse*, of being amidst things as they are in all their open-ended potential. It is in absence that we find potential – we anticipate what we might be but at present are not – as well as dissolution, in anticipating our ageing, or our death. It is through this anticipation that we disclose our own being, we are a thrown project; an undertaking through which disclosure we make of the world a place of such disclosure for other entities. In being known through disclosure we are not known simply as an entity but as an entity who is becoming.

We encounter Van Gogh's peasant shoes already knowing the equipmental nature of shoes generally, and having seen representations of shoes, their form and their component parts, and having groped into imperfect traditions associated with the agricultural lives of ancestors. What is being revealed here is not the specific utility of the shoe but the abundance of being by which this utility is possible:

The equipmental quality of equipment was discovered. But how? Not by a description and explanation of a pair of shoes actually present; not by a report about the process of making shoes; and also not by the observation of the actual use of shoes occurring here and there; but only bringing ourselves before Van Gogh's painting. This painting spoke. In the nearness of the work we were suddenly somewhere else than we usually tend to be.[45]

We tend not to be there because, as *Dasein*, we typically encounter things as being with (in the sense that we behave in the acceptable, usual ways of everyone, and so anyone) and as readiness to hand (we understand things as they are, and have been, used). Our intellect takes us out of this mode of being; we abstract from entities properties, types and the like, to make sense of our lives through the use of structures built by our reason. This is one way of encountering things as they are present, indifferent to any specific encounter. What Ruskin and Heidegger (as well as Bergson) wish to remind us of, however, is our tendency to elevate this mode of abstraction as particularly true, or accurate, at the expense of our appreciating dwelling. Gothic sculpture and Van Gogh's clogs do the contrary, taking us away from our technologically ordered and intellectualized condition. In encountering these works of art we confront a world that is not simply an accumulation of ready-to-hand things, nor something that we imagine, or invent, so as to superadumbrate things with transcendent generalities. What distinguishes the work of art from the entity we term a pair of clogs, therefore, is that whereas the clogs are brought forth in order that their nature be then ignored (they become serviceable pieces of equipment), or that they are brought forth to be analysed in terms of their material form and dimensions, Van Gogh's work brings forth something whose thingliness is revealed by what is implied rather than what is explicitly stated. It is this kind of paradoxically distanced emotional involvement, this near-documenting of things, this thoughtfulness and attunement, that are required if we are to understand what we mean by the real experience of strategy.

In summary, this chapter gives rise to two points of issue with Nonaka and Toyama's understanding of strategy as distributed *phronesis*. First, whilst *phronesis* is the kind of engaged awareness that is often overlooked by strategy researchers wanting to understand strategic experiences from within, it is not the kind of awareness that can be articulated and codified by individual leaders and their followers in the ways suggested. It is not in the gift of an individual to articulate or dispense *phronetic* awareness to others, because a whole host of evaluative and historical scene-setting has to occur in order for any *phronetic* engagement to make sense. Equipmental awareness remains immanent to a system nested in other systems and the possible relations, affects, motivations and outcomes of action and thought in such system-bound systems are always latent; what occurs is always absorbed by what potentially could occur but that remains unarticulated. Second, *phronesis* and its associated *praxis* extend beyond a simply pragmatic relationship with things; the manner of appropriate awareness of things is governed not just by their being tools we are able to use but also by their being things-present-in-themselves, distinct from our pragmatic use of them. *Phronesis* is a capacity to attend to what is appropriate for things-in-themselves as much as things-in-use, and a willingness to accept that things-in-themselves are always much more than what they appear to be; a concealment that draws us on. The manner of style of dwelling involves a bringing forth of things that can be equipmental (things understood as *pragmata*) but also *phronetic*, alive to non-productive, non-equipmental life as a latent, concealed source of potential. To dwell is to act unthinkingly in the wider swim of wider system influences, therefore to be aware of how *poiēsis* breaks down on occasion and to be able to recognize the creative potential erupting from the indifferent pure presence of things as they are outside our relationships with them. Researching and understanding this condition, therefore, is not confined to an abstracting analysis of our relationship with things as equipmental habit or the intellectual recovery of habit. It can also involve a kind of bringing forth exemplified by the Gothic sensibility and in works of art such as Van Gogh's clogs, in which the equipmentality of things in the constantly moving, open-ended world into which we are thrown is made visible and remains unconcealed, rather than hidden in use, and in being so we can see hints of things other than their being just equipment. To research strategy, then, is to get at how we ourselves, and others and other non-human things, appear as ready-to-hand equipment, to understand how this readiness to hand breaks down when things no longer act as fully functioning means to know ends and to appreciate the range of possible responses to this breakdown, whether they are: efforts at pragmatic recovery (*technē*); efforts at sense-making involving intellectual abstractions (*episteme*); or a loosening of effort associated with a continual encounter with things presenting themselves on their own terms, which is what Heidegger regards as the proper condition of there (*da*) being (*sein*) (*phronesis*). In the next chapter we begin to suggest one way in which this might be done by understanding strategic practice using the metaphor of wayfinding.

6   Strategy as 'wayfinding'

[W]e know *as* we go, not *before* we go (ambulatory knowing). . .the world is *not* ready-made for life to occupy . . . It is rather laid out along paths of movement. . . To find one's way is to advance along a line of growth, in a world. . .whose future configuration can never be fully known.

Tim Ingold, The Perception of the Environment, *pp. 230–31*
(*emphasis in original*)

In the previous chapter we identified two distinct modes of engaging with the world strategically, which we termed building and dwelling. In the building mode the agent-strategist is presumed to construct mental representations of the world prior to any practical engagement with it. The dwelling mode of engagement, on the other hand, consists of local adaptations and ingenuity in everyday practical coping, which constitute the kind of micro-strategizing associated with the practice approach to strategy. In acting strategically on an everyday basis, therefore, an agent is acting purposively to deal with immediate concerns at hand but doing so in habituated ways that are consistent with and reinforcing his or her own sense of identity. He or she is also aware, potentially, of the limits of this pragmatic engagement, and of how things might be encountered other than simply as equipment for human ends.

Whereas in the next chapter we develop the sense of strategic limit brought about by dwelling amid things phronetically, *in this chapter we begin to develop the dwelling approach by introducing the notion of strategy as a process of wayfinding, in contrast to the conventional idea of strategy-making as a navigational process. Whilst the latter view presupposes the strategic actor to be detached and surveying his or her individual circumstance from a 'bird's-eye' point of view, the wayfinding view treats the agent as intimately immersed in and inextricable from contexts, and, as such, his or her actions emanate from within the constantly evolving circumstance. Here strategy-making is about reaching out into the unknown and developing an incomplete but practically sufficient comprehension of the situation in order to cope effectively with it. Prospective rather than retrospective sense-making is involved. What this implies is that strategy is continuously clarified through each iterative action and adjustment and not through any predetermined agenda.*

159

Strategic positioning and navigation

In business theorizing, strategy provides one of the more obvious candidates for a world view still informed by a building mode of explanation. Strategy invokes images of conscious intention, deliberate forethought and rational planning, and it is the presumed scope and coverage of such strategic activities that provide a kind of organizational duvet through which those who live and work in organizations are presumed to derive their purpose and meaning. Strategists are deemed to be knowledgeable agents who, being in possession of clear purposes, theoretical principles and technological means, can bring about intended outcomes by the proper mobilization of available expertise and resources. This overtly means–ends form of thinking has it that the correct job of strategy is to establish clear corporate destinations, plot an efficient course of action to arrive at the destination specified and use organization to align contractual and governance structures in such a way as to exploit fully the range of available resources, given the knowledge that other strategists in other organizations and institutions will be attempting to do likewise. In this caricature of strategy-making the analogy often adopted is that of cognitive mapping and of *navigation*. The strategist is often likened to the captain of a ship, who, using established maps and models of the environmental situation, knowingly specifies the intended destination, plots the course to be taken and steers the corporate vessel successfully towards its predetermined destination.

This image of strategy-making as a navigational process involving map-using is exemplified in particular by some of the most compelling questions incessantly asked and widely popularized by strategy textbooks; questions such as 'Where are we now?' and 'Where do we want to go?', locations that are ostensibly asked by management practitioners and consultants alike. The knowledge being sought here is knowledge of where individual bodies of people are, where they might go and how this direction can be pursued within a wider navigable territory of well-known, less well-known and unknown circumstances that present the potential for, and obstacles to, reaching the destination. According to this widespread and dominant view, the answer to the questions posed may be found through recourse to models, maps and classifications that represent the topology of the strategic terrain to be negotiated. These 'cognitive maps' of strategic realities present the external environment as an even, stable surface to be occupied, controlled and manipulated at will. Knowing where one is, therefore, entails identifying one's current position with a corresponding location on the model or map and then attempting to move from one location to another by means of it.

Whether one employs one of the popular two-by-two strategy matrices, such as that developed by the Boston Consulting Group (BCG) or Michael Porter's 'five forces' model of industry attractiveness, the intention is to identify a suitable competitive position for the organization vis-à-vis the industry sector and then to navigate one's way towards it. In this regard, the idea of strategy-making as a navigational act has been either explicitly or implicitly incorporated into the mindsets of strategy theorists, and now through the widespread influence of Master of Business Administration (MBA) programmes into the consciousness and awareness of would-be strategy practitioners.

Tim Ingold, citing the work of Edwin Hutchins, suggests that navigation 'is a collection of techniques for answering a small number of questions, perhaps the most central of which is "Where am I?"'.[1] According to Hutchins, what we need to have in order to feel that the question may be satisfactorily answered is some form of representation of the space to be negotiated; a map, whether inscribed externally on a piece of paper or internally in the mind. Through the use of this map one can then establish a coherent set of correspondences between what is shown on the map and what one observes in one's own surroundings. Only then can the questions "Where am I?" and "Where do I want to go?" be answered. Ingold suggests a sympathy between this view and that of Alfred Gell, who maintains that the act of navigation 'consists of a cyclic process whereby images generated from maps are matched up against perceptual information, and perceptual images are identified with equivalent coordinates on a map'.[2] For both Hutchins and Gell, therefore, navigation, reduced to its bare essentials, is a quintessentially cognitive task that we all face all the time as we find our way about, be it on land, at sea or even in the air. Navigational techniques may vary and the complexity of each situation encountered may differ but none of this alters the fact that

[w]hen the navigator is satisfied that he has arrived at a coherent set of correspondences he might look to the chart and say 'Ah yes; I am here, off this point of land.' *And it is in this sense that most of us feel we know where we are.* We feel we have achieved a reconciliation between the features we see in our world and a representation of that world.[3]

Navigation, therefore, is predicated upon the pre-existence of maps and charts, which, in turn, presumes the capacity for a detached surveying of the terrain to be navigated. As Ingold points out, though, this imaginative act of achieving a reconciliation requires that we have a 'bird's-eye point of view' – something not normally attainable save from an aircraft overhead or through modern satellite means. In effect, this abstract and deductive capability for achieving such a reconciliation is not a natural endowment but something learnt and internalized. This would explain why a passenger on a ship not trained in the techniques of navigation may be quite unable to achieve this reconciliation and 'may confess to being baffled by maps and charts. He cannot, in other words translate from his on-board experience of motion as moving through a surrounding space to the depiction of motion on the chart as that of an object moving across a space.'[4] Navigators, on the other hand are so accustomed to thinking of movement in navigational terms that they find it difficult to imagine the perception of this movement from the ordinary experience of the passenger himself.

What navigators have learnt to do is to internalize a technologically governed building world view in which navigation is perceived as a mode of movement involving the intermediary of an ordering map. With the means of such a map, a person situates him- or herself on the ground through a comparison to 'a location in space, as defined by particular map coordinates'.[5] Such a locating activity is devoid of any historical narratives or memory traces of the place that might have resulted from prolonged inhabitation over time. They do not dwell, but simply measure dimensions in time and space. In navigation there are, basically, places designated by the map and the non-places in-between. Through the map as a navigational aid it is possible to 'specify where one is – one's current location – without regard to where one has been, or where one is going'.[6] By connecting points on a map, navigation allows a person to move from place to place at will, since these identifiable places have been translated into grid coordinates such that it offers a flat projection of the terrain one is attempting to negotiate. It is this stubbornly held notion that the questions 'Where are we?' and 'Where do we want to go?' must be answered in spatial terms – as expressed in terms of coordinates or as a point along a sequence of points, à la Bergson's extensive manifold – that severely restricts our understanding of how ordinary people move around and get by on a day-to-day basis.[7]

Similarly, in thinking and representing the strategic situation in terms of positions and locations on maps and models, there is a presumption that strategy-in-practice must be conceived solely in building terms. Here the relationship of the strategist with the world is understood as seeking a general representation of the world as something distinct from him- or herself, and consisting of fixed resources spread out across territories, amenable to canalizing and to movement so as to bring about closure between known start and end points. This is a general view realized by removal from the world. It is a view the strategist believes to be all-sided, an overview. It is a map of markets and market opportunities, more or less complete, dependent on the accuracy and penetration of information sources, the complexity of territorial environments, the capacity and robustness of the tools being used, and so on. For Heidegger, this strategist's view is not all-sided but one-sided; not because there is an omission on the map, so to speak, or because navigational reason is inevitably bounded, but because it is a mapped view abetted by machines and controlled by the singular interests of solitary, well-ordered humans who are themselves part of the scene – isolated things to be ordered as potential means. The world is understood as an amalgam of events and things that present themselves to the strategist's perception and remain amenable to his or her perception because of increasingly sophisticated mediation, such as mapping technologies.[8] As we suggested earlier, in acting this way the character of the strategist is an expression of a more general epistemological relationship that we occidental humans tend to have with our world. We elevate our consciousness; both in ourselves, as the mind governs the body, and collectively, as the world is represented as mute heap of things/events against which we human beings presume to exercise some form of conscious, unilateral challenge. The strategist is a condensed characterization of an epistemological tendency to regard ourselves in opposition to our surroundings, a peculiarly modern figure whose skilful trope is one of reducing the world to isolated variables held in plotted relations across given territories.

In this chapter we explore the metaphor of 'wayfinding' in strategy-making as an alternative to navigation, and show that thinking of strategy in navigational terms, with its *spatial* and technical ordering emphasis, derives from a building world view whilst wayfinding, which is associated with a dwelling world view, points to the inherently durational character of strategy emergence in practice. Following Ingold, we make clear distinctions between the activities of *mapping, map-making* and *map-using*, and show how the process of mapping as wayfinding is *performative* rather than *inscriptive* and that it precedes both the activities of map-making and map-using (navigation). Thus the experience of moving from one place to another comprises the opening up and closing of vistas and things such that the environment is progressively disclosed to the advancing observer in the course of ambulation. In other words, strategic wayfinding is characterized not as a plotted sequence of static positions but as the coming-into-sight and passing-out-of-sight of various contoured and textured aspect of the environment. In this way, we can begin to conceive of strategy-in-practice not as a process of locating positions using pre-established reference points but as a dynamic, evolving and self-referential process of discovery and self-clarification that is never complete because things are always turning away.

Knowing as we go: mapping, map-making and map-using

Whilst both Hutchins and Gell and many others view navigation and wayfinding interchangeably, insisting that this capability is necessarily reliant on the establishment of internal or external 'maps', Ingold argues persuasively for an important difference between navigation and *wayfinding*. Unlike navigation, which presupposes knowing '*before* we go', wayfinding involves knowing *as we go*: an 'ambulatory' form of knowing.[9] For him, '[n]avigation (or map-*using*) is as strange to the ordinary practices of wayfinding as is cartography (or map-*making*) to ordinary practices'.[10] This is because, in wayfinding, the question 'Where am I?' is not answered in terms of location in space but, rather, in terms of the sense of familiarity and comfort that we feel in knowing where we are. It depends on the 'attunement of the traveller's movements in response to the movements, in his or her surroundings of other people, animals, the wind, celestial bodies, and so on'.[11] For instance, the Micronesian seafarers relied on the position of the sun and the movement of the waves to aid them in finding their way from island to island. Ingold's argument is sustained by his reading of a classic paper on the subject of Micronesian seafaring by Thomas Gladwin, which describes how, at every movement during the voyage, the mariner is attentive to 'a combination of motion, sound, feel of the wind, wave patterns, star relationships, etc.' that, through a comparison with internalized observations from past experiences, is unthinkingly translated into 'a slight increase or decrease in pressure on the steering paddle'.[12] Unlike the trained navigator, with his charts, compasses and even satellite navigation instruments, the Micronesian seafarer 'feels his way towards his destination by continually adjusting his movements in relation to the *flow* of waves, wind, current and stars. In this respect, his activity does not differ in principle from the terrestrial traveller who responds to the flow of perspective structure as he journeys through a landscape ... [E]very journey is remembered as a movement through time rather than across space'.[13] Similarly, in the case of the Umela tribe in Papua New Guinea that Alfred Gell himself studied, the dense and continuous forests required sensory perception to be more auditory than visual. In the thickly covered forests, the Umela 'travelled with eyes downcast, looking for thorns and obstacles on the path while they "surveyed" their surroundings with their ever-receptive ears'.[14] Hearing for the Umela is the primary sense for detecting and assessing events and situations. The multitude of sounds heard in the midst of the forest – the winds, trees, flowing water, etc. – were all crucial to Umela wayfinding activities. No maps of any sort, whether internal or external, were required for them to make their way successfully through the dense forest. In both the cases of Micronesian seafarers and Umela travel, an 'ambulatory' form of knowing that is distinguishable from navigational understanding appears to characterize the kind of wayfinding skills that are acquired *in situ*. In both instances, action and comprehension radiates outwards from the situation an individual finds herself in. The difference between navigation and wayfinding, therefore, is precisely that paralleled by the distinction between building and dwelling that we have previously made.

Ingold suggests that the subtle, but vital, difference between navigation and wayfinding can be illustrated by the two alternative but familiar everyday situations. Let us, first, imagine that you and a companion are walking through unfamiliar terrain equipped with a map of the area. You reach a scenic spot and your friend asks you: 'Where are we?' You scan the terrain, refer back to the map, look for correlating features, and then finally indicate a point on the map and say: 'We are here.' This is the typical instrumental approach to answering the question 'Where are we?'. Consider, alternatively, that you are walking with your friend, not in unfamiliar terrain this time but around the countryside where you have lived and been brought up. When your companion asks 'Where are we?' you may at first state the name of the place, but, very quickly, you follow up with a personal story about your own association with the place, the people you knew, the things that happened there as a part of your growing up, and so on. In this second instance, you have no need to consult a map, not because you already have a map in your head, so to speak, but because your present whereabouts are intimately linked to your life history and your experiences and the way that they have shaped your personality, identity and predispositions. It is not about fixing your location in space using some established reference point. In the first scenario, you have little or no knowledge of the terrain; you are a 'foreigner' to the land, a 'visitor' or a researcher trying to understand the practice of strategy-making. For those who know the country first-hand (so to speak), however, the question 'Where are we?', or even 'Where shall we go?', are not found in reference to the map but in relation to their past experiences and in relation to the narratives acquired within the context they found themselves in, and hence how they have shaped their identities and aspirations. 'As someone who has lived in a country, and is used to its ways, knowing where you are lies not in the establishment of a point-to-point correspondence between the world and its representation, but in the remembering of journeys previously made, and that brought you to the place along the same or different paths.'[15] In the first scenario, using a map to locate where we are and where we might go incurs a lack of flexibility that is often problematic, notably in moments of breakdown, when the occurrence of unexpected events demands that people break from the map of standardized and specialized distinctions and behave more flexibly, looking to absorb the unfamiliar experience by renegotiating norms. This requires a different ordering of difference and a different understanding of maps and metaphors. Here what is being represented is a shifting scene *within which* we find ourselves.

Unlike the act of navigation, wayfinding implies progressing tentatively and incrementally reaching out from one's situated circumstance, using oneself, and not some independent external point, as the basis of reference. For the wayfinder, the territory is boundless and bottomless, using self-referential devices to express experience there and then as he or she moves *through* the landscape. Wayfinding precedes navigation. In a fascinating and exhaustively researched piece of work, Gavin Menzies, a retired submarine captain in the Royal Navy, argues convincingly that the 'new worlds' were discovered well before Bartolomeu Dias rounded the Cape of Good Hope in 1487, before Vasco da Gama reached India ten years later and certainly before Christopher Columbus first sighted land in the modern Bahamas.[16] Menzies shows that these latter achievements owed much to the influence of Henry the Navigator, the Portuguese prince whose base in south-west Portugal served as an academy for explorers, cartographers, shipwrights and instrument makers. What Menzies astonishingly and controversially reveals, however, is that Henry himself had had access to the knowledge and understanding of a group of mysterious master mariners who had discovered these new lands and oceans without leaving any trace of their own identities. In his own epic voyage to discover the intriguing source of this knowledge of the oceans and lands, Menzies came to the 'incontestable proof' that it was the ancient Chinese mariners who had explored the world long before the Europeans did so. Using nothing more than lodestone compasses that they had discovered showed a consistency of direction wherever they were, hourglasses of sand (ten hourglasses to a day) to measure their lived time, and the stars to guide their passage, they set out from the Longjiang shipyards in southern China on their epic voyages of discovery during the reign of Emperor Zhu Di (1402–1421). It was the Chinese seafarers, then, who first explored the oceans and new lands, and provided narrative accounts that were then converted into navigational aids for the subsequent 'discoveries' made by the Europeans.[17]

These colourful Chinese accounts 'passed from da Conti to Fra Mauro and from him to Dom Pedro of Portugal and Prince Henry the Navigator'.[18] They were invaluable to the subsequent achievements of the Portuguese, but these achievements might never have taken place had the rudimentary decorative charts produced by the Chinese as aids to their recounting and storytelling not been produced first. These were never intended as maps but as aides-memoires for the retelling of their voyaging experiences.

The central point we wish to make here is that without first engaging in wayfinding, without the painstaking task of noting, internalizing and memorizing each little success in wayfinding, as the example of the Micronesians and Chinese seafarers shows, no map could possibly exist and navigation as map-*using* would not be possible; the dwelling world view has to precede a building world view. The activity of wayfinding precedes both map-*making* and map-*using*. This is because the wayfinder's understanding unfolds over time through the accretion of many different experiences, with the result that every place encountered 'holds with it memories of previous arrivals and departures, as well as expectations of how one may reach it, or reach other places from it'.[19] To account for this wayfinding mode of engagement, characterized by its 'knowledgeable ambulating', Ingold introduces the notion of *mapping*, as a third term that cannot be accommodated by the dichotomy between map-using (navigation) and map-making (cartography).

Ingold's concept of 'mapping' is to be strenuously differentiated from the commonly held notion of 'cognitive mapping', which pervades much of the literature in the social sciences and the strategy literature in particular, and it shares much with Ruskin's notion of Gothic building work. For Ingold, mapping is a physical activity more akin to the performance of storytelling. 'The traveller or storyteller who knows as he goes is neither making a map nor using one. He is, quite simply, mapping.'[20] Something like this is expressed by the artist and map-maker Tim Robinson:

For me, making a map was to be a one-to-one encounter between a person and a terrain, a commitment unlimitable in terms of time and effort, an existential project of knowing a place. The map itself could hardly then be more than an interim report on the progress of its own making.[21]

Mapping is similar to a speech act whose appropriateness and sense remain intimate to the space in which it is uttered, whereas map-making involves acts of prescription whose detail and technical finesse come to subsume the less articulate experience of dwelling. In other words, it is only when the map itself, rather than the situated performance of storytelling, becomes the focus of attention, instead of being just an aid to the latter, that mapping gives way to map-making. At this point maps are outputs of *poiēsis*, they cease to be 'by-products of story-telling, and are created instead as end-products of projects of spatial representation... [M]apmaking suppresses, or "brackets out", both the movement of the people as they come and go between places (wayfinding) and the re-enactment of those movements in inscriptive gesture.'[22] As regards an awareness of the world, the distinction is telling. For Ingold, the wayfarer literally 'knows as he goes'; there is no distinction between movement and cognition, and, whereas the navigator goes across a territory from one isolated point to another, the wayfarer builds up understanding from an irreversible array of wandering experiences.[23]

This is what must have happened with the rudimentary charts of the Chinese in the hands of the Portuguese. What were recorded as aides-memoires for recounting experiences at sea became, in the hands of the Portuguese, valuable navigational aids. That which was performative, transient and communicated in context is rendered a permanent fixture through the act of inscription; *scripta manent, verba volante* (scripts are permanent, words spoken fly away). It is, therefore, this fine line between performance and inscription that differentiates Ingold's 'mapping' from map-making. One consists of an involved, active perceptual engagement with one's experiences, the other a detached translation of that experience into a permanently recorded form. In the transition from the narration of lived experience to the recorded document, the map 'slowly disengages itself from the itineraries that were the conditions of its possibility'. For some time afterwards, these maps would continue to be illustrated with pictures, landforms, people and beasts of various descriptions, winds and currents, etc., but gradually these storied maps were dismissed as quaint decorations, so that the spatial map eventually 'won out over these pictorial figurations, eliminating all remaining traces of the practices that produced it'.[24] At this point, the map takes on a life of its own, detached from the very phenomena, experiences and activities that brought it into being in the first place; the representation has superseded the living reality, 'so the flow of a river along to the sea becomes a line cutting across a plane – a boundary even'.[25] A fallacy of misplaced concreteness ensues, so that the map or representation is mistaken for reality itself.

The Phillips machine

Bringing our discussion right back into the realm of economic and organizational strategy, the distinction between map-making and mapping is played out quite well by the development of what became known as the Phillips machine. Anxious to restore the fortunes of ailing, post-war European economies, the British economists Dennis Robertson and John Maynard Keynes had been embroiled in an ongoing dispute as to how economic demand could be stimulated and then managed through mechanisms of money supply and circulation. Alive to the intricacies of this argument, two economist-engineers, named Bill Phillips and Walter Newlyn, came up with a novel response that they felt would overcome the traditional limitations of representing and understanding economic phenomena using static entities, locations and linear movements. In the place of formulae and curves came Moniac, a three-dimensional simulation device the two men had knocked up in a garage in Croydon, south-east England, in 1949. As with Dr Maerten's boots, post-war austerity meant for a somewhat makeshift first version, glued together, as it was, from a trove of detritus, including bits from old dolls, mothballed Lancaster bombers and broken clocks. The result was a complex array of tanks, valves, pipes and pumps filled with, and emptied of, water of different colours. The tanks represented deposits of money, such as savings or government reserves. The valve-regulated flow of water in the pipes linking the tanks represented money moving around the economy. The flow rate simulated different levels of taxation, interest rates, import and export levels, employment levels, etc. The level of water entering the system was governed by the supply curve, and that leaving the system was governed by the demand curve. Changing the flow using tapering valves and cams represented changes to these values over time that were marked on paper by pens driven by moving water levels. For Newlyn and Phillips, the value of this analogue simulator lay in its ability to convey the emerging relationships in a multivariable, and at times non-linear, system of the functionally dependent variables that went to make up a general economy.[26] They had, in effect, built an animated and controllable map of an economic territory. By replicating changing economic conditions in compressed time, the system gave an accurate (4 per cent tolerance) account of how an economy or economies might behave in real time. It was, for example, by using the machine to ponder how dynamic and complex economies might be stabilized that Phillips began to think about and formulate the intimate relationship between unemployment and wage levels, along with the associated actions and proportional controls needed to balance these variables.

Newlyn and Phillips were engineering-minded; they believed that their machine was an important contribution to the emerging economic discipline of managing production and consumption through the provision of controls. For all its concrete ingenuity, though, it never really coped with the complexity of real economic life. The assemblage of moving parts, multicoloured flows and definite readings gave an impression of how things were and might be, but its testimony was rarely borne out. To assess its worth as detailed 'map', however, is to mistake what, for Newlyn especially, became the real impact of their machine. It was not so much the accuracy or otherwise of its predictions but the almost visceral quality of its representation. For Newlyn, the worth of Moniac lay in its returning those who used it back towards what we have identified as a 'wayfinding' mode. Of course, these students and researchers were not participating in an economy, as they remained intellectually engaged in a representation of it, a bracketing off, yet they began to get a sense of how one part of a system was reliant on other parts, and the entire system on other systems, and that this reliance was ceaseless and inherently open-ended. Those who used the machine 'felt' themselves closer to this thing called the economy in a way that those using formulae to carry out far more nuanced simulations simply did not. The almost preternatural flows of red water, the inexorable tracing of ink on mute graph paper, the sound of escaping air – all of these physical and visual effects conspired to render a dynamic account of mutually interrelated economic variables combining and recombining over time. The machine was impressive because a previously entirely conceptual entity called an economy was being witnessed in a physical state of becoming. This state was still an abstraction, but like all good abstractions it pinpointed and condensed elements of experience held in some kind of relational balance, rather than removing them for isolated inspection. In this the machine worked to upset its own concrete authority as a controlling, ordering device; it became a storytelling device into whose plastic tanks the experience of living with an economy was transformed into one of active rather than passive perception.

The active nature of perception

The relationship between wayfinding understood as inscriptive move-ment and active perception finds eloquent expression in the works of the ecological psychologist J. J. Gibson. For Gibson, perception is a form of practical action and not a passive cognitive activity involving the mere registration of sensations. To perceive something is to actively create a distinction through the bounding of phenomenal experience without thereby presuming oneself separate from the other systems by which that experience is sustained. In this way, the environment is not perceived from any particular framed perspective, or indeed from mul-tiple points of view, but instead takes place along a specific path of observation. Rejecting the notion of navigation by means of cognitive maps, Gibson proposes a 'theory of reversible occlusion' in which one makes one's way around by experiencing the specific sequence in which the surfaces of the environment come into or pass out of sight along the particular path travelled.[27] Take, for example, the experience of entering into a town centre: the façade of buildings, the road ahead rising up to meet you, and all the elements that draw your attention comprise what Gibson calls a 'vista'; these are the city dwellers whom de Certeau noted from atop the World Trade Center. As you turn the corner into another street a new set of surfaces, previously unseen, looms into view, while those of the original vista disappear from sight. The passage from one vista to another, during which the former is gradually occluded while the latter opens up, constitutes what Gibson calls a 'transition'. Thus the experience of travelling from one place to another comprises the opening up and closing of vistas. In this way, the environment is progressively disclosed to the moving observer, who knows as she goes.

Considering this active perception is how Ingold is able to characterize wayfinding 'not as a sequence of point-indexical images, but as the coming-into-sight and passing-out-of-sight of variously contoured and textured surfaces'.[28] This physiological becoming and passing away is itself nested within wider environments of tradition and physical things. In being under way we have expectations. Our own history and wider ancestry has taught us how certain states of affairs afford us certain spaces of disclosure; streets allow us to move, lamp-posts to see in the dark, pavements to walk safely two abreast (or even, as in the city of Bath, four abreast, as the mannered Georgian couples walked past one another without unseemly shuffling), and so on. The vistas and transitions are themselves influenced by our own perceiving physiology, but also by the behaviour of other parts of our own human system, as well as its own history of previous behaviours and their effects, along with the influence of other systems and their histories. This interplay of systemic influence makes for a constrained but not constraining view of perception. Each of us cannot decide what to notice; our active engagement with our wider environment is one of affordance, yet in being under way in the world each of us has a unique empirical sense of how this occurs, and is upset. This is what is meant by being active within our systemic environment; we are mapping rather than conforming to maps. De Certeau talks of this active engagement as 'bricolage'. Bricoleurs are people for whom life is not something that can be forced into their own system demands, or those of any other system, but that instead is an experience of coping across the demands made by multiple, interpenetrating systems and subsystems. Bricoleurs accept their condition without trying to impose an alternative condition from outside, as it were. Rather, they use what they find as vistas and transitions arise; there is no planning because there is no way of knowing what will become ready to hand, and what will break down.[29] They are not constrained in these actions, however; they instil in the wider systems a sense of personal spirit; they enliven them by finding opportunities for expression where others simply find waste and frustration.

The theatre director John Doyle, for example, worked in the perennially hard-up world of British repertory theatre. The constraints were obvious: small budgets, limited space, earnest but often intrusive amateur support and technically limited stagings. These were unavoidable; so putting on Stephen Sondheim's *Sweeney Todd* required ingenuity. The actors would double up as musicians, the staging would be homespun, rehearsals would take place in a fish and chip shop, the effects were wrought through blank contrasts rather than technical wizardry and showy sets, the delivery was pared down, the publicity was negligible because of legal fears associated with multi-tasking actors breaching union rules and health and safety stipulations. The proper space of the musical was completely disrupted by the forces of necessity. Out of such constraints, however, came critical acclaim and the creation of a new musical form. Despite the move from an intimate space to the neon-gilded boards of Broadway, Doyle kept faith with his style. He shocked and then won round the audience, winning awards and new commissions (including opportunities to work with Sondheim himself), influencing film-makers and working in new genres.[30] Working within constraints meant that nothing much else was possible; the strategy lay with an imaginative appreciation of how such constraints are replete with potential.

Doyle was wayfinding rather than navigating, and it is this kind of experience that we feel best expresses one aspect of the dwelling mode of strategic practice that is so often overlooked. Wayfinding is about the experience of living in an organizational territory and apprehending situations in terms of their potential rather than their positions: an aesthetic rendition of a place created through skill at suggesting both the continuity and alternation of elements; the overall sense of being both open and plain, yet suggestive and latent, where things are understood as tools we use to get along, but are not entirely confined by this use, as we on occasion become aware of their being potentially different – unknown, even. Organizations are typically populated by navigational routines that are regulative; they tend to look to the specific and fixed in ways that concentrate organizational activity within the narrowing confines of measured performance, compliance, control and risk reduction. Wayfinding routines are appreciative; they encourage mapping, a widening of awareness of events, and in so doing expose strategy practitioners to the potential of being under way that is the lifeblood of any organization. The strategic impress is not about a narrowing focus but a widening reach, a creative willingness to tolerate ambiguity and to cope with the frustrations of not being in full control. Where navigational routines suggest strategy to be the pre-planned, efficient movement between previously identified points, wayfaring initiatives are animated by an ever open environmental sensitivity that allows for detours, lingerings and directional changes. This is the strategic skill of the bricoleur.

Graeme Obree: the case of a bricoleur

In the mid-1990s the cyclist Graeme Obree broke onto the international scene. He became a world champion, twice, and began to break world records that had stood for generations. What was surprising about his success was that he came from nowhere (well, the British time trialling scene, which in the world of professional cycling is very close to being nowhere). British 'time triallers' are a close-knit, localized community whose achievements rarely translate across to the main stages of the sport on the European continent. Within this community Obree stood out. He was good, very good. In the late 1980s and early 1990s he was British time trial champion and had broken the British hour record. He typically won whatever race he turned up for, his competitive edge sharpened like a keenly edged harrow that had been ploughing up and down the trunk routes of the United Kingdom with tenacious, tireless rhythm. Time trials are typically run over distances ranging from ten miles to 100 miles, preferably on flat, featureless ground so as to encourage an equivalent flat, featureless riding style. The trials often start at dawn, ostensibly to avoid traffic, but there is something about the grey chill of an early morning torn by a solitary figure that lends itself to what we might call an existential attraction for lonely, aesthetic performance: one road, one position, one person, one measured time, no salutary distractions. Amongst cyclists, exponents of the time trial, or 'testers', as they are known, are a somewhat diffident breed, preferring the monotonic whirr of their training rollers to conversation with less serious racers. Idle chit-chat before a race interrupts the preparation for isolation, and preparation is all. The equipment must demonstrate optimal balance between aerodynamics, weight and efficiency of motion (cost is an outlier); the food and drink intake must be analysed for calorific content and absorption rates, and biorhythms electronically assessed beat by beat. Chance is excommunicated. It is not by chance that you race, meet your demons and still win; it is through a deliberate, acutely managed architecture of individual power.

Obree, however, was somewhat different. For a start, he did not use the normal range of a tester's tools. There was no heart rate monitor, no strictly controlled diet, no personal trainer or riding plan. In training he rode long, knee-busting slogs on the unsteady tarmac of the Ayrshire hills until he was knackered, and, being miles from home, was forced to ride some more just to get back. He did have some rollers for when the weather was too foul to ride, but these he made from an old sit-up-and-beg shopping bike. He was not indifferent to tools, but related differently to them. Tools could be found other than at the bike shop. Staring at a washing machine spin at thousands of revolutions a minute, he wondered whether the drum bearings would be smoother than those found in a typical bike, so he dismantled the washer, found the bearings and stuck them into his bottom bracket (the part where the pedal cranks rotate in the bike frame). He thought about aerodynamics, and his position on the bike, and wondered whether the standard position of a cyclist dictated by the bike frame could be improved. He had previously experimented by simply turning the handlebars of a standard bike upwards, but, not content with simply adapting existing bikes, he built a new one. The contraption (using a few more bits of the washing machine, some metal found by the roadside, and the handlebars from a child's BMX bike) had a narrow bottom bracket, bringing the legs closer together but necessitating an X-shaped frame to make room for the closely aligned knees. The geometry threw the rider upwards in the lower half and then encouraged the upper body to bend over, almost hunched, with the handlebars tucked invisibly somewhere under the upper chest and the head thrust to the fore, like the prow of a Norse king's ship. It looked uncomfortable, inelegant, but intuitively Obree understood the aerodynamic benefits. He just had to retrain his body to cope. Obree was a true bricoleur; someone who not only made do with what he found but who had the savoir-faire to experiment with alternatives when more obvious tools were already available. Chance was something not to be resisted but to be integrated through empirical experiment into his regime.

Obree was distinct in his personality as well. He had set out in 1992 to break a world record of twenty years' standing for the hour, set by Francesco Moser. This was considered the blue ribbon event in cycling: how far could a cyclist go on a wooden, circular track in one hour? The record had been held by those who occupied the pantheon of cycling, Jacques Anquetil, Eddy Merckx and Francesco Moser amongst them – great untouchables adorned with *palmares* bought with pain and lit with the unquestioning adoration of entire European communities. So what was a reclusive Scot, literally unknown outside the testing community in

Britain, thinking about when he decided to take on their mantle? Well, for a start, he was thinking very little about them; he was thinking about himself, obsessively. At root he saw no distinction physically between himself and Mercx or Moser; what mattered was the experience of enduring effort. The object of one's intention is your object; it is a directly felt expression of endeavour. The object, therefore, is like Gibson's vista: it lives through your own effort, your own ongoing path. In Obree's world of cycling, the vista called 'world record-holder' was brought into being through the experience of suffering pain. Pain was something Obree had a good grounding in and was something he did share with his wider time-trialling community. 'Testers' are used to suffering. Indeed, there is an acutely phenomenal sense amongst many 'testers' that they suffer pain in a particularly raw form. Some will go so far as to etch motifs about pain into their handlebars; maxims urging them to ignore the hurt as they stare downwards onto the bars, mile after mile. They appear almost as a Jungian collective; a cult group of human beings who compensate for the ease with which many of us can avoid and so forget basic human sensation. To push the Jungian analysis a little further, whilst undoubtedly sensing pain, there is no guarantee that the testers can then feel good about the pain, or that they can understand any purposive hue by which the pain resonates with the sense of its contributing to a life being led. Often it seems it is pain for pain's sake, a self-referring relationship mediated by a linear calculation of the time it took to move from A through B and back to A. 'I did the twenty-five miles in fifty-nine minutes' (less than an hour is the benchmark for a reasonably good tester). Here there is a sense of belonging; of not being excluded. Pity the tester who always and for ever remains outside the hour. There is not necessarily anything else, however. What seemed to mark Obree out was his awareness of pain as something that could be transcended, a transition to something else opening up. It was the singularity with which he felt this that was his peculiar gift.

He first broke the world record for the hour in Norway in 1993. Norway is a good place to go test yourself: not quite Søren Kierkegaard's existentially bleak flatlands, but close enough. Ludwig Wittgenstein built a hut in Norway to write without precedent. Obree built a bike to ride there, without precedent. He had booked a day's slot on the track at Hamar. On the evening of Friday 16 July he made his attempt, and failed. The judges began to pack up and the audience drift away in the wake of failure. He insisted on going again, though. He found that the rules allowed for a twenty-four-hour window for the attempt, and insisted the begrudging judges remain. He drank water all night, forcing himself to wake up so that he could stretch and prevent his muscles going rigid with the memory of effort. At 9 a.m. on the following morning, on little sleep, he had a second go, and this time extended the record by half a kilometre (51.59km). Asked how he coped with the pain, he simply mentioned it was effort, not pain. He intuitively grasped the value of understanding pain as effort; pain was an undertaking, a wayfinding, a thing that could be related to differently. In his autobiography, he describes how he had thrown himself onto a bike early in life literally to ride away from other human beings; to escape the conditions of being bullied because of his dad's job as a 'copper' and from his own bouts of depression.[31] The bike does this; it is an apotheosis of self-sufficiency, in which a well-loved machine will unhesitatingly and quietly mediate intentional being into momentum. As you ride a bike and start to ride it well, there are moments when it becomes an affirmation of life devoid of separation and distinction; you ride through the earth unthinkingly rather than across it. There is no need to account for who you are in others' terms, in language, even. Your characteristics give way to your being. The effort put into the bike can take you out of your socialized, represented self into what we earlier called Heidegger's disclosing self, where you simply are ever-shifting endeavour.

Obree's 1993 record stood for only one week. Strangely, a fellow native of the backwoods that was the British time trialling scene, Chris Boardman, set a distance of 52.27km in Bordeaux. Boardman, though, had not been an unknown. His talent had found full expression in the previous year's Olympic Games in Barcelona, when, on a visually striking carbon fibre bike, he had eclipsed all competition to win the 4,000m track pursuit title. Unfairly, many put Boardman's dominance down to the technically advanced and hugely expensive machine he rode, a world away from Obree's home-brewed bricolage. The distinction was hard to avoid however. Boardman had been meticulous in his preparation, had used computers, trainers and sponsors to ensure he had eliminated any chance of not succeeding. He had applied a direct, known strategy to record-breaking, and it worked. Obree's response was to find yet more effort. A few weeks later he went on to win that year's 4,000m pursuit world title, beating Boardman in the semi-final. Barely ten months later, still in his weird-looking tucked position, Obree was back on top of the hour record, upping the distance to 52.713km. After this the International Cycling Union (UCI), the governing body of cycling, took note of Obree. Here was something of note. Rather than embrace his achievement, though, the UCI took umbrage at his maverick ways and tried to prevent him from riding in his now famous position. First it changed the rules governing bike geometry, stipulating that the saddle had to be at least 5cm behind the bottom bracket, meaning that the forward hunch Obree had used was now a much harder position to occupy on the bike. Obree took this rule change in his stride, by putting the saddle back the required length and then competing in the first rounds of the 1994 world track championships. He won these easily. Before he could ride the subsequent rounds, though, the UCI officials at the championships simply banned him from taking any further part in the meeting. They stopped him riding, literally making up a new rule on the spot that there had to be 'daylight' between the arms and the body. Nowhere did this stipulation about daylight appear in the rulebook. When asked afterwards why they had banned Obree mid-flight, they invoked a Kafkaesque justification that 'extraordinary' equipment was not allowed; that and, it seemed, extraordinary people too. It was simply a case of an organization wanting to rid itself of a threatening insurgent who came at them using detour.

As is the way with true bricoleurs, Obree not only responded, he did so with wit, brio and lingering effect. In *Swann's Way*, Marcel Proust remarks that often the greatest works of poets are composed when they are facing the tyranny of rhyme, when they have to work within the confines of established structures. Obree did the same. He became a great poet. If the rules stipulate daylight then daylight it shall be. Lots of it. He created a new position. This time using conventionally available bike tools, but in a novel mix that meant the handlebars and hence arms extended well beyond the front axle of the bike, meaning that there was as much daylight as was possible between the arms and torso. He had developed what was to become known as the 'superman' position. Despite the tucked position and 'X' frame used in his original record-breaking being one of the most impressive and successful innovations in track cycling, Obree did not wed himself to his original ingenuity, nor did he lament its being banned. His wayfinding eschewed such fixity, even when what was fixed was itself born of his own detouring and oblique line of flight. In 1995 he won the 4,000m pursuit world title, but this time as superman. So arresting and effective was his new position that 1996 witnessed a crescendo of imitation among his peers, culminating in Chris Boardman's breaking of the hour record in the style of Obree's 'superman'. Boardman's record of 56.375km still stands.

Yet again the UCI stepped in, however. With the certainty of their rule-bound world ruffled by all this innovation and flux, they stipulated in October 1996 that the handlebar of a bike could not extend beyond the front hub by more than 15cm, effectively ridding any further aping of Obree. The UCI was once more looking to rid itself of the troublesome maverick. Obree himself had become so notorious by this time that many professional cycling teams were clamouring to sign him up. The teams realized that because of the protestations of the UCI, and Obree's remarkable responses, he was a bankable 'performer'. He had always done things alone, working on record attempts as single projects and scraping around for odd sponsors. Now this solitary wanderlust was no longer necessary. The detours had seemingly paid off. He had gained access to a previously inaccessible world, if only as a fashionable outsider with deep talent. He quickly became disillusioned with the teams themselves though. What he encountered was another organizational obstruction, though this time rather than being written down in the rulebook of bike design it was the unwritten rule of drug-taking. Obree had a history of depression, even trying to take his own life a number of times. Cycling had been a way of helping him cope with this; of allowing him to dispense his own remedies. Now teams were wanting his signature, but with the contract came the expectation of regular doping programmes. Cycling was so rife with doping that few people believed he had achieved what he did without drugs. They just assumed he was on them too. The outsider was bemused, then angry, and finally just disappointed. This organizational norm was one he felt unable to respond to as a bricoleur. There were teams and riders running clean (Boardman's being one of them), but Obree said he witnessed too much of the other side, the dopers, to want to continue; his singularity was lost to what he personally experienced as a more insidious tyranny than any formal rule.[32] The proper space in which he now found himself was not somewhere he wanted to be, and, rather than effect a new relationship with things, he refused to test himself any further. Where the blazers in the UCI could find no grip to control this bricoleur, the ethos of doping had. The irony, of course, is that Obree was expunged from the world of professional cycling by the inactivity of the UCI rather than by any deliberate strategy; it was the organization's lack of thoroughness in the control, prosecution and punishment of drug use rather than its tinkering with the rules that engendered the intolerable conditions.

Unlike navigation, a wayfinding orientation captures the richness and quality of lived experiences that are inevitably missed out on with any form of cognitive mapping activity. This is not simply because of the 'coarseness' of the mapping grid provided; it is because, however refined the grid may be, it is incapable of capturing the *movement* involved in wayfinding, where the world comes into being only through our engagement with it. Obree's story shows how our own movement through our surroundings contributes to the richness and variety of that lived experience. In the cartographic world, on the other hand, 'all is still and silent. There is neither sunlight nor moonlight; there are no variations of light or shade, no clouds, no shadows or reflections. The wind does not blow, neither disturbing the trees nor whipping the water into waves. No birds fly in the sky, or sing in the woods; forests and pastures are devoid of animal life; houses and streets are empty of people and traffic.'[33] So Ingold echoes Whitehead's comment about the impotency of measurement in its encounter with the radiance of a sunset, and expresses the difference between those who map out spaces and those who express themselves in spite of these spaces. The world of cartography and navigation is one devoid of life in all its richness and variety. Wayfinding, unlike navigation, depends upon the attunement of the wayfinder and his or her response to the movements he or she observes in his or her specific surroundings. He or she grows and reaches out into the environment along the paths he or she makes, advancing along a line of growth whose future configuration can never be fully known or understood. Here strategy, like perception and mapping, is an active and exploratory process of information pick-up and passing away that extends well beyond the mental, and even bodily, skin of any one human individual, top management team or even single organization.

Wayfinding the Google way

On 19 August 2004 the internet company Google went public with an initial public offering of US$85 per share, raising close to US$2 billion in the largest technology offering ever. Within a year the stock had soared to well over US$300 per share and Google came to be worth more than US $80 billion by 2005.[34] Google represents an unplanned and unanticipated phenomenon, the success of which has been unprecedented in this day and age. Indeed, a measure of its achievement is that within a space of ten years it has transformed the way of life of hundreds of millions of people all over the world, who cannot today realistically contemplate how they would go about their daily need for accessing information were Google to cease to exist as an internet search facility. Moreover, the word 'Google' has come to describe what it means to 'search' on the internet. The insatiable quest for instant information on virtually every conceivable topic in more than 100 languages is what has catapulted Google into a global phenomenon that some claim parallels the knowledge revolution created by Johannes Gutenberg's invention of the printing press in the fifteenth century.

The genesis of Google lies in the very Gothic characteristics of curiosity and error. The curiosity came from Larry Page, one of the founders, who had written a programme that told him how many other websites were rubbing up to his own. This interest in who was interested in him soon extended beyond the personal, and, together with Sergey Brin, he launched a more comprehensive bibliometric assessment of web pages. Top-ranking is a perennial human concern, and Page and Brin tapped into this almost Darwinian urge with algorithmic aplomb, creating a dynamic map of the connectivity of internet web pages. The error came in the naming of the search engine they then designed to use this programme, responding to search queries by looking for where the search terms appeared on a web page and in what criterial form (the criteria including the headline, the typeface and repetition, and never ever how much those who ran the web page were prepared to pay Google), along with the relative connectivity of the websites on which those terms appeared. Like the open-source community, what worked best was not down to a cabal of website editors but a shifting, democratically aligned mass of users. The sheer expanding scale of the computational operation warranted a name conveying something unfeasibly big, something like 'googol', the mathematical term for ten to the power 100. It was misspelt as google, however, and google, not surprisingly, was still available as a domain name. So Google it became, heralding a far more powerful and system-sensitive search technology than had previously been available. The ranking did not come from expert assessment but through an internet version of the invisible hand; the order arose spontaneously from continuously applied, individual searching activity.

Like the search engine itself, there was no God's-eye view of how such an endeavour was going to earn money. Google began as a technical device that searched the internet and whose prowess then attracted the likes of Yahoo! and Netscape to help run their portals. Revenue streams for Google itself were something of an afterthought, and they came from a very simple, unassuming and low-cost source: ad-words. Revenue came as an ad-on, literally. Attending the results page of each search Google began to append 'sponsored links'. Firms would bid for words that they felt were apposite in some way to what they were selling, and each time the link was followed from a search page the agreed fee was levied. Again, there was no attempt at imposing a pricing structure, so the fee followed emerging, shifting search patterns, and it would typically be measured in cents, depending on the level of use. Thus the earning stream went almost unnoticed, a financial tracery from web crawler to an immensely sophisticated ad business, its information and communication technologies echoing the ever-expanding reach of a nested system of users and computational processes. If its architecture resembled an increasingly intricate rose window in the east elevation of a Gothic cathedral, the relationships being fostered between users increasingly resembled the kind of intimacy found between worshippers. In symbiotic combination, the ranking search engine and ad-words mediated between buyers and producers in ways that tapped into almost unconsciously expressed wants. Providing the search terms gave expression to the desires and needs of those doing the search, the associated ad-words became a tradable extension, reinforcing or embellishing what the human searcher was interested in with linked products and services. As more people searched, and clicked on related ad-words, more revenue was earned, without any marketing, or strategic positioning, or public investment – and, if search pages could carry sponsored links, then why not other web pages, such as bloggers and small business websites with which revenues might be shared? The only job was to enhance the sophistication of the search engine in order that the ad-words became better targeted, and more nuanced in their appeal, without their becoming seditious or disguised. This was Google's unique offering, its singular 'trick', and even this was never specified or touted as such. The subsequent phenomenal rise of the firm has been subject to reams of testimony and analysis; by 2008 Google was taking, on conservative estimates, over three-quarters of all search-related advertising revenue in the world, and carried a market capitalization of US$150 billion.

All this was achieved without explicit navigation or strategic destination. According to Eric Schmidt, the current CEO, management always takes second place at Google; it acts as an under-labourer, a flattened and minimal servicing of the problem-finding and problem-solving experiences of its engineers, who work in loose, 'small-room-sized' teams or pairs. The decision-making is taken by crowds. In an echo of Athenian democracies, where the ideal number for a city state was a crowd sufficiently small that each of their faces could be made out from a single vantage and where each betook upon him- or herself the responsibility of legislating for the *polis*, Google requires decisions to be subject to debate, dissent and then collective resolution from within what remains today, at least, still a relatively small firm, given its global presence.

As if to preserve its own sense of identity, Google's managers have rarely committed to or made the firm reliant on any other organization. The use of equipment is a good case in point. The computing power needed to make copies of the internet and allow searches was originally provided by networked computers at the University of Stanford. Page and Brin used what they had and could beg and borrow, and simply continued in this tradition of dispositional bricolage. Even now, Google continues to be serviced by networked, cheap servers rather than centralized, hierarchically governed mainframes. These are built by Google people from white boxes installed with a range of different chips from different manufacturers, and run using bespoke versions of the Linux open-source software. The network is called the 'cloud'. It is spread around the world, is ubiquitous, is infinitely adaptable; its power resides in an interacting, composable system of tens of thousands of logo-less processors and storage systems that are continually being updated. Many other companies can simply not operate like this; it is outside their intellectual, cultural and psychic capacity. In the words of Gary Hamel,

What the laggards [incumbents trying to adapt to a changing world] have failed to grasp is that what matters most today is not a company's competitive advantage at a point in time, but its evolutionary advantage *over* time. Google gets this.[35]

Even with public listing in 2004 Google retained a sense of maverick singularity. Its newly adopted mission statement, seemingly devoid of bathos, was 'to organize the world's information and to make it universally accessible and useful'. This is Bergson's 'irregularly expanding rubber balloon' made commercially manifest. Within the ambit of this unconfining mission comes an unending, rhizomic growth of lines of flight: Froogle; Google Scholar; gmail; Google Earth; Google News (which came about after an engineer wrote a web-crawling programme for himself and colleagues that would gather together news items relating to 9–11 without him having to enter search terms actively); and, more recently, an open-sourced browser called Chrome. Employees are the firm, and their only job is to look for ever new modes of, and reasons for, human–machine interaction that might be predicated by variants of the ubiquitous Google sobriquet. People are encouraged to work on projects and problems that interest and excite them and are given time to pursue these independently, and mistakes and dead ends are regarded as grist to this ever-turning mill of innovation. Ideas are tested straight away; there is no waiting for something to be refined and tweaked by its author as a fully formed creation. Instead, the nascent programmes are launched into testing labs, where multiple peer review, user interaction and feedback grow the programme organically, and in unpredictable ways. Even outside developers are courted and their suggestions worked on.[36] This blend of maverick and collective internal innovation sustains growth. Outside influence is courted, but typically from smaller, maverick operations for which Google is a natural bedfellow. On being asked whether Google would acquire other firms, Schmidt has been quite firm:

I would think so. But small. The likelihood of us doing big things is pretty low because we'd have to assimilate the culture. Nobody works the way we do. The Google culture makes sense if you're in it, and no sense if you're not in it.[37]

Google exemplifies the art of wayfinding from within an embedded set of dwelt circumstances. Innovation is not a non-imitable asset, it is not a niche market position and it is not a powerful occupation of territory;

it is a wayfinding attitude to life of infinite flexibility – period. To innovate is to acknowledge, absorb and respond to an ever-shifting array of opening and closing experience without recourse to relying on the explicit, the codified and the orthodox. Strategically, the challenge for Google is how to maintain the accompanying spirit of being under way. Preserving a sense of open-ended and often unmanaged innovation in an economic system expectant of specified share prices and revenue streams, in a political system inured to post-9/11 paranoia, in an environmental system experiencing unsettling changes in climate, and in a social system increasingly versed in confrontation is about preserving a restless, knowledgeable system-in-systems. In our terms, the strategic challenge for Google is one of wayfinding in which Google's employees are constantly attuning themselves to the shifting tenor of wider systems. Their productions have to become, in part, akin to those of Ruskin's Gothic sculptors. The value of Google is not just in the search capacity itself but what the searching activity reveals about the lives of those doing the searching. Of course, this puts much of the onus of Google's potential on preserving a relationship of trust, at least to the extent of preserving such levels as are necessary for people to continue to use the system and, in such use, more or less wittingly divulge information about themselves.[38] The mission statement of organizing the world's information is somewhat misleading; it is information about people, not the world per se, that is being disclosed, and one system's sense of legitimate accessibility and utility differs from another. Disclosing details of the browsing habits of political dissidents; storing searchable personal data files from social websites; facing subpoenas to hand over search data to third-party organizations; resisting demands from financial analysts for guidance notes and greater third-party transparency of its activities and technology; and being expected to confront hierarchically ordered, hostile behemoths such as Microsoft are just a few of the roughly contoured surfaces coming into sight.

To give just one instance of what such wayfinding might entail, *Business Week* carried an article on the work of one Google engineer, Christophe Bisciglia.[39] He had opted to use his unsupervised innovation space to work on an educational project to teach new programmers how to think and work with the immense potential offered by the Google cloud. Bisciglia created a small cloud of forty computers, enlisted the help of some colleagues and members of the computing department at his old university in Washington and began talking to new Google intake about the firm's MapReduce software designed to break up tasks, distribute the micro-tasks across the cloud and then reassemble these into coherent responses. This works so well because the cloud consists of identical boxes installed with the same systems producing very reliable, stable responses across the cloud; the greater the scale required the more the number of boxes required.[40] One of the many obstacles was that Google was unwilling to afford access to the intricacies of one of its critical pieces of software; it did not want MapReduce to be taken into a public arena, even if it was to teach a course called Google 101. So Bisciglia adapted and used a simpler, open-source version of Map-Reduce called Hadoop that had been designed by a small start-up called Nutch that had been acquired by Yahoo!, wanting to instil some of the Google method into its own systems. Students learnt how to think about programming using a cloud rather than isolated systems, and word spread, as did demand for the reputed data-crunching potential of a cluster networked in Google's unique manner. Bisciglia recognized that forty computers were insufficient for such a demand; different departments and different universities wanted access to a system to run ever more complex analyses of data that they had previously been unable to approach because of the sheer logistics. In stepped IBM, whose experience of using open-source systems in large-scale applications gave Schmidt and Bisciglia access to an architecture on which to run Google-based standards of cloud computing across a number of US and then global universities, all of which would continue to invest and develop the application in accord with Hadoop, and hence MapReduce. The cloud gave each university access to supercomputing capacity that hitherto had not been imaginable, and in comparison with which even the web looked tiny, all run by an ever-expanding cluster of peers using systems with which they were familiar.

From running an education course, Bisciglia has exposed Google to an unfurling strategy of fundamentally changing the manner in which we understand computing. Rather than using solitary machines in fixed locations owned by the users, programmers and end users will start to programme and navigate globally available cloud space. There is no need for a computer as we know it, as mobiles will work just as well, or public terminals; there is an organic dissolution of the mediating device as people connect more and more directly with their own and others' information held, analysed and transformed online. More creatively, smaller organizations such as new ventures will be able to use Google applications freely to store data, manage e-mails, authenticate customer accounts and create websites, leaving them free to concentrate on why they went into business. For Google, this locks systems into its systems: its applications, programming language, servers and other products and services. There is no indication as to where this will lead, how much cloud space will be available and what it could be used for, and what part

Google will play in its further development. Bisciglia himself admits that he had no strategy in mind when he first thought of the course; he simply wanted a break from the routine of programming and felt that returning to a university environment to run a course would be a reasonable option. The result has been to place Google at the heart of a fundamental realignment with how we relate to computing as a practice. There has been no intervening, pre-planned design in any of this, simply a willingness to let people experiment and to go, collectively, where these experiments might take them.

Others disagree, however. Richard Stallman, about whom we wrote earlier in relation to the emergence of open-source programming, has argued that cloud computing does not have the same kind of arresting logic as open source. Indeed, it might be nothing more than a well-designed marketing campaign, in which companies such as Google try to enlist users in such a way that they become not just entrenched customers wedded to a specific hardware but also suppliers of valuable data, in the forms of pictures, e-mails and documents, that can be further exploited by those 'holding' it on their systems. For Stallman, cloud computing is nothing new; it is simply a way of redescribing what lots of computer people knew how to do anyhow. The difference is the hype.[41] If nothing else, criticisms such as this put Google on notice that wayfinding is not effortless, and how the world comes into being as we are under way differs depending on who is engaging; there are different perspectives on what is coming into, and going out of, sight. Wayfinding therefore requires an ability to reflect consciously on one's habits, to adopt what we mentioned earlier was a near-documentary style of bringing experiences into some kind of suspension. For example, if Google is a firm that never relies on other organizations, how is that experience of independence reconciled with the possibility that cloud computing will make consumers excessively reliant upon it? This is a sideways glance at, and appreciation of, how the firm might look in its ongoing everyday activity when no one is really looking. It is not a presentation of the firm but an awareness of its presence amongst other things as it continues to be under way.

7   The silent efficacy of indirect action

> The history of strategy is, fundamentally, a record of the application
> and evolution of the indirect approach... The indirect approach is as
> fundamental to the realm of politics as it is to the realm of sex.
>
> *Basil Liddell-Hart*, Strategy: The Indirect Approach, *pp.xix–xx*

*In the last chapter we argued that wayfinding provided a different and almost
counter-intuitive take on what it means to act strategically. The underlying
spirit of wayfinding is a sense of the positivity of incompleteness: one is under
way, and in being under way the ends of one's actions emerge as one goes along.
We only know as we go. Contrary to the navigational mindset, this openness and
absence is not something to lament or correct; indeed, it is not a limitation at all,
but a part-expression of our natural condition of dwelling that has steadily been
hidden from us as we have become more and more technologically advanced.
As the examples of Graeme Obree and Google show, the existence of an as yet
indefinable space (something that is yet to be ordered technologically) constitutes
a realm of potentiality that allows wayfinders to establish an authentic imprint
on unfolding situations and, in so doing, to unexpectedly effect a dramatic
change in the course of events through their ingenuity and local coping actions.*

*In this chapter, we return to our initial observation that somehow, paradox-
ically, it is these locally initiated spontaneous responses, the ad hoc 'making
dos', that often, surprisingly, generate longer-term sustainable outcomes than
more deliberate and direct forms of intervention. Indirect, unspectacular
actions often prove more efficacious, and the efficacy of such indirect forms of
action have been well understood by students of military warfare and politics,
both in the East and the West. They point us away from a preoccupation with
grand gestures and spectacular interventions to quieter forms of timely and
seemingly inconspicuous actions that nevertheless make a material difference to
eventual outcomes.*

Direct and indirect approaches to strategy

In a study of the Western model of war, the ancient-military scholar
Victor Davis Hanson maintains that it was the ancient Greeks, around

the seventh century BC, who first insisted on the superiority of a face-to-face frontal clash between armies as the most effective way to engage in battle. According to Hanson, it was from this period onwards that a new structure, the *phalanx*, was introduced, in which two bodies of heavily armed and cuirassed hoplites were arranged in lines, and made to march in step to the rhythm of sound and to advance in tight formation towards the enemy, with no possibility of fleeing from direct head-on confrontation. The only proper form of warfare was one involving this frontal clashing of the phalanxes in broad daylight, so as to ensure that nothing underhand was done to mar the nobility of the encounter. To win by any other means, such as through the art of harassment or evasion or through the use of devious manoeuvres such as ambush, dodgings and skirmishes, was to 'allow...one side to "cheat" in a victory achieved by some means other than their own bravery in battle'.[1] According to François Jullien, some accounts of Alexander the Great suggested that he 'refused to achieve victory "through the wiliness of brigands and robbers whose sole desire is not to be noticed"'. The Greeks thought that it was only a 'hand-to-hand battle at close quarters which was truly decisive'.[2] Skill in strategic manoeuvres and the use of cunning and deceit were rejected in favour of the supreme display of courage exhibited at the crucial moment of encounter. Moreover, all arms that were able to inflict injury from afar, such as arrows, javelins and other projectiles, were rejected and despised, 'because they killed from a distance and without regard to the personal merit of the fighting men'.[3] Additionally, this form of brief, direct and decisive confrontation between two armies on the battlefield was deemed more desirable because it promised to do away with the potentially ravaging effects of a long and protracted war. Hanson argues that this model of war did not die with the Greeks. For him, writing in 1989, the Americans in Vietnam in the 1970s were the most recent prisoners of this heritage. Today, we might add that the invasion of Afghanistan and Iraq are further examples of the continuing unquestioned faith in this spectacular, confrontational approach to war. This obsession for the dramatic and spectacular is deeply infused in almost every aspect of modern Western life, particularly in the United States, and, with that country's vast reach and global influence, it is becoming increasingly prevalent in virtually every other part of the world as well.

François Jullien makes the observation that there is a certain homology existing between the form of strategic engagement involving the phalanx on the battlefield and the underlying organizational strategy of modern Western institutions: both are united through 'the uniformity of equipment, the equivalence of position, and even the types of behaviour involved'. Although some might argue that the use of the military metaphor has long outworn its application in business organizational contexts, nevertheless what has been retained is a continuing penchant for a directness of approach in dealing with business affairs. It therefore appears that the 'phalanx...with its choice of a frontal approach' indicates a core aspect of Greek culture that has been wholeheartedly embraced and incorporated into the overall attitude of the modern West. Thus, the 'face-to-face confrontation of the phalanxes on the battlefield [has] an equivalent in the face-to-face discussion' around which modern democratic societies operate.[4] What is ubiquitous in Western democracy is a receptivity and willingness to embrace open dissent, public debate and the art of persuasion as the founding basis for societal progress. In this preference for direct engagement, it is not unlike behaviour on the battlefield. For Jullien, the '*agonistic* structure of armed confrontation' is paralleled in the social structure of the theatre, the tribunal, and the assembly: '[W]hether in the dramatic, the judicial, or the political realm, the debate manifested itself like a force pressing for or against something, in which the upper hand was gained only by sheer strength and number of arguments either side amassed.'[5] Hence, if a homology exists it is because both the military phalanx and the institutions of society share the same confrontational habitus or predisposition in their preferred mode of engagement; one that leads them to orient themselves and to make decisions in terms of directly confronting and overcoming difficulties and obstacles technologically, whether by sheer physical force or by the force of logic and persuasion. This is why, in oratory and debate, the face-to-face confrontation of speeches is intimately bound to the Western model of democracy. The natural attitude, born of this legacy, is to emphasize transparency of intention, openness of confrontation and the direct and deliberate mobilization of available resources and capabilities to achieve the desired end.

In sum, we can say that the direct and deliberate approach to strategy-making and execution that has become the leitmotiv of business strategy theorizing draws its inspiration from these ancient Greek roots. This directness in approach has its downside, however. We have seen in our earlier discussion how Dr Martens eventually declined, due in large part to strategists adopting a more and more direct and deliberate attempt to capitalize on the brand that had unintentionally and unwittingly been developed. We have seen how large-scale planned interventions have had very limited success in effectively rehabilitating the lives of ordinary people in the case of the Asian tsunami victims, and we have seen how large-scale forestry planning in the German forestry sector in the eighteenth and nineteenth centuries led unexpectedly to a stripped-down forest devoid of a diverse habitat for wildlife and the crucial development of the undergrowth in order for soil-building processes to take place. We have also seen how, in the case of the Swiss bank UBS, which had gradually built a strong reputation on wealth management and private banking over several decades, the desire to emulate the spectacular successes of the American investment banks led its strategists to directly address a perceived deficit of talent by recruiting from and imitating those very banks it admired, with the subsequent catastrophic consequences that ensued. Within the context of the global financial turmoil in 2008, one almost universal observation can be made of those financial institutions that have failed. All of them, from the Icelandic banks such as Landsbankinn to the demutualized British building societies such as Northern Rock, Bradford and Bingley and HBOS, as well as US investment banks such as Lehmann Brothers, had grown too quickly and aggressively, borrowing money extensively from the international money markets to facilitate their rapid expansion. Their short-term achievements were spectacular – and so was their downfall.

Even the recent attempts to rescue the world's financial system and prevent it from a global meltdown are couched in spectacular and gargantuan terms. The summary talks at the 2009 G20 summit in London spoke of these governments incurring additional borrowing amounting to US$5 trillion as a result of having to respond to the credit crisis, and of granting the International Monetary Fund additional facilities of US$1.1 trillion.[6] People remain totally enamoured of the presumed efficacy of direct spectacular interventions. There remains a widely pervasive commitment to the belief that the best approach to adopt in dealing with affairs of the world is to confront, overcome and subjugate the external world to conform to our will, control and eventual mastery. We still build without acknowledging how we might better dwell; we still favour the order and finish of the Renaissance over the edginess of the Gothic; we still navigate with plans rather than wayfinding as we go. Victory is accomplished by overcoming the opposition through either a *surplus* of resources (in the case of the battlefield, the corporate venture or even the rescue of the financial system) or a *surplus* of argument and evidence presented (in the case of open debate or of academic claims made). Jullien puts it well:

This figure of confrontation highlights the structure of the antagonistic *thrust*. […] Once two lists enumerating the advantages of the two sides of an argument have been established like two opposing phalanxes one settles the question merely 'by saying which list is longer or presents greater advantage' …

Confrontation and calculation are thus the basis of this conflict of words, and it is always by *surplus* – of arguments presented, not of secret obliqueness – that a victory is won.[7]

Recall Shackle's point from chapter 1 about how in commercial life we can use probabilistic reasoning to isolate the possible from the less impossible, but from amongst the group of outcomes labelled 'possible' we recur to evaluation in which we distinguish the good and the bad, the desirable and undesirable. Shackle was suggesting that, too often, researchers and some strategists conflate these two modes of engagement, presuming that strategic evaluation can take place probabilistically, when experience of commercial life shows it cannot be confined to nice Gaussian curves. Jullien is pushing further at the implications of this technical tendency, because, even when it is accepted that strategic judgements are being based on evaluative rather than statistical criteria, these evaluations are versed in ideas of quantity or surplus, in which the desired wins out over the undesired (revenue and profit, the weight of argument, the number of votes, and so on). What Jullien then goes on to show is that this weighty confrontation of positions and arguments aimed at confining the world to events and things that can be articulated as means linked to desirable outcomes is neither universally accepted nor the only possible mode of strategic engagement available. Indeed, such spectacular forms of intervention aimed at generating desired outcomes often unintentionally generate negative consequences.

The downsides of spectacular strategic interventions

In his detailed comparison between spectacular action and silent transformation, Jullien asks provocatively 'Is there anything in reality that can be attributed to a particular person and identified as his or her action?' and suggests that the ancient Chinese thinkers very probably thought not, for they 'considered human behaviour, like everything else, in terms of a regulated and continuous process'.[8] Human agency is subordinated to the impersonal transformational forces that exist beyond human comprehension; a natural propensity exists in the configuration of things and situations. Jullien proceeds by elaborating on the difference between active strategic action and the process of silent transformation.

To start with, the explicit aim of active intervention is the overpowering of an adversary; in warfare, for instance, the aim is the elimination of the enemy, while, in a free market situation, strategy is directed at overcoming the threat of competition in business. In both instances it involves the active seeking of the *destruction* of the opposition. On the other hand, from a transformation point of view, the objective is *deconstruction*, the gradual reconfiguration and open integration of multiple potential lines of conflict. In the former, the efficacy of action is direct, in that the means employed are expected to produce the desired outcome most expeditiously. Cause and effect are closely coupled: success can be traced to specific actions taken; rewards such as bonuses are readily assigned to specific individuals who are deemed to have 'performed' well. Nevertheless, the overall endeavour may be overly risky and incur hidden, as yet unaccountable costs. On the other hand, the efficacy of silent transformation, because it is slow, indirect and almost unnoticed, becomes progressively irresistible, and ultimately it is absorbed into a way of life. Despite this, the dominant Western myths have always tended to elevate heroic action and spectacular intervention over patience, passivity and apparent non-intervention. This is something that the Chinese, for instance, have not widely embraced. The Chinese language, for its part, does not categorically oppose the active and passive voices. Sympathizing with this attitude in dealing with human affairs, Jullien, in language that echoes Bourdieu's notion of habitus, writes:

Take, for example, efficacy through influence, which results from conditioning... how can that be attributed to ourselves? We do not 'choose' to be so, nor does it come about as a result of some kind of 'violence' against us... It is both integral to us and at the same time inclines us to such behaviour. The active–passive divide, as defined in our Western grammar books, is too narrow to apprehend this. For whatever 'inclines' me is neither within me nor imposed upon me, rather it 'passes through me'. Where action is personal and refers back to a subject, this transformation is *trans*individual, and its indirect efficacy dissolves the subject.'[9]

In the West, especially from the Renaissance onwards, with the introduction of the notions of contingency and causality, action and efficacy have come to be more closely associated than ever before. With the human world increasingly seen to be characterized by instability, ephemerality and mobility, the taking of bold action to arrest and fix this inherently ambiguous situation has come to be seen as the only means of controlling our own future and destiny. Such bold intervention carries with it its own problems however. Spectacular strategic action is external action that decisively intervenes into, and hence interrupts, the natural course of things. It is, as such, an *intrusive* initiative.

Because it impinges from outside...it is always to some degree external to the world and is therefore relatively incompatible and arbitrary...for by forcing itself into the course of things, it inevitably, to some degree, tears at the tissue of things and upsets their coherence... [I]t inevitably provokes elements of resistance, or at least of reticence...that...block and quietly undermine it. The shock that it thereby produces is deadened, makes little impact, and its effects are absorbed.[10]

Moreover, such action from the outside, because it intervenes at one moment and not another, tends to attract attention. By artificially forcing the course of things it also forces itself onto our attention, thereby becoming an 'event' to be accounted for. Its '*asperity*...provides a hook on which to hang a story', yet, according to Jullien, this spectacular aspect 'is simply the counterpart to its lack of impact upon reality; its *arti*- and *super*ficiality. In short it is just like an epiphenomenon that momentarily appears, like a shower of spray, against a silent background of things, and then is gone. The tension that it produces may well satisfy our need for drama...but it is not efficacious.'[11] On the other hand, silent transformation occurs through its tireless continuity and pervasiveness, and that is what makes it eventually effective. Transformation, because it is continuous and operates at a mundane everyday level, normally passes unnoticed. The skills and knowledge are absorbed unconsciously and applied *in situ* and *sponte sua* from moment to moment. As de Certeau insists, the knowledge of ordinary practitioners 'is as blind as that of lovers in each other's arms'.[12] The efficacy of such everyday coping actions is all the greater the more discreet and unnoticed it is.

Mētis as spontaneous indirect action

The existence of such indirect and spontaneous forms of everyday coping, widely acknowledged by the scholars of ancient China, is not entirely unknown to the West. Its specific form may differ but the underlying approach remains the same. It was a non-deliberate coping strategy widely practised by the 'weak' during the pre-Socratic period, when Homer's *Iliad* and Hesiod's *Theogony* held sway, but since then it has been overlooked or obscured in most influential accounts of ancient Greek history. In their classic work, Marcel Detienne and Jean Pierre Vernant identify this form of unreflective practical knowing called *mētis*, which combines intuition, foresight, feint and a sense of opportunism.[13] They argue forcefully that, although such a form of resourcefulness played a major role in Greek culture and mythology and held an important influence on Greek values and beliefs, it has, curiously, never been subject to study by ancient Greek scholars. Even Aristotle had nothing to say about it. *Mētis* is conspicuous by its absence in the literature.

In Greek mythology, Mētis was the goddess of prudence, cunning and craftiness and, given this array of earthly insight, became known as the most knowing of all beings. She became the first wife of Zeus, who, having lain with her, was then beset with male paranoia and fear that she was pregnant and therefore soon to bear a child potentially more commanding and impressive than himself. Being a Greek god, the response was swift, resolute and brutal: he ate her. Cannibalism is about absorbing the character and powers of the consumed, so it would be Zeus himself and not the child that benefited from his wife's skill. In his *Theogony* (886), Hesiod describes the scene thus:

> Zeus, as king of the gods, took as his first wife Mētis, and she knew more than all the gods or mortal people. But when she was about to be delivered of the goddess, gray-eyed Athene, then Zeus, deceiving her perception by treachery and by slippery speeches, put her away inside his own belly. This was by the advices of Gaia (Earth) and starry Ouranos (Sky), for so they counselled, in order that no other everlasting god, besides Zeus, should ever be given kingly position. For it had been arranged that, from her, children surpassing in wisdom should be born, first the gray-eyed girl, the Tritogeneia Athene; and she is the equal of her father in wise counsel and strength; but then a son to be King over gods and mortals was to be born to her and his heart would be overmastering: but before this, Zeus put her away inside his own belly so that this goddess should think for him, for good and for evil.[14]

Hesiod then recounts, however, how this all-consuming Zeus was unable to contain what he had swallowed and found the goddess Athena, Mētis's child, spring forth, fully formed and armed, from atop his head. Mētis's offspring is thus born under the skein of deception and of a cunning circling back, in which the mother exploits her apparently inactive and stationary originating point to sustain and complete a pregnancy and offspring more powerful than any that would have occurred by normal means. From such a beginning, *mētis* never deviates; it is alive with shadow and the blink of lightning fall; a cunning that comes from being woven into shapeless, shifting tolerances; it is surprise set fast in an aspic of redundancy.

It is perhaps not surprising that something so shaded as *mētis* has resisted academic analysis. Homer can talk of it through example. Book XXIII of the *Iliad*, for example, describes a chariot race that pits a young Antilochus, the son of Nestor the Sage, against Menelaus (the king of Sparta).[15] Unfortunately, although the boy is very skilled, his horses are not as fast as those of his adversary. The young man appears bound to lose. Placed at a disadvantage, Antilochus instinctively recalls his father's words: 'It is through *mētis* rather than through strength that the wood-cutter shows his worth. It is through *mētis* that the helmsman guides the speeding vessel over the wine-dark sea despite the wind. It is through *mētis* that the charioteer triumphs over his rivals.' Weaned on such a diet of practical wisdom handed down from his father, the young man takes advantage of a sudden narrowing of the track, which had been worn away by storm rains the night before, and drives his chariot obliquely across in front of that of Menelaus. The manoeuvre takes his adversary by surprise, forcing the latter to rein in his horses, whereupon, seeing his adversary's momentary disarray, Antilochus quickly capitalizes on the advantage gained to outstrip him and win the race. The rhetorically crafted tale evokes *mētis* through appeal to drama, messy tales of unlikely advance that cannot be easily converted into generalizations and typifications. We learn of the fickleness of *mētis* as much as its potential; its coming by surprise and how, on occasion, it speaks of a world that can be heard but not enlisted. Western epistemological pursuits have, therefore, concentrated their attention mainly on explicit theoretical knowledge, which is viewed as more rigorous, robust and reliable.

It is in the classic work of Marcel Detienne and Jean Pierre Vernant that *mētis* begins to find sustained consideration, though even here the texts remain *intaglio*.[16] Like magicians only too aware of the dangers in discussing their trade, exponents of *mētis* pass over most opportunities to elaborate on their serpentine trickery, if indeed they notice such invitations as opportunities at all, given the inevitable recourse to hints, allegories and myth. In reducing *mētis* to some form of classificatory rigging, equating it with a persistent urge to avoid directness, eschew objectives and ridicule truths, Detienne and Vernant are not engaging in definition so much as suggesting a spirit of approach. Like their subject, they hesitate before declaring anything definitive; the prose deliberately and suggestively stutters towards and then away from explanation with the regularity of a fast-moving tide.

First, *mētis* involves a complete submission to circumstance, an intimacy so tight that the difference between the known and the knower collapses. In many ways, like *phronesis*, *mētic* knowledge simply is the expression of the affective power of what exists in the potential of things rather than just things known about and enlisted in the service of explicitly known ends. There is no reaction, no riposte; the knower simply expresses the inevitably tendency of what is there and remains ever vigilant of the changes to what is there. Second, *mētis* is prejudice: the awareness of the sagacity of ancestry; the accumulated wisdom and cunning of unregulated genealogy in whose branches we are able to leap with an unplanned fleetness of foot. Without prejudice we are empty, left with the responsibility of having to design responses without relief. Prejudice is the wellspring of collective achievement from which responses, like Athena, can come askance, but ready-made. Third, *mētis* is movement: the labile world shown and reshown in irreversible unrest. Exponents of *mētis* display a capacity for suppleness, an ability to extricate themselves from circumstances to which they remain enamoured, aware as they are that there is little to distinguish unblinking commitment from crass brute force. They flow through events like water, bending to the shape of emerging and passing histories with an alacrity and accuracy that come from the direct and immediate apprehension of phenomena rather than general reflections upon them. Any pathway is an action itself; there are no routes waymarked, only a constant negotiation of passageways that close as soon as they are breached. Finally, *mētis* is cunning: a duplicity and shadow play found in reversals, counter-factuals, disguises, mazes and camouflage.

Mētis operates on the cusp of its own dissolution. *Mētistic* beings operate in a world of becoming, coping with whatever arises immediately, and without qualm or resentment, but decidedly, where decision is not a choice amongst a known set of options but the capacity to judge in the future using figments of their imagination. Detienne and Vernant are careful to distinguish *mētis* from indifference, or fatalism. Exponents can influence events, their cunning can bind the experience of others, but not in ways that are logical or even demonstrable, because they are acting immediately, and with regard to an as yet unformed future. *Mētistic* knowledge is an economy of force, an ability to use the presence of what exists (including the powers of others) to ensure and enhance one's own persisting presence as what exists unfolds. This enhancement is not necessarily visible; where others look to perform on the surface of events, to gild their world with success, the *mētistic* value the persistence of life itself, not things that persist. There is no grip for the regulations of the ego and the preservation of a solid character; the *mētistic* is he or she who remains constantly and acutely aware of the context of context of context, a world without end occupied by balance and repose rather than distinction. It is simply hubris to suppose that achievements and acquisitions count; indeed, it is in the singular pursuit of such that strategists often fail, wedded as they become to a certain rigid framing of their experience.

As well as loosening the hold of immediate and obvious achievement as a mark of distinctiveness, it also loosens the idea of any hierarchy of human ability. *Mētis* is something all of us can learn, because it is in us all, lurking beneath the architecture of human rationality, and even our customs of reasonableness. As biological organisms, humans have unconsciously acquired, through the evolutionary process, this survivalist instinct involving a 'mindless' practical coping, which has remained theoretically unexamined since the time of the ancient Greeks. That such *mētic* qualities are more universal than generally acknowledged has led de Certeau to observe that they correspond to an ageless art which has not only persisted through the institutions of successive political orders but...present in fact a curious analogy, and a sort of immemorial link, to the simulations, tricks, and disguises that certain fishes or plants execute with extraordinary virtuosity... They [the qualities] maintain formal continuities and the permanence of *a memory without language, from the depths of the oceans to the streets of our great cities.*[17]

Mētis is a kind of internalized coping capability involving a 'memory without language' or representation. By its nature, then, the more we know about it the less it is what it is; the *mētic* belongs on the edges of silence. One good example of its primordial character is further illustrated by Detienne and Vernant:

The frogfish is a sluggish creature with a soft body and a hideous aspect. Its mouth opens exceedingly wide. Nevertheless it is a possessor of *mētis* for all that and it is *mētis* that procures its food. What it does is crouch, motionless, deep in the wet mud. Then it stretches out a little fleshy appendage which grows below its lower jaw; the appendage is thin, white and has an unpleasant smell. The frogfish waves it about continuously, using it as a bait to attract small fish. As soon as these catch sight of it they fall on it in order to seize it. Then, imperceptibly, the frogfish draws this sort of tongue back towards it and continues to wave it gently about a couple of finger-lengths away from its mouth. Without the slightest suspicion that it is a trap the little fish follow the bait. Soon they are swallowed up one after another within the wide jaws of this huge mouth... The domain of *mētis* is one ruled by cunning and traps. It is an ambiguous world composed of duplicity and deceit.[18]

Although Detienne and Vernant equate *mētis* with deliberate 'duplicity' and 'deceit', and hence imply conscious intentional action on the part of the frogfish, the use of this example elicits a kind of universal commonality of being, a common sense of dwelling that has been gradually refined and 'unconsciously' passed on from one generation of frogfish to another. Moreover, this kind of primordial 'knowing' is made more understandable from the *dwelling* world view that we spoke of earlier. This links *mētis* with *phronesis*, both being predicated upon the direct bodily acquisition of skills in a manner that does not involve conscious learning or explicit articulation and that as much as it reveals the world accepts its remaining concealed. *Mētis* operates on the unexpressed premise that both language and reality cannot be understood (or manipulated) in straightforward ways but by means of 'subtlety, indirection, and even cunning'.[19] In other words, its very efficacy is dependent upon it remaining unnoticed, unstated and unacknowledged. Paradoxically, the moment it is declared and noticed it loses its potency. It is, therefore, tempting but misleading to reduce *mētic* intelligence to 'know-how'. Nor is this *mētic* intelligence a deliberate and reflective form of knowledge.

Rather, *mētic* intelligence is, to use the words of Pierre Bourdieu, a consequence of habitus: a style, demeanour, and culturally mediated set of predispositions inscribed onto material bodies that result in a propensity to act in a manner congruent with the demands of a shifting and evolving situation. Experienced within the practice of business strategy, Philippe Baumard suggests that this 'furtive, discretionary' form of knowledge allows its exponents to 'escape puzzling and ambiguous situations'.[20] Baumard talks of its being a knowledge or awareness that is versed in obliquity, from the merest hints and small happenings to situations can be read and anticipated. Sherlock-Holmes-like, the response to the riddles of crime is not one of deduction from apparent clues but imaginative leaps between snippets of data wrested from unlikely and murky places.[21]

Throughout we have suggested that obliquity is the very atmosphere of doing strategy. Reading feint messages, being curious and remaining alive to diverse perspectives and second-order effects are the very stuff of what George Day and Paul Schoemaker identify as a basic strategic virtue, namely vigilance.[22] To be vigilant is to remain alive to vague and diverse and seemingly minor occurrences; it is to look beyond the abstract confines of data-based analysis; it is to absorb contradictions; and all of this is *mētis*. It becomes a cultivated *art* for reversing unfavourable or disorienting or even unrecognized situations into ones replete with potential that involves alertness, sensitivity and a peculiar disposition that is particularly attuned to emerging opportunities contained in unfolding circumstances.

The strategy of indirectness

Emphasizing the strategic resonance of the surprising capacity for vigilance, for reversing fortunes through indirect and circuitous actions, enabled Liddell-Hart to assert: 'Its [the indirect approach's] fulfilment was seen to be the key to practical achievement in dealing with any problem where the human factor predominates, and a conflict of wills tends to spring from an underlying concern for interests.'[23] This indirectness is fuelled by the kind of habituated duplicity demonstrated by the frogfish, an economy of effort whose perfect expression would be to realize an outcome without any intervention other than just being.[24] These sentiments are clearly reminiscent of the writings of the ancient Chinese military strategist Sun Tzu in his *Art of War*, which have become widely read in strategy practitioners' circles but which, curiously, hardly feature at all in business strategy texts.

Military exponents of the need for cunning and the economy of effort it implies are typically associated with those fighting or commenting on unconventional or guerrilla wars, in which asymmetrical power forces a weaker party to harry, disrupt and confound the enemy through pragmatic tactics of incursion and avoidance. For Mao Zedong's guerrillas, for example, the general tactic was to 'avoid the solid, attack the hollow; attack; withdraw; deliver a lightning blow, seek a lightning decision', and in so doing exhaust rather than confront the enemy. As Colin Gray notes, Mao's guerrillas could pass imperceptibly through Chinese society; their disguise was their common guise. An alternate form of unconventional style comes with the use of special forces; clandestine, self-sufficient units of professionals licensed to act outside the boundaries drawn by conflict. Surprise comes from their dormancy, their being in the most ordinary and so unexpected places, their disrespect for the niceties of a well-run engagement.[25]

It was to experiencing and elaborating on indirect engagement that T. E. Lawrence attributed the 'success' of the Arab campaign during World War I, in which his part was retrospectively recounted in his book *Seven Pillars of Wisdom*. In deliberate planning, forecasting, and making sense of a territory, an army is always being placed as though confronting its territory. It is always visible, and in being made visible it is always struggling to blend in with its environment and maintain advantage. Lawrence did not decry the use of such direct engagement, only – like Bergson – the singular reliance upon it. In an entry on 'guerrilla warfare' in the 1929 edition of *Encyclopaedia Britannica*, he sets out for the reader a narrative that goes a little way to conveying what he felt was the alternative, indirect approach. Strategy – which as an officer 'in charge' of Arab units he recognized as defining his job as such – he describes as 'the synoptic regard which sees everything by the standard of the whole'.[26] For Lawrence and the Arabs, the campaign was governed by an entirely purposive endeavour: to recover and live freely in their own land. Faced with the rubric of writing an entry for an encyclopaedia, Lawrence classified this human endeavour into a triptych – the algebraic mode; the biological; and the psychological – all of which could be understood as something indirect rather the confrontational. By algebraic, Lawrence means the mechanical, calculable or what we have been calling the navigational: the identification of fixed conditions, of mapped geographies and of unfeeling objects such as hills and munitions. The Arabs' algebraic calculations were primarily territorial. They did not use the calculation to best occupy the land, however; rather, they used it to better understand how their opposition, the Turks, were too few in number to do so, giving the Arabs space to roam, by which they would become 'an influence, a thing invulnerable, intangible without front or back'. The Turks could control only that which they occupied or could 'point a gun at'; all else was Arabian.

By biology, Lawrence talks of waste, or wear and tear; the consideration of life and death. Here Lawrence speaks of a need for reserves, an economy of engagement preserving a dormant source of influence that can be awakened and deployed in a flash before vanishing into dust. At the risk of essentializing, Lawrence describes the Arab army as being a loose confederation of tribes with each tribal member contributing on his or her own turf and terms; they could not be ordered outside the native tribal unit, nor would they persist with the army outside their territory. So the Arab army was being constantly renewed, was a shifting haze, undisciplined, its unity entirely organic, expressive and animated by the vivid efficiency of tribal groups bound by unspoken honour. Such a force could not afford human wear and tear; the fighters had not been compressed into typified units; they retained a human face; individual loss rippled through the tribe. They therefore waged war on machines rather than men; they attacked train lines, fuel depots, food stocks, which depleted the enemy with a minimum of face-to-face engagement.

This leads to the third mode, psychology, by which Lawrence means the arrangement of the minds of one's own soldiers, the minds of the opposing forces and the minds of the nations supporting the engagements. The purposive disposition of the Arab mind was one devoted to the idea of freedom: to die for freedom was the thing; the enemy was simply incidental. In contrast, the mind of the Turkish soldier, being an occupant, was beset with anxieties of preservation, of holding the visible, detailed, geographical line. Arab strategy therefore cohered into imposing upon the Turks the expense of having to maintain a passive defence (they were holed up in the coastal town of Medina), to make life uncomfortable but not so impossible as to drive them out into direct confrontation. The Arabs used fast, small, mobile camel parties to harry defensive lines, forcing the Turks into a steady expenditure of assets without offering any target. The battle was fought only by one side; the Arabs had nothing material to defend or to lose; they had speed and surprise rather than 'hitting power':

Most wars are wars of contact, both forces striving to keep in touch to avoid tactical surprise. The Arab war should be a war of detachment: to contain the enemy by the silent threat of a vast unknown desert, not disclosing themselves till the moment of attack.[27]

The desert was like the sea, without lines, a space of immanence without bases or fixed points, affording opportunities to raid and retreat at will, taking as much of the war as one wanted, retreating rather than pressing home; an engagement of strokes rather than strikes. The outcome was inevitable; slowly the Turks withdrew into themselves, eating themselves away in pensive inaction. It was only the final assault by the British – forcing the Turks into fighting and then a hurried surrender – that undermined this strategy of indirectness, the British phalanx denying the Arabs the sense of having won the war without fighting any battles.

Reflecting on Lawrence's campaign, Liddell-Hart recognizes how the guerrilla strategy of avoidance, mobility and dispersed ubiquity can bring more powerful opponents to their knees, but at the cost of a seeping moral duplicity and an exposure to the effects of such a strategy upon oneself. Though the victory may be apparent, those inured in a guerrilla spirit are often unable to sustain any peace; the legacy of 'illegitimate' action looms over the polity like an unwelcome but unchallengeable shadow. The nomadic lifestyle and long-cultured attitude of defiance sit uneasily with the civic endeavour of creating acceptable institutional processes.[28] This suggests another reason why *mētis* has been often overlooked: it is the seemingly clandestine nature and apparent deviousness of 'cunning' that make it morally opaque and hence unworthy of serious study and scholarship.[29] An admission of *mētis* puts us on notice that giving oneself over to the twists and turns of events will involve us in beguiling and furtive actions alike. This might be acceptable in the context of war, in which a 'needs must' mentality prevails above personal qualms about the effects of cunning, but in other contexts its expression is more ambivalent. Lawrence himself was acutely aware of this. Arriving at Damascus with the Arabs, who had been promised their freedom if they threw in their lot with the British, Lawrence realized they were themselves going to be tricked. Unable to bear the ruin of this betrayal, Lawrence resigned, withdrew from the political subterfuge and, taking a new name at random picked from a telephone directory, enlisted in the air force as 'Aircraftsman Shaw', a common rating. W. B. Yeats tells the story of an encounter he had with Lawrence, asking him how he felt about his desert campaign. Lawrence responded to Yeats thus: 'I was an Irish nobody.' (Pause.) 'I did something.' (Pause.) 'It was a failure.' (Pause.) 'And I became an Irish nobody again.'[30] Lawrence's strategic action brought enduring repute gained through a persisting resistance to being elevated in one position for too long, both militarily and personally. This avoidance and the cunning it required were bought at a price. Lawrence felt that he, in turn, was the victim of British *technē*, an unwitting instrument of a machine-like, pragmatic colonial disposition. His values, reflected in the war of liberation, were left emptied, as the Arabs were refused the political and spiritual presence they had been expecting.

Lawrence's tale is as disturbing as it is attractive; the skilful strategic display of *mētistic* indirectness and economy brought its own devils. What Lawrence argued was lost was what we might call, following Aristotle, a capacity for *phronetic* reasonableness, or appropriateness, brought about through a basic stability of character. This stability is not so much a constancy of roles or preference for a certain status or resources but a more basic constancy of attitude, whereby we are able to accept that all modes of strategic engagement, including the *mētistic*, have their own limits, their own contradictions, that need to be acknowledged rather than excused. Too consistent a display of duplicity, no matter how habitual, confines strategy to a mealy, somewhat insidious promotion of short-term singular interests, of the kind we discussed earlier when financial speculators used new technical tricks such as financial shorting to earn revenue deviously simply by betting on the demise of others. Shorting could be described as a *mētistic* trick, an immediate response to ever-shifting circumstances demonstrating a preparedness to win through avoidance, but one that has been unchecked by *phronesis*. Its very singularity and intense selfishness has led to its being labelled a somewhat dubious practice. It is not a common enemy that is being exploited but the potential projects of a wide range of others, many of whom have little influence in the speculative systems in which they find themselves indirectly embroiled. If all we have is cunning, then we get back to the very crude state of nature abstractions that belie what it is to live in a state of dwelling.

Towards a strategic blandness

What, therefore, besides the negative approach of harrying, opportunism and avoidance, one might ask, is the real alternative to spectacular strategic intervention? The answer, François Jullien[31] suggests, is a certain strategic *blandness*; a strategy-less strategy, in which indirectness, *phronesis*, *mētis*, complexity, curiosity and spontaneity persist without any one dominating. To understand and recover the bland is to abandon positions, to withdraw from stated preferences, to shy away from once fervidly held commitments, and instead nurture a curiosity for everything in whose meanderings our actions and thoughts eschew both infatuation and indifference. From sayings and doings informed by blandness there can be no determining outcomes that do not always supersede themselves. Jullien talks of blandness as the achievement of sages: achieving a balance of invisibility, going through the world unnoticed, is the work of gifted and knowledgeable people able to resist the temptation of hanging on to whatever presents itself as fixed and so distinct from the flow of life. We are getting closer to the kind of release that Heidegger speaks of as learning to dwell amid things whilst still confined by the pragmatic and theoretical frame of our ordering technology.

Stimulated by early Chinese thinkers, Jullien suggests an alternative way of conducting the withdrawal from everyday life that does not involve a cutting off from the very dwelling that sustains us. Rather than expend intellectual energy building theories and classifications from whose precarious height we attempt to view the world, it is better to remain within it, but obliquely, refusing to remain in any one position in that life. The knowledge project becomes something very different: a centred, dynamic perception of the bland. The bland is the source of this, our only world and from which all things and states unfurl and to which all things and states return.

The bland does not utter the things of the world – does not paint the world – except at their point of assimilation back into the undifferentiated where they shed their distinctive traits, integrate their differences, and give rein to their propensity for fusion.[32]

The clamour of colours, objects, possessions, symbols and their being named disposes us against such blandness; the flavours of life provoke attachments and jealousies not readily given up. Jullien wishes us to relinquish a little, to cleave to movement without wishing for destinations, to taste without craving more, and so to know whilst eliding from the characterizations we so often give to experience. It is a call for us to go unnoticed, to blend in with what is immanent and leave no residue, to be outwardly dull and yet inwardly resonant. The withdrawal amounts to a constant shuffling of hands, an oscillation of concentration and dilution, hard and soft, passion and disinterest.

It appears paradoxical, but it is only by passing through the insipid and the bland that the vivid values and the intensities of taste and colour can appear; the bland is the origin of all the world. Nurturing the bland is not, then, akin to Aristotle's golden mean; it is not the advocacy of moderation in all things by adherence to which we achieve a steady pattern of considered adaptability to situations.[33] Rather, it is the movement, the passing through, the ever so temporary occupation of experiences. To recall our earlier comments on Heidegger's *interesse*, it is a placing that we can incite and influence but only with the prospect of removal, a presence amid presenting things only to have them withdraw. The bland is not itself a position but the residue of this constant breathing with a life that is part of us and that it is not in our gift to look down upon and possess. The occidental knowledge project, of which strategy tends to be a part, is an attempt to resist this movement, to isolate and move towards a desired position of distinction; a preoccupation that in its being asserted and reasserted in codified objectives removes us from the free play by which we nourish our lives.

If we go back to our earlier etymological discussion of strategy – or *strategos* – being the 'art of the general' (understood in two distinct senses) then blandness offers us a completely different sense of what might be meant. Our argument has been a steady reiteration of the impossibility and undesirability of trying to understand the general as though it were an overview of things, a general picture of a territory in which entities are known, placed and moved about like pieces on a chessboard. There are too many contingencies, too many alternative limits, too many system influences, and the pursuit is too debilitating, for such an intellectualized picture ever to emerge fully. That our intellect and navigational habits encourage us to think otherwise is to our detriment. If we approach the general as blandness, however, we command a sense of the whole understood not as what is but as what might be; we become ever sensitive to the weak signals and little things from which distinctive experiences unfurl. The art of the general becomes less an overarching knowledge of things reached through a specific mode of intellectual withdrawal, whose assertive severance proves increasingly costly, than a persistent nourishing of a life by being amongst things and always under way with these things in all their plenitude. There is a reversal of strategic intent here, as it becomes a joining of things through movement rather than arresting or bracketing off experience: it is being strong and then weak; using the intellect and then intuition; understanding the intimacy between dwelling and building.

Bland strategies eschew fixed images, goals, and instead acknowledge the inherent 'lack' in all things, overcoming the human preoccupation with nice representations, with distinctive statements, with focused ideas, with the addictive attachments induced by strong flavours. On Jullien's terms, a good strategist is akin to one who feeds life without demanding that it conforms to an idea and who recognizes the inherent danger of persisting relations:

The sage does not allow his conduct to be encumbered by knowledge, stuck in agreements, bogged down in virtues or hobbled by success.[34]

This upsets the mantra of strategists and strategy researchers recommending the occupation of niches, distinctiveness, scarcity, aloofness. Strategic homilies are versed in a concern with an organization's differentiation, its separateness from its environment. Every effort is put into instructing its members on how to attain and maintain such visibility in the seething competitive environment, much like a rock stuck fast in a pummelling sea. Performance is all about sustaining this distinctiveness, preserving a life understood in terms of resistance, barriers, protection. The purpose is to maintain a position above the waterline, beneath which poor performers are plunged and the average gently slip. Here strategy is about achieving notable or even spectacular distinctiveness.

From Jullien's perspective of the bland, good strategy goes unnoticed. What carries greatest force is not what is most distinct but what is minimal and most invisible:

> True efficacy is always discreet; conversely, the ostentatious is illusory. Sage and strategist alike reject spectacular and superficial acts in favor of an influence that operates profoundly and over time.[35]

Strategists who look for the spectacular and the distinct are often wanting praise; they are enamoured with what is most distinguished rather than with realizing effective influence through apparently minute actions. Distinction can come with successive attempts to structure, organize and control lives through the creation of institutions, but often this is done by avoiding or resisting, rather than understanding, the flow of life. In this resistance the effects might be instant and evident, but they will not last, because they are wrought in opposition and separation. The huge firm will collapse under the weight of its buildings, its legacy costs, its procedure-induced boredom; the detailed phalanx of soldiers will stutter and then stop, devoid of purpose in the wake of enemies who remain fleet of foot; the ordered hierarchy of political officers will become brittle and then wither as it gradually loses touch with the human concerns upon which it was distantly founded.

Invisibility often carries the most resonant and persistent of influence. Take memorials such as the Cenotaph in London's Whitehall, built by the architect Edward Lutyens. The author Robert Musil notes how most public monuments seemed to repel attention, to elicit the indifference of a busying mass so inured to the elevation of national notables that all monumental embodiment suffers from a paradoxical invisibility: 'Most of us show the same attitude to these statues. One considers them – like a tree – to be a part of the street, one would be immediately struck by their disappearance, but one does not look at them and one does not have the slightest idea whom they represent.'[36] Lutyens' design embraces rather than resists this relationship, but it does more than is typical of a monument, and certainly a bronze statue: it lets absence resonate throughout the tree-lined avenues of power; the absence of the lives lost under the direction of brittle causes so that other lives might be better lived. Rather than lament the invisible character of monuments, therefore, Lutyens exploits it; it was precisely the nameless and featureless quality that the Cenotaph was expressing, its innocent, blank walls absorbing the cold indifference of real, non-human life. There is no better *in memoriam* to the lost dead than an empty, faceless plinth that irradiated its viewers with silence in spite of the clamour. The Cenotaph now stands as a pigeon-stained, stone island held fast amongst eddies of diesel and drifting, brightly dressed tourists. It is largely ignored; long-lived wreaths decorate the base, a permafrost of collective memory circuiting the nation's gravestone. The less evident its quality the greater its capacity to endure and grow into the interstices of foraging humanity, however; it is its very stillness that ensures it endures.[37]

Exponents of the bland are looking constantly to relate things, to open each thing to other things, to expose the 'vivid variety' of the plain and everyday. Such is the way with Herman Miller, a US furniture manufacturer operating out of Zeeland, Michigan. Its incorporation and subsequent global expansion have been, and remain, rooted in an assiduous attention to its roots, or what Hugh De Pree, a descendant of the firm's founding family, calls the 'life and lore of one company'. For De Pree, what sustains Herman Miller is not a well-drilled divisional structure, savvy marketing or an enviable diversity of product offerings but a perennial insistence on an organized life in which people experience open relations, have their talent nurtured, are able to share ownership and are encouraged to undergo what the Herman Miller designer George Nelson has described as 'the dirty work of creativity'. Recounting the atmosphere during the 1950s, when Herman Miller was producing arguably its most iconic furniture, George Nelson said:

The real assets of Herman Miller at this time were items one never finds on balance sheets: faith, cheerful indifference to what the rest of the industry might be up to, lots of nerve, and a mysterious kind of interaction that had everyone functioning at top capacity while always having a good time.[38]

Another designer at Herman Miller, Charles Eames, described such creativity as a curiosity and attention to detail in articulating and responding to the problems of function and utility *within* constraints. The constraints are those of material properties, price, time, expectation, techniques, enthusiasm, and so on; constraints whose very obstacles stimulate creative thought, by which they transform into opportunities.[39] For Eames, the notion that function and utility could ever be exhausted was an anathema; the designer simply had to keep acknowledging the ever-shifting pattern of purposes and constraints, and those who ran the firm similarly recognized such.

Strategic efficacy is found in escape from positions, from commitments and from objectives. These establish opposition and separation from other systems and risk pathology, whereas blandness is perception constantly opening up to new states, new paths, new things. This is the seat of creativity: the ability to absorb contradiction, to display an array of character and a multiplicity of traits, none of which dominate and all of which can be brought into play without any inner fixation that blocks the renewal of one's self. To effect such blandness requires a strategist constantly to enjoin alternatives, opposites, and so moderate and challenge specific virtues, abilities and tastes; to become inscrutable, durable.[40] This takes us back to Ruskin's Gothic character: the ability to create and absorb contrasts without apology, to encounter anxiety without the urge to restore uniformity. It is in the constantly changing contrasts of the Gothic frieze, say, that the foliage of plants is seized in all its propensity, which means that it should be seen not merely as 'form' but also as a continuing process.[41] This dynamism of contrast and reciprocity was most ably demonstrated by Ruskin's hero, J. M. W. Turner. In the summer exhibition of 1832, held at London's Royal Academy, John Constable's entry was *Opening of Waterloo Bridge* – a radiant, opulent burst of cherubic sky, foliage-clad stonework and river barges strewn with bunting and resounding with the shrill cheers of a new industrial age. Next to it hung a plangent, muted seascape by Turner (*Helvoetsluys*, now in Tokyo's Fuji Art Museum). At the time, it was common for artists to put finishing touches to their work *in situ* (varnishing days), and Constable had been working hard on embellishing his piece when Turner came in and, looking over Constable's back, stared intensely at the two paintings side by side. He eventually left, came back in with his palette, put a small daub of red lead on his shifting grey sea, and departed, silently. The effect transfixed Constable, whose own painting had been rendered little more than decorative noise in the wake of Turner's stunning economy of effort: 'He has been here,' said Constable, 'and fired a gun.' Turner returned a few days later to glaze his painting and changed the daub into a small buoy.[42]

Bland strategies are not so much attempts at acquiring or influencing resource bundles in their relations to one another as they are about recognizing the restrictions in becoming too enamoured with them. It entails a potential for maintaining an alertness or lightness of touch. This lightness, however, can also itself become too habitual, too devouring of identity. Jullien's project is one of using a growing and deep familiarity with a foreign world view in order to reflect upon the habitual projects of Western people that typically go unnoticed. These projects can then be held up for scrutiny; their naturalness is unconcealed; we are thinking about them. This is not the same as being inherently critical of them *en masse*. Indeed, Jullien finds the oriental habits upon which he elaborates as potentially debilitating as Western ones. The skilled exponent of the bland finds ultimate expression in the annihilation of otherness and an accompanying liberation from the perishable body and petty, personal concerns. This is as utopian as a Platonic ideal. Neither project offers the possibility of another side so no possibility exists of contradiction, counter-assertion and difference, as all is harmless, harmonious, endless. Hence our advocacy of blandness in the company of *mētis*; the latter intercedes and disrupts harmony, meaning that blandness is something moved towards without being reached.

More tellingly, we might recall both Bergson and Heidegger, for whom intellectual and pragmatic engagement remained vital to a flourishing life. Giving oneself over entirely to unthinking intuition and thoughtful dwelling belittles the achievements of those who have constantly striven to resist their history by defending themselves against it, or contradicting it. This is why, for example, Heidegger's later work admits a persisting need for otherness – the anxiety of being in the presence of things in themselves – which he himself in his National Socialist 'phase' failed to acknowledge, with such bad consequences for himself and others. Jullien's wariness in the face such extreme blandness, such a sacrifice of individuality and character to wider historical energy, is telling.[43] The bland is advocated as a counterblast to the intellect. Considering the bland is not about advocacy of a completely different, alternative world view but about 'deranging' the technological tendency of the West to use the intellectual project to do something similar. Bateson talks of this tendency as an urge to become conscious of more and more of the world (to confine the world to static assertion by constantly revealing new states of affairs). Jullien elaborates on an alternative tendency of the East to become less and less conscious of oneself as separate from the world. Such an awareness of the bland is what Heidegger was reaching after with dwelling; an awareness that the knowledge we use to guide our projects and activity is not confined by already visible end points. A bland strategy is one infused with the kind of knowledge that looks ahead to that which is still invisible and which might be brought into visibility through our projects. For Heidegger, this takes us back to the goddess Athena, the bright-eyed one born of Mētis yet whose cunning is refined with humility. The knowledge of which Athena speaks is, for Heidegger, an acknowledgement of limits, where limits are not outlines, or constraints, but the gathering of something into its own in order that it appears full, in order that it merges into presence.[44] The bland, then, is a means of ridding strategy of the unreflective egoistic conceits of a scientific method and its technological expression, in which what is made present is always confined to what can be located, fixed and analysed in advance. The overt designs of strategists manifest in targets, positions, goals and the like are tempered with an understanding of belonging in which what is being made present is always something coming to fruition, whose limits are not well-defined end points but a bringing into being something that has not yet appeared, and that might be held together, amid other things also holding themselves together. This is what we are hinting at by considering how strategy might be made more akin to dwelling rather than just building; this is what we are reaching after with 'strategy without design'.

Epilogue: Negative capability

Throughout this book we have endeavoured to become what Elias Canetti calls writers – *Dichter* – whose role it is to explore and comment upon experience without fixation. The writer does not collect or build things, but tries to encounter and absorb them as they are, in all their inconsistency and contradiction, and all their latency and potential. The writer is not someone who propounds models if by such are meant institutional designs and outcomes that are deemed desirable irrespective of circumstance. This is the impetus behind our advocacy of strategy without design, a deliberately tense title – unattainable, of course. We all use designs all the time. This book is designed using chapter structures and attributions; it recommends states of affairs; it uses structured arguments to attempt to elicit sympathy. Being without design acts as an impetus, however; it encourages endeavour by those for whom it resonates to strive towards it, ways of thought without the prospect of an end point, or even a resolution. It is in the striving that we experience plenitude, that new qualities arise. For the economist Thorstein Veblen, something akin to this striving, this resistance to fixed goals and ideals, was expressed in his oft-used phrase 'Whatever is, is wrong'. The more entrenched, orthodox and generally established an idea was the greater the likelihood of its being wrong, because, whilst its appropriateness was always an upshot of our future-oriented activity, its formal or accepted sense languished in unexamined academic and commercial habit.

It is an arresting notion that, as soon as they are pronounced, ideas suffer an irreversible redundancy as the events from which they emerge recede into the annals of history. What is disturbing for Veblen is not only that we avoid recognizing this intellectual decay but that we actively combat it by wishing to preserve ideas, diverting critical attention away from the idea itself and towards its more fruitful application and exploitation. Veblen, always an animated man experiencing what he found to be an animated world, was inherently suspicious of these attempts. It is ideas that we should be wary of, especially the well-received ideas that have become naturalized, unnoticed and devoid of troubling movement. All too often we recur to these ideas to seek what Veblen calls a comforting spiritual stability; they become institutionally sacred. In contrast, productive ideas are will-o'-the-wisp insights that afford us a reorientation of experience but at the expense of discomfort, of having to maintain a lithe and circumspect mien. They do not concern what is (which is only ever a conduit for what is no longer) but what might be.

Strategy without design is not simply a resistance to orthodox models, however. The phrase 'Whatever is, is wrong' comes from the essay 'On paradox and common-place', written in 1822 by William Hazlitt. It is part of a pair, the other phrase being, as is the way with the *near*-symmetry of pairs, 'Whatever is, is right'. These two statements belong to two types of individual identified by Hazlitt, both of whom are the cause of much social malaise. The one is forever directed to the torpid warmth of the usual, the other, the lover of paradoxes, to the dancing heat of the novel:

The one stickles through thick and thin for his own religion and government: the other scouts all religions and all governments with a smile of ineffable disdain. The one will not move for any consideration out of the broad and beaten path: the other is continually turning off at right angles, and losing himself in the labyrinths of his own ignorance and presumption. The one will not go along with any party: the other always joins the strongest side. The one will not conform to any common practice: the other will subscribe to any thriving system. The one is the slave of habit: the other is the sport of caprice. The first is like a man obstinately bed-rid: the last is troubled with St Vitus's dance. He cannot stand still, he cannot rest upon any conclusion. 'He never is – but always to be *right*.' [1]

What matters in strategy without design is that both stances are avoided. Productive ideas might be those that render us homeless and stripped of habit, that instil in us a sense of the uncanny, yet their productivity resonates only because of the prepossessing weight of conformity and agreement against which they can strike. The ensuing insights arise *intellectually and imaginatively* as descriptive skits, flying and dying like sparks issuing from repeated strikes against orthodoxy. There is no sense of where these truths might locate or lead us, no objective towards which they steer, no resolving power by which they might end speculative endeavour. The sparks are flying, and keep flying, and the weight of agreement keeps resonating with the blows.

Strategy without design is about embracing the uncertain, the ambiguous and the unknown as a pervasive human condition without persistently hankering for clarity and certainty, whether that certainty is found in the most ancient and comforting of traditions or the most recent of fashions. As such it involves the internal cultivation of a certain 'negative capability', an enduring quality *of individuals* that the poet John Keats expressed in a letter to his brother sent at Christmas in 1817: 'Negative capability, that is, when a man is capable of being in uncertainties, mysteries, doubts, without any irritable reaching after fact and reason.'[2] In strategy, the term 'capability' is generally associated with the positive ability to act, to intervene with confidence, to be notable in one's capacity to bring about desired outcomes; so much so that the idea of a negative capability appears somewhat paradoxical. The word 'capability', however, actually derives from the Latin root *capabilis*, meaning 'able to hold' or 'to contain'. Negative capability thus implies *containment* and the capacity to *endure* rather than the capacity for active intervention: the cultivated resilience to resist premature closure in the face of vagueness, uncertainty and equivocality. Containment implies suspending judgement, dispersing attention and resisting the tendency to gravitate all too quickly towards recognizable forms of comprehension associated with positive capability, whether this is a capability of the intellect or of intuitive belonging.[3]

Such an ability to resist premature judgement and closure is encapsulated in the Japanese industrialist Konosuke Matsushita's notion of the *sunao* mind, which he insisted was a vital quality for good management. *Sunao* is a Japanese word that is used to denote meekness, tractability or an open-hearted innocence and naïvety: an untrapped mind that is free to adapt itself effectively to changing circumstances.

The untrapped, open mind – *sunao* – of which I often speak is a temperament that allows one to see things as they really are. Without this open, receptive mind, we lack true strength. We have made it a regular management policy at Matsushita Electric to cultivate this *sunao* mind, in the conviction that it enables us to perceive the real state of all things in society.[4]

Matsushita acknowledges that this *sunao* mind bears a certain resemblance to zen which, with its austere lifestyle and stress on meditation, seeks an encounter with pristine reality in all its blandness and undifferentiated state of becoming. Negative capability also requires this emptiness itself to be treated with curiosity, however, to be considered against the shadows of alternatives; to consider how this emptiness of mind takes us to the edges and in so doing constitutes a renewal of who we are, as substantial beings-in-the-world with our own unique projects for which the world unaccountably makes room.

Strategy without design is about making room, the limits of which are not boundaries, but the edges where things begin their essential unfolding. Strategy without design is building for the dwelling of things, notably our self amidst other selves and other things. This is what it is to practise the art of the general: not to cover and control life from above, but to bring forth things by cultivating the things that grow, and constructing the things that do not. Heidegger used the term 'clearing' to describe this. The clearing is neither physical nor the expression of an individual or group of human wills, but the place of persisting encounters of things expressing themselves as we work with them habitually in our everyday lives, and as we on occasion stop to encounter them, unconcealed as disclosing things-in-themselves. Confronting the world simply as a stock of strategic resources, as an assemblage of mute objects defined entirely by ideas (their degree of utility; their dimensions; the length of time they persist) forecloses us from things; it flattens the world into the singular, ordered and destructive designs of men. Strategy without design is a willingness to think about what is unthought and unsaid whilst freeing us from both the obstinacy of the commonplace and the iridescent glare of the new. It requires us to face things as things, without recording or representing or analysing these things, so that we meet the world as something other than a vast collection of resources and that we understand ourselves as something other than an isolated, rational, separated collector of these resources.

Notes

PREFACE

1 Henry Mintzberg and James A. Waters, 'Of strategies, deliberate and emergent', *Strategic Management Journal*, 1985, 6(3), pp.257–272.
2 Edwards N. Luttwark, *Strategy: The Logic of War and Peace*, 2001, Cambridge, MA: Belknap Press, p.2 (emphasis in original).

INTRODUCTION

1 In Eliot Weinberger (ed.), *The New Directions Anthology of Classical Chinese Poetry*, 2003, New York: New Directions, p.32.
2 See www.grameen-info.org/bank/GBGlance.htm.
3 Muhammad Yunus, *Banker to the Poor*, 2003, London: Aurum Press, p.9.
4 Muhammad Yunus, *Banker to the Poor*, pp.4–5, (emphasis added).
5 Jim March, 'A scholar's quest', 1996, Stanford Graduate School of Business, www.gsb.stanford.edu/community/bmag/sbsm0696/ascholar.htm.
6 Richard Branson, *Screw It, Let's Do It: Lessons in Life*, 2007, London: Virgin Books, pp.39–40.
7 Richard Branson, *Screw It, Let's Do It*, p.51.
8 Robert Michels' book *Political Parties: A Sociological Study of the Oligarchical Tendencies of Modern Democracy* (1966, New York: Macmillan) describes how, once in power, political movements founded on radical ideas will begin to converge with established values and interests, eventually betraying their own principles, not necessarily consciously, but because of a gradual, pragmatic dilution in order that they remain in power. Michels has extended this argument from parties to all forms of social organization, suggesting that the tendency of institutional engagement to compress individuality and difference was akin to an unbreakable 'iron law'. Michels himself became deeply suspicious of social reformers and those advocating institutional intervention to bring about human betterment, eventually becoming an apologist for fascism on the somewhat sanguine grounds that its exponents offered no false hope. Friedrich Hayek also suffered disillusion and frustration when witnessing the failure of consciously designed reform in his native Austria, but unlike Michels he felt that organized life did not necessarily collapse into what he emotively termed 'institutional serfdom'.
9 Basil H. Liddell-Hart, *Strategy: The Indirect Approach*, 1967 (rev. edn.), London: Faber and Faber, pp.xix–xx.

10 Herbert Simon, *The Sciences of the Artificial*, 1996 (3rd edn.), Cambridge, MA: MIT Press, pp.33–34.

11 Philip Ball, *Critical Mass: How One Thing Leads to Another*, 2005, London: Arrow Books, p.183.

12 Malcolm Gladwell, *The Tipping Point: How Little Things Can Make a Big Difference*, 2000, London: Little, Brown, pp.141–142.

13 Malcolm Gladwell, *The Tipping Point*, p.134.

14 Magora Maruyama, 'The second cybernetics', *American Scientist*, 1963, 51(3), pp.163–167.

15 In 2008 it was €540,000 per employee, while GM, for example, was €420,000 (from which high welfare costs have to be further accounted for and Volksweger only €310,000), and had the highest earnings before interest and tax in absolute dollars of any high-volume manufacturer. In all this, however, one has to be careful not to eulogize the firm uncritically, which would be falling into the very trap that Toyota's people seem capable of avoiding.

16 *Business Week*, 10 November 2006.

17 MSNBC, 24 April 2007.

18 MSNBC, 24 April 2007.

19 Toyota spokesman Paul Nolasco, BBC News, 24 April 2007.

20 'Toyota looks to the return of family values', *Financial Times*, 20 January 2009.

21 Takahiro Fujimoto, *The Evolution of a Manufacturing System at Toyota*, 1999, New York: Oxford University Press.

22 Simon Caulkin, 'Toyota's never-to-be-repeated all-star production', *Observer*, 2 December 2007.

23 Pierre Bourdieu, *The Logic of Practice*, 1990, Cambridge: Polity Press, p.x.

24 Muhammad Yunus, *Banker to the Poor*, p.14.

25 Amartya Sen, *Development as Freedom*, 1999, Oxford: Oxford University Press, p.xiii.

26 Daniel Curran and Herman Leonard, *Recovery in Aceh: Towards a Strategy of Emergence*, 2005, Harvard Business School Working Paper no. 05-082, p.3 (available at www.hbs.edu/global/research/asia/articles.html).

27 James Scott, *Seeing Like a State*, 1998, New Haven, CT: Yale University Press, p.19.

28 All quotes from James Scott, *Seeing Like a State*, p.20.

29 Nassim Nicholas Taleb, *The Black Swan: The Impact of the Highly Improbable*, 2007, London: Penguin, p.xxv.

30 Nassim Nicholas Taleb, *The Black Swan*, p.131.

31 Nassim Nicholas Taleb, *The Black Swan*, p.132.

32 Amartya Sen, *Development as Freedom*, p.15.

33 Amartya Sen, *Development as Freedom*, p.xiii.

34 Samuel Huntington, 'The clash of civilizations', *Foreign Affairs*, 72(3), pp.22–49.

35 Paul Rogers, *Towards Sustainable Security: Alternatives to the War on Terror*, 2007, Oxford: Oxford Research Group (available at http://oxfordresearchgroup.org. uk/work/global_seciruty/war_on_terror.php).

36 Basil M. Liddell-Hart, *Strategy*, 1991 (2nd rev. edn.), New York: Plume, p. xvii.
37 Pierre Bourdieu, *The Logic of Practice*, pp.52, 82.
38 Pierre Bourdieu, *Outline of a Theory of Practice*, 2002 (1977), Cambridge: Cambridge University Press, p.73.

CHAPTER 1

1 Hobbes' design of the covenant is an explicit attempt to impose an artificial, foundational organizational form that he has designed from reason. Hobbes used the analogy of drawing a circle: in experiencing circles we are unable to tell whether it is a true circle, but in designing them we are sure each time, at least insofar as we can conjecture how a circle could have been caused, having demonstrated such through reason. Being a conduit between natural and artificial conditions (a foundational institution), the covenant is one such design of reason. The covenant is not the outcome of prudential discourse between agents but the rational imposition of Hobbes acting as a social philosopher (akin to how an architect imposes form upon matter to create a building). Hobbes, then, designed the leviathan as a response to what he believed was the inability of evolutionary human engagement to arrive at lasting peace. The leviathan has to create and sustain order by constantly working away at the prudential excess of naturally avaricious persons (see Ted Miller, 'Oakeshott's Hobbes and the fear of political rationalism', *Political Theory*, 2001, 29(6), pp.806–832). Quentin Skinner (*Reason and Rhetoric in the Philosophy of Hobbes*, 1996, Cambridge: Cambridge University Press, pp. 358–375) argues that, to do this, Hobbes suggested the leviathan employ rhetoric. Rhetoric involves: acting in a clear and consistent manner; making direct appeals to the imaginative capability of the audience; and being understood as an entity worthy of being heard. This means that the leviathan has to avoid the contempt of the agents, appear as a person or body in whom agents can place their trust, and command a clear, inspiring vision of the social good.
2 Ronald Hamowy, *The Political Sociology of Freedom: Adam Ferguson and F. A. Hayek*, 2005, Cheltenham: Edward Elgar, p.39.
3 Heraclitus, quoted in Philip E. Wheelwright, *Heraclitus*, 1974, New York: Atheneum, p.29.
4 Philip Wheelwright, *Heraclitus*, p.36.
5 Heraclitus, quoted in John Mansley Robinson, *An Introduction to Early Greek Philosophy*, 1968, Boston: Houghton Mifflin, p.90.
6 Graham Parkes, *Heidegger and Asian Thought*, 1987, Honolulu: University of Hawaii Press, p.106.
7 *Tao Te Ching*, in W. T. Chan, *A Source Book in Chinese Philosophy*, 1963, Princeton, NJ: Princeton University Press, p.139.
8 *Tao Te Ching*, in W. T. Chan, *A Source Book in Chinese Philosophy*, p.148.
9 *Tao Te Ching*, in W. T. Chan, *A Source Book in Chinese Philosophy*, p.170.
10 Chuang Tzu, in Joseph Spengler, *Origins of Economic Thought and Justice*, 1980, Carbondale: Southern Illinois University Press, p.57.
11 Adam Ferguson, *An Essay on the History of Civil Society*, 1966 (1767) (ed. Duncan Forbes), Edinburgh: Edinburgh University Press, p.122 (emphasis added).

12 Bernard Mandeville, *Fable of the Bees*, 1924 (1714) (ed. F. B. Kaye), Oxford: Clarendon Press, p.142.

13 Adam Smith, *Theory of Moral Sentiments*, 1976 (1759), Oxford: Clarendon Press, pp.184–185 (emphasis added).

14 Adam Smith, *An Inquiry into the Wealth of Nations*, 1976 (1776) (eds. R. H. Campbell and A. S. Skinner), Oxford: Clarendon Press, p.456.

15 Gavin Kennedy, *Adam Smith: A Moral Philosopher and His Political Economy*, 2008, Basingstoke: Palgrave Macmillan, p.224.

16 Gavin Kennedy, for example, suggests that the metaphor was a limited 'poetic device' borrowed from attempts in classical literature to describe divine intervention, and used by Smith to arrest the attention of readers. Its subsequent rise to prominence through the latter part of the twentieth century and its being coupled to an advocacy of laissez-faire is regrettable, because it masks a proper understanding of Smith's work, in which he spoke at length on the duties of governments and on the collective nature of human society.

17 Claude Frédéric Bastiat, *Essays on Political Economy*, 2007 (1848), New York: Bibliobazaar, pp.43–90.

18 Claude Frédéric Bastiat, *Fallacies of Protection*, 2006 (1845), New York: Cosimo Classics, pp.104–105 (emphasis added).

19 Claude Frédéric Bastiat, *Fallacies of Protection*, pp.104–105.

20 Peter Ackroyd, *London: The Biography*, 2000, London: Chatto and Windus. Ackroyd is content to recognize and map the migrations without seeking an explanation. Why the fur- and feather-dressing trades concentrated around Hoxton gave way to galleries and artist studios, and why furniture dealers still persist on Tottenham Court Road despite the influx of electronic goods outlets, are rhythms that seem to resist causal analysis: 'Like much else in London there is no surviving rhyme or reason to elucidate its secret and mysterious change' (p.127).

21 Henry George, *Protection or Free Trade: An Examination of the Tariff Question, with Special Regard to the Interests of Labor*, 1949 (1886), New York: Robert Schalkenbach Foundation, p.56.

22 Carl Menger, *Investigations into the Method of the Social Sciences with Special Reference to Economics*' 1985 (1883), New York: New York University Press, p.146.

23 Friedrich Hayek, *Individualism and Economic Order*, 1948, Chicago: University of Chicago Press, pp.86–87 (emphasis added).

24 Friedrich Hayek, *Individualism and Economic Order*, p.87.

25 Friedrich Hayek, *Individualism and Economic Order*, p.77.

26 Claude Frédéric Bastiat, *Essays on Political Economy*, p.43 (emphasis added).

27 Frank Knight, *Risk, Uncertainty and Profit*, 1921, Boston: Hart, Schaffner & Marx (available at Library of Economics and Liberty website: www.econlib.org/library/Knight/knRUP1.htm; retrieved 6 January 2006). Though Joseph Schumpeter (*History of Economic Analysis*, 1997 [1954], London: Routledge, p.303) attributes the formulation of this distinction much earlier, to the Swiss mathematician Daniel Bernoulli, for whom the riskiness of deciding upon a future course of action was a function of its (calculable) diminishing marginal utility understood as a function of the accrued wealth resulting from

that course of action. See Daniel Bernoulli, 'Exposition of a new theory on the measurement of risk', *Econometrica*, 1954 (1738) (trans. L. Sommer), 22(1), pp.23–36. Risk was understood as a function of peoples' awareness of the final outcomes associated with a range of possible decisions. The economist George Shackle suggests that risky scenarios are rare and rarefied; found in casinos, perhaps, where the odds associated with the turn of a card were calculable (probability), or in closed markets, where all available options were presented for selection (stated preferences). In economic life as it was lived it was uncertainty and not risk that prevailed, making economics itself a difficult undertaking, given that it had to speak meaningfully of a turbid, shifting world.

28 Ludwig von Mises, *Human Action*, 1949, London: William Hodge, p.105.
29 George Shackle, 'Policy, poetry, and success', in George Shackle (ed.), *On the Nature of Business Success*, 1968, Liverpool: Liverpool University Press, pp.2–38, p.36.
30 Ulrich Beck, 'The terrorist threat', *Theory, Culture and Society*, 2002, 19(4), pp.39–55.
31 Herbert Simon, *The Sciences of the Artificial*, pp.50–55.
32 Herbert Simon, 'Strategy and organizational evolution', *Strategic Management Journal*, 1993, 14(S2), pp.131–142.
33 Alfred North Whitehead, *Process and Reality: An Essay in Cosmology*, 1929, Cambridge: Cambridge University Press, p.58.
34 George Shackle, 'Policy, poetry, and success', p.3.
35 Herbert Simon, 'Can there be a science of complex systems?', in Y. Bar-Yam (ed.), *Unifying Themes in Complex Systems: Proceedings from the International Conference on Complex Systems*. 1997, Cambridge, MA: Perseus Press, pp.3–14.
36 Eric Raymond, 'Open minds, open source', *Analog*, 2004, June–July; see http://catb.org/~esr/writings/analog.html.
37 Gift-giving has a long human history, something Raymond picks up on using the work of Marcel Mauss (*The Gift*, 2002 [1924], London: Routledge). For Mauss, gift-giving is an ancient form of exchange in which the commodities being exchanged are riven with symbolic status, collective identity and expectation. Whilst money has been shorn of the more visceral elements of transacting, it retains common lineage with gifts insofar as it affords some of its bearers a capacity for what Thorstein Veblen called 'conspicuous consumption'. These are what Veblen termed the 'leisure class', who spend on 'costly entertainments'. These gatherings (not just parties, but product launches, charity gatherings) are versed in a sense of collective conviviality, but they also serve the more invidious end of sustaining the leisured, unproductive classes by enhancing their reputation amongst potential peers:

> The competitor with whom the entertainer wishes to institute a comparison is, by this method, made to serve as a means to the end. He consumes vicariously for his host at the same time that he is witness to the consumption of that excess of good things which his host is unable to dispose of single-handed, and he is also made to witness his host's facility in etiquette. (Thorstein Veblen, *The Theory of the Leisure Class: An Economic Study of Institutions*, 1899, New York: Macmillan, p.89)

Where in the past the leisured class had been aristocratic, the twentieth century saw the rise of business leaders, financiers, investment bankers and the like looking to control and acquire flows of money without getting involved in production. Their roles were entirely ceremonial. These were distinct from the engineers, such as software developers, the producers of goods immersed in technology. Whilst gifts remain distinct from the accrual of material wealth, therefore, they are not entirely separate; indeed, for Veblen they are indicative of what is perhaps most wanting in our current economic system, namely the stranglehold of finance over the productive process of efficient technological production. Given Veblen's work, what Raymond means by 'gift' is not synonymous with the kind of gift or potlatch (a conspicuous display or even destruction of wealth to demonstrate the wealth and status) identified by Mauss and then Veblen. This distinction is implied by Raymond's explicit attempt to distinguish repute from fame, retaining a mannered, almost humble sense of what it means to display gifts. In this distinction, Raymond may have in mind the ancient Greek notion of repute discussed by Paul Nieuwenburg. Here reputation is not inherent within an individual but is realized in community agreement coupled to the phenomenological sense of shame accompanying those brought into disrepute. This fear of disrepute, or shame, argues Nieuwenburg, explains how in acquiring virtues of character the learner becomes immersed in community morality. Disrepute reflects bad character (an inability to deliberate and contribute) coupled to an ignorance of community wishes. Repute and knowledge are therefore bound up with public action: it is people's activities that undergo judgement from others and by which their repute if assessed. This means that a concern with reputation cannot be feigned, because such knowledge requires sincere acts of deliberation. It also implies that the audience is party to the creation of repute; it is a lack of discernment (*paideia*) amongst the audience that provides the famous with their lifeblood (Paul Nieuwenburg, 'Learning to deliberate: Aristotle on truthfulness and public deliberation', *Political Theory*, 2004, 32(4), pp.449–467).

38 Ragu Garud, Sanjay Jain and Philipp Tuertscher, 'Incomplete by design and designing for incompleteness', *Organization Studies*, 2008, 29(3), pp.351–371.

39 For a fuller discussion, see Charles Leadbeater, *We-think: Mass Innovation, not Mass Production*, 2008. London: Profile Books. Leadbeater identifies five principles for successful we-think projects: they have a core; they attract a mix of perspectives; they exhibit suitable connections; they afford ordered collaboration; and they create. When expanded upon, it is far from clear how these principles remain distinct, and, indeed, are often cited in support of one another, yet a lingering sense of the distinctiveness of we-think remains (pp.68–88).

40 Katherine Hayles, *Chaos and Order: Complex Dynamics in Literature and Science*, 1991, Chicago: Chicago University Press.

41 J. P. Crutchfield, J. Doyne Farmer, Norman H. Packard and Robert S. Shaw, 'Chaos', *Scientific American*, 1986, 255(6), pp.46–57, p.56.

42 Ilya Prigogine and Isabelle Stengers, *Order out of Chaos: Man's New Dialogue with Nature*, 1984, New York: Bantam Books.

43 The slowing down was first voiced in a paper published in *Nature* by Harry Bryden, Hannah Longworth and Stuart Cunningham, 'Slowing of the Atlantic Meridional Overturning Circulation at 25°N', *Nature*, 2005, 438, pp.655–657. Subsequent testing and review is being undertaken in the United Kingdom by the UK Climate Impacts Programme. For more details, see Anna Steynor and Craig Wallace, 'The Gulf Stream – Atlantic Meridional Overturning Circulation: observations and projections', 2007, www.ukcip.org.uk/index.php?option=com_content&task=view&id=158.

44 Ruth Curry, Bob Dickson and Igor Yashayev, 'A change in the freshwater balance of the Atlantic Ocean over the past four decades', *Nature*, 2003, 426, pp.826–829; followed by G. S. Jones, P. A. Stott and N. Christidis, 'Human contribution to rapidly increasing frequency of very warm Northern Hemisphere summers', *Journal of Geophysical Research – Atmospheres*, 2008, 113, January; available at doi:10.1029/2007JD008914.

45 David Parker and Ralph Stacey, *Chaos, Management and Economics*, 1997 (3rd edn.), London: Institute of Economic Affairs. This insight has been developed by many other theorists. For example, W. B. Arthur, S. Durlauff and D. Lane (*The Economy as an Evolving Complex Adaptive System*, 1997, Reading, MA: Addison-Wesley, pp.1–13), in developing a complexity perspective to understanding the economy, have identified several key features that resist traditional mathematical formulation in economics. They are: (a) the dispersed nature of interactions; (b) the absence of a global design or controller; (c) continual adaptation on the part of individual elements; (d) the perpetual novelty of arrangements; and (e) out-of-equilibrium dynamics. Together these features make up what they term *adaptive non-linear networks*, which spontaneously form themselves without any centralized planning or design. See also K. I. Vaughn, 'Hayek's theory of the market order as an instance of the theory of complex, adaptive systems', *Journal des Economistes et des Etudes Humaines*, 1999, 9(2/3), pp.241–256, and K. I. Vaughn and J. L. Poulsen, *Is Hayek's Social Theory an Example of Complexity Theory?*, 1998, George Mason University Working Paper in Economics no. 98.07. Other interesting studies include: P. Anderson, 'Complexity theory and organization science', *Organization Science*, 1999, 10(3), pp.216–232; S. L. Brown and K. M. Eisenhardt, 'The art of continuous change: linking complexity theory and time-paced evolution in relentlessly shifting organizations', *Administrative Science Quarterly*, 1997, 42(1), pp.1–34; J. P. Davis, K. M. Eisenhardt and C. B. Bingham, *Complexity Theory, Market Dynamics, and the Strategy of Simple Rules*, 2008, working paper, //web.mit.edu/~jasond/www/complexity.htm; Bill McKelvey, 'Avoiding complexity catastrophe in co-evolutionary pockets: strategies for rugged landscapes', *Organization Science*, 1999, 10(3), pp.249–321; and Tor Hernes, *Understanding Organization as Process: Theory for a Tangled World*, 2007, London: Routledge.

46 See Ralph Stacey, *Strategic Management and Organizational Dynamics*, 2007. London: Prentice Hall, pp.260–290.

47 Ralph Stacey, *Strategic Management and Organizational Dynamics*, p.183. Stacey continues (p.197): 'If there is design, it is the basic design principles of the (emergent) system itself, namely a network of agents driven by iterative nonlinear interaction. What is not included in the design are the emergent

patterns which this interaction produces. There is inherent order in the complex adaptive system which evolves as the experience of the system, but no one will know what that evolutionary experience will be until it occurs.'

48 David Parker and Ralph Stacey, *Chaos, Management and Economics*, pp.92–94.

CHAPTER 2

1 Gregory Bateson, *Steps to an Ecology of Mind: Collected Essays in Anthropology, Psychiatry, Evolution, and Epistemology*, 1972, New York: Balantine, p.440.

2 Friedrich Hayek, *Individualism and Economic Order*, pp.13–14 (emphasis in original).

3 Nishida Kitaro, *An Inquiry into the Good*, 1990 (1921) (trans. M. Abe and C. Ives), New Haven, CT: Yale University Press, pp.19–26.

4 Gilles Deleuze and Félix Guattari, *What Is Philosophy?*, 1996, New York: Verso, p.66.

5 John Berger, *Ways of Seeing*, 1972, Harmondsworth: Penguin, pp.62–84.

6 Clifford Geertz, *The Interpretation of Cultures*, 1973, New York: Basic Books, p.5.

7 Tim Ingold, *The Perception of the Environment: Essays in Livelihood, Dwelling and Skill*, 2000, London: Routledge, p.175.

8 Joseph Rykwert, 'House and home', *Social Research*, 1999, 58(1), pp.51–62.

9 Theodore Schatzki, 'The sites of organizations', *Organization Studies*, 2005, 26(3), pp.465–484, p.466.

10 Emile Durkheim, *The Rules of Sociological Method and Selected Texts on Sociology and Its Methods*, 1982 (ed. S. Lukes), London: Macmillan, p.39.

11 Karl Popper, *The Open Society and Its Enemies*, vol. II, *The High Tide of Prophecy: Hegel, Marx and the Aftermath*, 1945, London: Routledge, p.91.

12 Pierre Bourdieu, *The Logic of Practice*, p.46.

13 Anthony Giddens, *New Rules of Sociological Method*, 1986, London: Hutchinson, p.76.

14 Margaret Archer, *Realist Social Theory: The Morphogenetic Approach*, 1995, Cambridge: Cambridge University Press, p.35, p.43.

15 Lars Udéhn, *Methodological Individualism: Background, History and Meaning*, 2002, London: Routledge, p.498.

16 Ludwig von Bertalanffy, *General System Theory: Foundations, Development, Applications*, 1968, New York: George Braziller.

17 Ralph Stacey, *Strategic Management and Organizational Dynamics*, p.40.

18 Theodore Schatzki, 'The sites of organizations', p.466.

19 Margaret Archer, *Realist Social Theory*, p.33.

20 Norbert Elias, *What Is Sociology?*, 1978, London: Hutchinson, p.13.

21 Robert Cooper and John Law, 'Organization: distal and proximal views', in S. B. Bacharach, P. Gagliardi and B. Mundell (eds.), *Research in the Sociology of Organizations: Studies of Organizations in the European Tradition*, 1995, Greenwich, CT: JAI Press, pp.275–301. Like Bourdieu, Elias uses the term 'habitus', and many subsequent writers have discussed possible tensions in how they construe our dispositional, background conditions. Elias is typically understood as offering greater latitude for subjective agency, whereas Bourdieu's habitus remains a structuring force over each of us. In our view,

what matters is not the degree of sovereign scope (as though structures and agents fight it out along a spectrum of control) but that both thinkers invoke habitus to suggest that any knowledge of how to act (including learning how to act) is neither a product of structure nor agent decision, but an accustomed sense of appropriateness acquired by being amongst institutions. Identifying habitus involves an epistemological reframing in which claims to know one's way about cannot be adjudged by any standards other than those being invoked in such knowledgeable activity.

22 Alfred North Whitehead, *Science and the Modern World.* 1985 (1926), London: Free Association Books.
23 Alfred North Whitehead, *Science and the Modern World*, pp.62–63.
24 Alfred North Whitehead, *Science and the Modern World*, p.64.
25 Alfred North Whitehead, *Science and the Modern World*, p.249.
26 Alfred North Whitehead, *Science and the Modern World*, p.248 (emphasis added).
27 Ludwig von Mises, *Epistemological Problems of Economics*, 1960, Princeton, NJ: Van Nostrand, p.130 (emphasis added).
28 Richard M. Ebeling (ed.), *Selected Writings of Ludwig von Mises*, 2002, Indianapolis: Liberty Fund, p.342.
29 Israel Kirzner, *Ludwig von Mises: The Man and His Economics*, 2001, Wilmington, DE: ISI Books, p.78.
30 Ludwig von Mises, *Human Action: A Treatise on Economics*, 1996 (1949), San Francisco: Fox and Wilks, pp.41–43.
31 Roger Bacon was known for studies in optics (in which puzzling illusions such as bending sticks in water and rainbows were brought into conjunction with theories of reflection and refraction) as well as statecraft (he translated and introduced an Arabic text on advice to would-be kings). His was an experimental attitude, inspired by his contact with a blend of Islamic scholars and Aristotle, that sought to dispel metaphysical truths associated with abeyance and contemplation, and instead advocated truth as something emerging from human rigour and curiosity (see Amanda Power, 'A mirror for every age: the reputation of Roger Bacon', *English Historical Review*, 2006, 121, pp.657–692.)
32 For a good and accessible introduction to the Vienna Circle, see Herbert Feigl, 'Positivism in the twentieth century: logical empiricism', in Philip Wiener (ed.), *Dictionary of the History of Ideas: Studies of Selected Pivotal Ideas*, vol. III, 1973, New York: Charles Scribner's Sons, pp.545–551.
33 An existing, well-argued and influential version of this theoretical idea is found in the rational, evaluative maximizer model (REMM) of human nature espoused by Michael Jensen and William Meckling ('The nature of man', *Journal of Applied Corporate Finance*, 1994, 7(2), pp.4–19). Their assumption is that no organizational theory can provide an explanation without acknowledging the nature and primacy of individuals in their essential features. It is people and their nature that influence and hence explain organizational and social life, economic life and political and cultural life. Of course, people's REMM state will alter given local circumstances: their stress levels, *force majeure* encounters, and so on. People do behave irrationally. Managers are

rude to potential customers and construction workers don't wear hard hats, but over time, and in sufficiently large settings, the REMM features are those that remain constant, if on occasion subsumed. Sophisticated, rational people will always adapt to and seek to influence their opportunity set, understood, basically, in terms of costs and opportunity costs. Rational people are optimizing choosers, and look to maximize the outcomes of their choices through purposeful action, conscious of a world in which their interests are not always synonymous with those of others. There are always trade-offs to be made. Altruism is one such trade-off: looking after the interests of others in the hope of a future outcome to which one can ally oneself peaceably and willingly.

34 Herbert Feigl (*Inquiries and Provocations: Selected Writings, 1929–1974* (Robert S. Cohen, ed.), 1980, Dordrecht and Boston: Reidel) finds that Carnap was investigating the possibility of extending the cognitive language of representation to cover human phenomena on the grounds that, ultimately, what was observed could be reduced to basic physical events/processes.

35 A. W. Carus (*Carnap and Twentieth-century Thought: Explication as Enlightenment*, 2007, Cambridge: Cambridge University Press) argues that, although early in his career Carnap was enthusiastic about the project of creating a unified language of science and truth, he became frustrated with repeated failures to provide sufficiently robust or hard concepts, and in response developed a method of explication in which replacing vague with precise concepts still took place but from *within* different logics, or frameworks, we create in order to get at the truth of things. These logics can be different (Carnap no longer elevates realist pure science as the unifying logic) and are themselves part of a wider, barely linguistic realm of pragmatic action in which our concerns are with getting things done rather than pursuing truth. In Carnap's later thinking this practical realm is allowed to intrude upon the logics of truth-seeking insofar as the rigour and precision of concepts have to have a use value in getting rid of the troublesome inconsistencies we experience in the practical realm.

36 Thorstein Veblen, 'Why is economics not an evolutionary science?', *Quarterly Journal of Economics*, 1898, 12(4), pp.373–397 (reprinted in Thorstein Veblen, *The Place of Science in Modern Civilisation and Other Essays*, 1919, New York: W. B. Huebsch, pp.56–81, p.73).

37 Filmed by Ian Sinclair, and mentioned in his *Lights out for the Territory* (1997, London: Granta Books, pp.97–98), where he also notes our obsession with, and anxiety over, the unknowable outcomes of weather patterns, suggesting a coinciding amplification of forces between the October storms in the United Kingdom in 1987 and the headless thrust into chaos of the financial markets: 'Forecasters blustered, and lost it. Paper fortunes dissolved.'

38 This description of clinical method comes from Gilles Deleuze and Felix Guatarri, who, in *Capitalism and Schizophrenia* (1988 [1972–1980], New York: Zone Books), reflect on our tendency to privilege the science of etiology above the processual project of symptomology. Investigating and naming symptoms brings to the surface our tendency to isolate and package phenomena in ways that fit our current purposes; it makes us conscious of

what ordinarily we are unconscious of; whereas etiology suppresses our awareness of this narrative involvement in what we call 'reality'. In privileging etiology we are privileging the isolation of unmoving entities held in linear connection and encouraging the view that this is how the world is, an amalgam of formally identified effects with knowable antecedents. We forget that initially the symptoms are uncertain (who, for example, would have recognized 'hearing voices' as schizophrenia prior to Alfred Adler and Sigmund Freud, or as heretical witchcraft prior to the Inquisition?) and bear the stamp of our own cultural impress.

39 Bateson elaborates using the Eden myth. Adam and Eve destroy the balance of life by taking it upon themselves to fixate on their own needs and to think purposefully, behaving in accord with common sense, but in unforeseen effect seeding the origins of dissolution as the system no longer runs in balance. The garden becomes skewed towards human purpose and human design, and so to sin.

40 Bateson uses the analogy with the governor, the name given to the thermostatic regulator found in steam engines, suggesting that it is more like a sense organ than a source of unilateral control; it is something that transforms input differences into output differences. In being so, it receives information about the behaviour of other parts of the system and is bound by that information, as well as by the effects of past behaviours (including its own). It is the total system that can be said to act, not the governor in isolation.

41 Herbert Marcuse, 'Liberation from the affluent society', in David Cooper (ed.), *The Dialectics of Liberation*, 1968, Harmondsworth: Penguin Books, pp.175–192.

42 Zygmunt Bauman, *Liquid Life*, 2005, London: Polity Press, p.18.

43 For a discussion of kitsch and camp orders of production, see Antonio Strati, 'The aesthetic approach in organization studies', in S. Linstead and H. Höpfl (eds.), *The Aesthetics of Organization*, London: Sage, pp.13–34, p.21.

44 Zygmunt Bauman, *Liquid Life*, p.33.

45 Italo Calvino, *Invisible Cities*, 1997 (1972), London: Verso, p.115.

46 The top-earning trader in 2007 on a list compiled by *Trader Monthly Magazine* was hedge fund manager John Paulson, who bet on the US house price decline and associated erosion of investment-grade mortgage bonds, making personally an annual return of around £1.87 billion, with his eponymous hedge fund netting an £11.5 billion gain in funds over the year (the latter figure being high enough to put the fund alongside Lebanon and Kenya in the 2006 World Bank's GDP rankings). Paulson had wit enough to counter the conventional wisdom that, spread nationally and over the medium term, property was always a sound investment. He thought the CDOs were more risky than assumed; they constituted 'the bubble' that he and his associates could short, along with buying the related credit default swaps that traders used to insure against debt going sour and that, given the apparent confidence in the lending market, were priced very cheaply. Paulson recognized the very early signs that aggressive, unchecked lending was taking place and that if he held out long enough, and kept his strategy as quiet as possible so that others did not emulate or counteract him, eventually the price of CDOs

would plummet and the price of swaps rocket, with his fund in pole position to earn revenues. Ethically, Paulson acknowledges his fund is making money from misery, but he points out that he simply reads and bets on trends, he doesn't make predatory loans or repossess homes. The effects of such activity remain, at the system level, deeply unsettling, however. Paulson's strategy is not so much predicting the future as following what he calls a rule of thumb: constantly watching for the downside and letting the upside take care of itself. Shorting on bonds such as CDOs is a way of betting that incurs minimal risk (Paulson estimates that with some bonds the risk was as little as a 1 per cent loss, set against a potential 100 per cent gain should the mortgage bonds become impaired). If his hunch that the credit market is overhyped bears out, he makes money – lots of it. If not, he loses very little, and looks for the next investment with a low downside and high upside. Recently, Alan Greenspan, former chairman of the US Federal Reserve and seen by many as one of the prime architects of the deregulation that pump-primed the credit system to such heady and unsustainable heights, was appointed adviser to Paulson's Hedge Fund, perhaps looking at the future revenue opportunities in shorting on credit card or auto loans, or shorting against banking and insurance company stocks? See Gregory Zuckerman, 'Trader made billions on subprime', *Wall Street Journal* (online), 15 January 2008; Anuj Gangahar, 'Greenspan joins NY hedge fund', *Financial Times*, 15 January 2008; and Steven Foley, 'The man who bet on the credit crisis' *Independent*, 17 April 2008.

47 Oliver James, 'A psychological analysis of the banking crisis', *Guardian*, 18 September 2008.

48 See R. Lowenstein, *When Genius Failed: The Rise and Fall of Long-Term Capital Management*, 2002, London: Fourth Estate.

49 Speech given by Marcel Rohner at UBS annual general meeting, 23 April 2008, Basel, pp.1–2; available at UBS.com (accessed June 2008).

50 Robert Chia, 'From complexity science to complex thinking', *Organization*, 1998, 5(3), pp.342–350; Murray Gell-Mann, *The Quark and the Jaguar: Adventures in the Simple and the Complex*, 1994, London: Little, Brown, p.33.

51 Haridimos Tsoukas, 'Forms of knowledge and forms of life in organized contexts', in R. Chia (ed.), *In the Realm of Organization: Essays for Robert Cooper*, 1998, London: Routledge, pp.43–66, p.47.

52 George Soros, *The New Paradigm for Financial Markets: The Credit Crisis of 2008 and What it Means*, 2008, New York: PublicAffairs.

53 Speech given by Marcel Rohner at UBS annual general meeting, 23 April 2008, Basel, p.2.

54 Speech given by Marcel Rohner at UBS annual general meeting, 23 April 2008, Basel, p.2.

55 In UBS's 2007 annual report, for example, there is a continuing lament for persisting ambiguity (UBS annual report, 2007; available at UBS.com, [accessed June 2008]): 'As seen in 2007, UBS is not always able to prevent losses arising from extreme and sudden market dislocations that are not anticipated by its risk measures and systems and affect sizeable inventory positions and therefore lead to serious losses. Value at Risk (VaR), a statistical

measure for market risk, is derived from historical market data, and thus, by definition, could not have predicted the losses seen in the stressed conditions in 2007.'

56 Speech given by Marcel Rohner at UBS annual general meeting, 23 April 2008, Basel, p.3.

57 Nick Mathiason, 'So long, farewell, auf wiedersehen: is it game over for Swiss banks?', *Observer*, 1 March 2009.

58 Gregory Bateson, 'Style, grace, and information in primitive art', in Gregory Bateson, *Steps to an Ecology of Mind*, pp.128–152, p.132.

59 See note 40.

60 Gregory Bateson, 'Style, grace, and information in primitive art', p.136.

61 Gregory Bateson, 'Ecology and flexibility in urban civilization', in Gregory Bateson, *Steps to an Ecology of Mind*, pp.502–514, p.505.

62 Gregory Bateson, 'Comment on part III', in Gregory Bateson, *Steps to an Ecology of Mind*, 2000 (rev. edn.), Chicago: Chicago University Press, pp.338–342.

CHAPTER 3

1 Johann W. von Goethe, *The Sorrows of Young Werther* (trans. T. Carlyle), 1774 (available at Project Gutenberg website: www.gutenberg.org/etext/2527).

2 Donald Hambrick and James Fredrickson, 'Are you sure you have strategy?', *Academy of Management Executive*, 2001, 15(4), pp.8–59.

3 Colin Gray, *Modern Strategy*, 1999, Oxford: Oxford University Press. Gray discusses seventeen, each of these always being in play (albeit to greater or lesser extents). Where the fungibility of these dimensions means prowess in one or a few is no guarantee of good strategic performance (policy outcomes being realized), weakness in any risks failure. They are grouped as: 'people and politics' (people, society, culture, politics and ethics); 'preparation for war' (economics and logistics, organization, military administration, intelligence, strategic doctrine, technology); and, finally, 'war proper' (military operations, command, geography, friction [chance and uncertainty], adversaries and time) (pp.24–26). Transposing these onto a consideration of the engagements of business life, we might arrive at the set of interrelated dimensions classified in the following table.

	Dimensions of strategy	Examples
Human environment	People	Cognitive capacities and patterns, such as means–ends reasoning or risk-taking. Theories of human nature (self-interested and individualistic?).
	Society	Institutional procedures such as legal frameworks, the role of the media, available social capital. The sanctity of the market: will contracts remain viable?

	Dimensions of strategy	Examples
	Culture	Prevailing values and ideas concerning economic exchange (e.g. whether entrepreneurship is valuable; usury is a sin; the state is a necessary evil).
	Politics	The executive and legislative theatres of influence in which the power to do things and power over things play out. Who is connected to whom? Which interests are in play in, say, proposals for investment in private health care systems? To this might be added the wider influence of the military stability of regimes. Will investments be safe?
	Ethics	The justice of exchange. The Western traditions of liberal rights (property titles), utilitarianism (maximizing the utility of the greatest number) and virtue ethics (leading an examined life). The Eastern traditions of balance (Confucian balance of emotional self – a sage-like neutrality; Daoists' balance of nature in which humans are but one element).
Trading conditions	Economics and logistics	Trade is inevitably constrained by the affordance of enabling factors. These include: costs of capital, availability of financing and legal expertise, transport infrastructure, data regulations.
	Organization	Institutional procedures that provide a modicum of stability and predictability. Rules of governance curtail the influence of individual judgement; design of the office and relations (feedback, review, etc.) between offices to which office-holders have to conform.
	Administration	Recruitment, training and preparation of employees; policies for career advancement; policies for resolving contractual disputes.
	Information and knowledge	Understanding the world view of others, an empathy with expectations of suppliers, competitors, regulators and customers. Information about oneself. This requires investment in learning (dynamic capabilities). Related is how this information on one's own organization is dispersed. Being known

	Dimensions of strategy	Examples
		to act predictably can be strategically important (for example, a reputation for litigation can prevent piracy of patents), as can the ability to conceal intentions and act unpredictably.
	Intellectual organization	Awareness of prevailing tendencies associated with models taught in business schools and advocated by policy-makers and consultants. Identifying five forces, conducting SWOT analyses, hedging investments, joint ventures, etc. within the organization. Developing shared inter-organization strategic vision using trade alliances; industry lobbyists; pan-sector, national alliances, etc.
	Technology	The available and emerging possibilities from science and engineering and the associated risks of investing/not investing.
Exchange	Operations	The tactical and operational actions by which goals and expectations are realized. The acquired skills and habits of operatives. The materials made available.
	Leadership	Quality of inspiration, clarity of instruction; reasonableness of expectation; provision of resources. Leaders can obviously detract from as well as enhance good strategic performance. For example, Robert Maxwell's narcissism at Mirror Group, Gerald Ratner's irony hitting Ratner's high street chain.
	Market territory	Geographical location (e.g. extracting hydrocarbons from oil sands, or beneath Arctic waters, or managing global supply chains). Changing markets (e.g. entertainment mediums; fashions).
	Friction, chance and uncertainty	Clausewitz's trinity of influence, whose force can rapidly become overwhelming. Friction comes from: asset specificity, contract length, conflicting sources of intelligence and manners. Chance occurrences, such as natural disasters. Uncertainty, associated with complex ecological systems of exchange.

Dimensions of strategy	Examples
Competition	Most obviously rival firms with whom advantage is being sought. Can also include foreign government/ international agencies. Adversaries learn from you; strategic effectiveness is only ever short-lived if the same strategy is always followed.
Time	Temporal sensitivity. Strategic ideas can be introduced too soon or too late. Also, time itself is a factor in strategy: waiting to follow first-movers, for example, and so learn from their mistakes.

Source: adapted from Gray, *Modern Strategy*, pp.26–43.

4 In the autumn of 2003 soldiers of the 372nd Military Police Company systematically, sadistically and illegally abused prisoners at the prison of Abu Ghraib, run by the US military, resulting in the isolation and prosecution of six suspects relating to offences of dereliction of duty and cruelty (see Seymour Hersh, 'Torture and Abu Ghraib', *New Yorker*, 10 May 2004). The investigation and, most significantly, pictures of these individuals' acts (sanctioned by a persistent institutional delegation of responsibility) may have marked not only the moment at which the United States and its allies began to lose their strategic grip on the war in Iraq but, more significantly still, the point at which it was unintentionally admitted that, for these nations, questions of morality were subject to a law of diminishing returns the following of which rides roughshod over the entire ethical edifice of Western liberal democracy.

5 Including, of course, the continuing relevance of Clausewitz himself, blind as his Enlightenment enthusiasm was to the dispiriting tendency of humanity to bend towards strife even where there is no apparent or obviously guiding material advantage. Security does not seem to be an equilibrium condition.

6 See Gregory Bateson, 'Ecology and flexibility in urban civilization', p.505, and 'The roots of ecological crisis', in Gregory Bateson, *Steps to an Ecology of Mind*, pp.496–501, p.499fn.

7 Friedrich Hayek, *The Sensory Order: An Inquiry into the Foundations of Theoretical Psychology*, 1999 (1952), Chicago: University of Chicago Press.

8 This theoretical fixing of entities will always run up against what the philosopher Nelson Goodman (*Fact, Fiction, and Forecast*, 1955, Cambridge, MA: Harvard University Press) calls 'the riddle of induction'. For any finite number of fixed points in a coordinate system representing pairs of values of two measurable quantities, an infinite number of curves can be drawn across the coordinates that yield different predictions regarding the behaviour or quality of these quantities. So we might, for example, infer from observation and experience that the price of goods in a market reflects a combination of

personal preference and availability; yet alternative hypotheses are always possible. This is not because of the possibility of exceptional evidence that has to be held in check by *ceteris paribus* conditions (of the kind presented by the discovery of black swans) but because, no matter what the evidence, we can always plot the relationship between prices, preferences and availability differently. The resulting trajectory may not be as smooth, and may describe possibilities that are less typical, but they can still have a logical hold if all we are relying on for establishing meaning is the conventional method of rational inference from observed (plotted) phenomena. The hypothesizing links between spatially finite bodies of data are always underdetermined. In addition to the inductive method of verification championed by the likes of the Vienna circle, then, we need another way of limiting the hypotheses that we isolate.

9 Brian Loasby, 'The ubiquity of organization', *Organization Studies*, 2007, 28(11), pp.1729–1760.
10 Friedrich Hayek, *Individualism and Economic Order*, p.23.
11 Friedrich Hayek, *Individualism and Economic Order*, p.8.
12 René Descartes, *Discourse on the Method of Rightly Conducting One's Reason and of Seeking both in the Sciences*, 1637 (available at Project Gutenberg website: www.gutenberg.org/etest/59).
13 Friedrich Hayek, *Individualism and Economic Order*, pp.6–7 (emphasis in original).
14 Friedrich Hayek, *Individualism and Economic Order*, p.13.
15 Friedrich Hayek, *Individualism and Economic Order*, p.13.
16 Friedrich Hayek, *Individualism and Economic Order*, p.15 (emphasis in original).
17 Martin Heidegger, *What Is Called Thinking?*, 2004 (1954) (trans. J. Glenn Gray), New York: Harper Perennial, p.5 (emphasis in original).
18 Alfred North Whitehead, 'The study of the past – its uses and dangers', *Harvard Business Review*, 1933, 11, pp.436–444.
19 Deirdre McCloskey, 'Bourgeois virtue and the history of P and S', *Journal of Economic History*, 58(2), pp.297–317, p.307. For McCloskey, Smith is an advocate of virtues such as justice, prudence, benevolence and propriety, all of which need to be balanced against one another within our commercial life. Gavin Kennedy suggests likewise in his *Adam Smith*, p.252.
20 Sumantra Ghoshal, 'Bad management theories are destroying good management practices', *Academy of Management Learning and Education*, 2005, 4(1), pp.75–91.
21 Richard Sennett, *The Craftsman*, 2007, London: Penguin Books, pp.155–177.
22 *Aristotle: Nicomachean Ethics, Book VI*, L. G. H. Greenwood, 1973 (1909), New York: Arno Press.
23 Philippe Baumard, *Tacit Knowledge in Organizations*, 1999, London: Sage, p.22.
24 Martha Nussbaum (*The Fragility of Goodness: Luck and Ethics in Greek Tragedy and Philosophy*, 1986, Cambridge: Cambridge University Press) recognizes how, at times, Aristotle in his discussion of *episteme* and *technē* does appear occasionally to use the terms interchangeably. It was perhaps with Plato that *episteme* acquired an honorific sense that distinguished *real* knowledge from mere opinion or belief. One's knowledge qualified as *episteme* only if one could give an adequate account of a phenomenon that traced its source or origin to

certain principles or causes and that established such explicit links with an expected degree of precision using logic and careful reasoning. Aristotle at times seems very aware of his predecessor's division, and at others happier to fall into more commonly accepted uses of *episteme*, which remain very similar to *technē*.

25 Joseph Dunne, *Back to the Rough Ground: 'Phronesis' and 'Techne' in Modern Philosophy and in Aristotle*, 1993, Notre Dame, IN: University of Notre Dame Press.

26 Joseph Dunne, *Back to the Rough Ground*, p.244.

27 Joseph Dunne, *Back to the Rough Ground*, p.263.

28 Joseph Dunne, *Back to the Rough Ground*, p.244.

29 Joseph Dunne, *Back to the Rough Ground*, p.268.

30 Joseph Dunne, *Back to the Rough Ground*, p.272.

31 Joseph Dunne, *Back to the Rough Ground*, p.266.

32 In this we distinguish our use of *phronesis* in organization studies somewhat from that used by Bent Flyvbjerg (*Making Social Science Matter: Why Social Science Fails and How It Can Succeed Again*, 2001, Cambridge: Cambridge University Press), for whom *phronesis* demands a consciously reflexive and evaluative stance in relation to the power and values manifest in the organized phenomena of human lives. Flyvbjerg emphasizes Aristotle's association of *phronesis* with the deliberation of things that are good or bad for human life, whereas for us *phronesis* is more a question of acquired style and manner than of thoughtful consideration on the utility of things.

33 We would like to note here that Martin Heidegger can talk of *technē* somewhat differently from this. In his 'Building, dwelling, thinking' (in *Basic Writings*, [ed. David Farell Krell), 1978 (1954), London: Routledge and Kegan Paul, pp.335–338), he talks of this form of knowledge as a way of letting something appear in the present, the knowledgeable construction of something that can be called 'present' because it brings forth other things, admits them. This seems closer to Dunne's reading of *phronesis* and *praxis*, in that it is far from being an abstracted, technical knowledge but, rather, a sense of craft understood organically, a willingness to work with things to create objects that have use value. What Heidegger objects to is not *technē* itself, which like *phronesis* is a knowledge of possibility rather than abstraction, but the way *technē* dominates *phronesis*. What marks the latter out for Heidegger is its avowedly anti-pragmatic vein, its being the kind of knowledge that allows the otherness of things to speak back to us outside our productive concerns, that affords us an awareness of things at their most distant and questionable. We discuss this in more depth in chapter 5.

34 Joseph Dunne, *Back to the Rough Ground*, p.273.

35 Gregory Bateson remarks how '[i]n the cliché system of Anglo-Saxons, it is commonly assumed that it would be somehow better if what is unconscious were made conscious. This view is the product of an almost totally distorted epistemology and a totally distorted view of what sort of thing a man, or any other organism, is' ('Style, grace and information in primitive art', p.136). It is not possible always to be aware of the primary processes by which we perceive things, nor even to be conscious of all the things we do perceive, without an ensuing constipation of being. Many of our messages are necessarily

unconscious – an economy of effort by which we husband our consciousness for the everyday job of getting on with life.

36 William James, *Talks to Teachers on Psychology, and to Students on Some of Life's Ideals*, 1912, New York: Henry Holt, pp.36–37.

37 John Ruskin, 'Modern painters, vol. I', in Edward T. Cook and Alexander Wedderburn (eds.), *The Works of John Ruskin*, vol. IV, 1903 (1844), London: George Allen, p.371.

38 Joseph Dunne, *Back to the Rough Ground*, p.263.

39 Joseph Dunne, *Back to the Rough Ground*, p.268, p.266.

40 Kant discusses purposiveness as a kind of direct or imaginative encounter with a thing that we judge on aesthetic grounds. There is no unity other than the thing itself: the thing does not exist for the purpose of something else; it is its own end. Purpose comes from within rather than being prescribed from without through comparison with a desired goal or an ideal type, though it still relies upon the judgement of a subjective will to make itself manifest. See Immanuel Kant, *Critique of Judgement*, 1914 (1790) (trans. J. H. Bernard) (2nd edn.), London: Macmillan, div. 1, sects. 10–11, pp.67–70.

41 Ernst Cassirer, *Kant's Life and Thought*, 1981 (1918), London and New Haven, CT: Yale University Press, p.321.

42 Joseph Dunne, *Back to the Rough Ground*, p.268.

43 Hubert Dreyfus, *Being-in-the-World: A Commentary on Heidegger's Being and Time, Divisional*, 1999, Cambridge, MA: MIT Press.

CHAPTER 4

1 Keith Ansell-Pearson and John Mullarkey, 'Introduction', in Keith Ansell-Pearson and John Mullarkey (eds.), *Henri Bergson: Key Writings*, 2002, New York: Continuum, pp.1–48, p.33.

2 Henri Bergson, 'The creative mind', in Keith Ansell-Pearson and John Mullarkey (eds.), *Henri Bergson: Key Writings*, 2002 (1933), New York: Continuum, pp.223–284, p.226.

3 Henri Bergson, 'Creative evolution', in Keith Ansell-Pearson and John Mullarkey (eds.), *Henri Bergson: Key Writings*, 2002 (1907), New York: Continuum, pp.171–204, p.188.

4 Keith Ansell-Pearson and John Mullarkey, 'Introduction', pp.5–9.

5 Much in the way of metaphysics has also traditionally attempted such a displacement from everyday practicalities, but only by turning us away from action and reality itself: a metaphysics of fleeing founded upon transcendent faculties that are distinct from the senses we use to experience this life. As Kant recognized, however, a metaphysics that relies upon transcendent faculties cannot exist, because we have no such faculty; we have only perception. Hence Kant's reliance upon our intellectual intuition to refine and compose our perception using unassailable categories: those foundational phenomena such as time and space without which knowledge could not sensibly persist. Kant realized that the status of these categories could never be proved, or, at least, that the proof was in their being continually accepted. Bergson, however, speculates on the nature of this acceptance, arguing that time and space are

often misconceived insofar as human beings tend to favour intellectual versions of the phenomena above intuitive ones. The use of images helps restore the balance, bringing the speculative back into favour (Henri Bergson, 'The perception of change', in Keith Ansell-Pearson and John Mullarkey (eds.), *Henri Bergson: Key Writings*, 2002 (1911), New York: Continuum, pp.248–266, p.254).

6 Bernard Bosanquet, 'The prediction of human conduct: a study in Bergson', *International Journal of Ethics*, 1910, 21(1), pp.1–15.

7 Indeed, no one thing can exist in isolation; things are primarily centres of action, partaking of the rhythm of duration, and what is interior and exterior is a matter of relation. Perception and feeling are intimately bound up with the plural conditions of existence in which a living mind/body finds itself (actions, recollections, dreaming, and so on) (see Keith Ansell-Pearson and John Mullarkey, 'Introduction', p.17).

8 Andrew Pettigrew, *The Awakening Giant: Continuity and Charge in Imperial Chemical Industries*, 1985, Oxford: Basil Blackwell.

9 Joe Orton calls this 'iterative grounded theory' in his paper 'From inductive to iterative grounded theory: zipping the gap between process theory and process data', *Scandinavian Management Journal*, 1997, 13(4), pp.419–438.

10 See Gerry Johnson, Leif Melin and Richard Whittington, 'Micro strategy and strategizing: towards an activity-based view', *Journal of Management Studies*, 2003, 40(1), pp.3–22; and Paula Jarzabkowski, *Strategy as Practice: An Activity-based Approach*, 2005, London: Sage, pp.4–5.

11 We are thinking especially of Karl Weick's view that better theorizing focuses on projects rather than 'fixed' entities (curiously called variables) as units of analysis, displays a ready-to-hand awareness of how people themselves engage in practices such as strategy in a ready-to-hand way, and that recognizes how concepts and activities are inseparably woven (see 'Faith, evidence, and action: better guesses in an unknowable world', *Organization Studies*, 2006, 27(11), pp.1723–1736.

12 For overviews, see Richard Whittington, 'Strategy as practice', *Long Range Planning*, 1996, 29(5), pp.731–735; Paula Jarzabkowski, *Strategy as Practice*; Paula Jarzabkowski, Julia Balogun and David Seidl, 'Strategizing: the challenges of a practice perspective', *Human Relations*, 2007, 60(1), pp.5–27; and David Seidl, 'General strategy concepts and the ecology of strategy discourses: a systemic-discursive perspective', *Organization Studies*, 2007, 28 (2), pp.197–218. Specific studies following what is a broad church of methodology and method include Dalvir Samra-Fredericks, 'Strategizing as lived experience and strategists' everyday efforts to shape strategic direction', *Journal of Management Studies*, 2003, 40(1), pp.141–174; Patrick Regner, 'Strategy creation in the periphery: inductive versus deductive strategy making', *Journal of Management Studies*, 2003, 40(1), pp.57–82; Sue Maitlis and T. Lawrence, 'Orchestral manoeuvres in the dark: understanding failure in organizational strategizing', *Journal of Management Studies*, 2003, 40(1), pp.109–139; Saku Mantere, 'Role expectations and middle manager agency', *Journal of Management Studies*, 2007, 45(2), pp.294–316; Saku Mantere and Eero Vaara, 'On the problem of participation in strategy: a critical discursive perspective', *Organization Science*, 2008, 19(2), pp.341–358; and Patrick

Regner, 'Strategy as practice and dynamic capabilities', *Human Relations*, 2008, 61(4), pp.565–588.

13 Richard Whittington, 'Completing the practice turn in organization studies', *Organization Studies*, 2006, 27(5), pp.613–634.

14 Richard Whittington, 'The work of strategizing and organizing: for a practice perspective', *Strategic Organization*, 2002, 1(1), pp.119–127.

15 Paula Jarzabkowski, Julia Balogun and David Seidl, 'Strategizing: the challenges of a practice perspective', p.19.

16 Pierre Bourdieu, *The Logic of Practice*, p.12.

17 Mahmoud Ezzamel and Hugh Willmott, 'Strategy as discourse in a global retailer', *Organization Studies*, 2008, 29(2), pp.191–217.

18 Ikujiro Nonaka and Ryoko Toyama, 'Strategic management as distributed practical wisdom (phronesis)', *Industrial and Corporate Change*, 2007, 16(3), pp.371–394.

19 Henri Bergson, 'Introduction to metaphysics', in Keith Ansell-Pearson and John Mullarkey (eds.), *Henri Bergson: Key Writings*, 2002 (1903), New York: Continuum, pp.274–282.

20 Charles Guignon talks of Heidegger's future-oriented characterization of agency in terms of projects as an 'ability to be' that can find expression only in the possibilities made available by existing practices in our ordinary world. In this way we arrive at Heidegger's concept of the clearing, the space in which things come to be as something of significance, notably where human agents – *dasein* – take a stance on being-in-the-world (see 'Introduction' in Charles Guignon [ed.], *The Cambridge Companion to Heidegger*, 1993, Cambridge: Cambridge University Press, pp.1–41).

21 Hubert Dreyfus, *Being-in-the-World*, pp.46–47.

22 Hubert Dreyfus, 'Reflections on the workshop on "the self"', *Anthropology and Humanism Quarterly*, 1991, 16(1), pp.1–28, p.22.

23 Hubert Dreyfus, *Being-in-the-World*, p.22.

24 Hubert Dreyfus, *Being-in-the-World*, p.17.

25 Pierre Bourdieu, *The Logic of Practice*, p.50.

26 Pierre Bourdieu, *The Logic of Practice*, p.61.

27 See, for example, Barry Barnes, 'Practice as collective action', in Theodore Schatzki, Karin Knorr Cetina and Eike von Savigny (eds.), *The Practice Turn in Contemporary Theory*, 2001, London: Routledge, pp.17–28, where he talks of 'acupuncture' as an example of how a set of predispositions, skills and modus operandi are transmitted through examples, techniques, postures and acquired mannerisms, often without recourse to cognitive representation.

28 Tim Ingold, *The Perception of the Environment*, p.3.

29 Tim Ingold, *The Perception of the Environment*, p.5.

30 Hubert Dreyfus and Stuart Dreyfus, 'Expertise in real world contexts', *Organization Studies*, 2005, 26(5), pp.779–792, p.788.

31 See Julia Balogun and Gerry Johnson, 'From intended strategies to unintended outcomes: the impact of change recipient sensemaking', *Organization Studies*, 2005, 26(11), pp.1573–1601.

32 Gerry Johnson, Leif Melin and Richard Whittington, 'Micro strategy and strategizing: towards an activity-based view', *Journal of Management Studies*, 2003, 40(1), pp.3–22, p.3.

33 Jeff Wall, 'A conversation between Jeff Wall and John Roberts', *Oxford Art Journal*, 30(1), pp.153–167, p.161.

34 Michael Fried, 'Jeff Wall, Wittgenstein and the everyday', *Critical Inquiry*, 2007, Spring, pp.495–526. Fried is careful to accept that absorption is never complete; indeed, this disjunct is necessary for aesthetic practice to gain any foothold. The artist is deliberately shedding prejudice in order to convey an absorbed intentionality in a way that we can never appreciate when we look, say, at other peoples' holiday snaps. The artist's skill lies in making the mundane come alive for itself.

CHAPTER 5

1 Tim Ingold, *The Perception of the Environment*, p.178.

2 Tim Ingold, *The Perception of the Environment*, p.168.

3 Pierre Bourdieu, *The Logic of Practice*, p.52.

4 Ikujiro Nonaka and Ryoko Toyama, 'Strategic management as distributed practical management (phronesis)'.

5 Gregory Bateson, 'The cybernetics of "self" ', in Gregory Bateson, *Steps to an Ecology of Mind*, pp.316–322.

6 For a fuller discussion on Heidegger's views on *praxis* and disclosure, see Joseph Fell, 'The familiar and the strange', in Hubert Dreyfus and Harrison Hall (eds.), *Heidegger: A Critical Reader*, 1992, Oxford: Basil Blackwell, pp.65–80.

7 Martin Heidegger, 'Building, dwelling, thinking', p.338 (emphasis in original).

8 Thomas Sheehan, 'Heidegger, Martin', in E. Craig (ed.), *Routledge Encyclopaedia of Philosophy*, 2003, London: Routledge (available at www.rep.routledge.com/article/DD027SECT4; retrieved 18 April 2007).

9 Laurent Thévenot, 'Pragmatic regimes governing the engagement with the world', in Theodore Schatzki, Karin Knorr Cetina and Eike von Savigny (eds.), *The Practice Turn in Contemporary Theory*, pp.56–73.

10 Hubert Dreyfus, *Being-in-the-World*, p.3.

11 We feel that the term *autopoiesis* is somewhat unfortunate, since, as we have argued, *poiēsis* is more associated with deliberately designed and planned production rather than spontaneous responsive actions and interactions, as the example in the quotation shows. It would have been more appropriate to call the second 'dwelling' form of engagement *autopraxis*, thus reflecting its thoroughly social and self-cultivating character.

12 Humberto Maturana and Francisco Varela, *Autopoiesis and Cognition: The Realization of the Living*, 1980, Dordrecht: D. Reidel, p.54.

13 Humberto Maturana and Francisco Varela, *Autopoiesis and Cognition*, p.54.

14 Pierre Bourdieu, *The Logic of Practice*, p.90.

15 Pierre Bourdieu, *The Logic of Practice*, p.62.

16 Pierre Bourdieu, *The Logic of Practice*, pp.52–53.

17 John Shotter and Arlene M. Katz, 'Articulating a practice from within the practice itself: establishing formative dialogues by the use of a "social poetics"', *Concepts and Transformation*, 1996, 1(2–3), 239–248; John Shotter, 'The role

of "withness" thinking in "going on" inside chiasmatically structured processes', keynote paper presented at 1st Organization Studies Summer Workshop, 'Theorizing Process in Organizational Research', Santorini, Greece, 12 June 2005.

18 Michel de Certeau, *The Practice of Everyday Life*, 1984, Berkeley: University of California Press, pp.91–94.

19 The phrase 'muddling through' as used here comes from Charles E. Lindblom in 'The science of muddling through', *Public Administration Review*, 19(2), 1959, pp.79–88.

20 Michel de Certeau, *The Practice of Everyday Life*, p.37.

21 Michel de Certeau, *The Practice of Everyday Life*, pp.37–38.

22 Hubert Dreyfus, *Being-in-the-World*, p.27.

23 Joseph Dunne, *Back to the Rough Ground*, p.272.

24 William James, *Some Problems of Philosophy: A Beginning of an Introduction to Philosophy*, 1996 (1911), Lincoln: University of Nebraska Press, pp.49–50.

25 Eric Abrahamson and David Freedman, *A Perfect Mess: The Hidden Benefits of Disorder*, 2006, London: Weidenfeld and Nicholson.

26 This incident, recounted by Ruskin from a letter written to him by Turner, has been disputed. No *Ariel* was found sailing out of Harwich, and Turner was only a very occasional visitor to that part of England. As an *imagined* fabrication, however, its power retains a visceral directness whose vagueness and chaos extend even to the question of its being experienced.

27 John Ruskin, 'Modern painters, vol. IV', in Edward T. Cook and Alexander Wedderburn (eds.), *The Works of John Ruskin*, vol. VI, 1903 (1856), London: George Allen, p.11.

28 John Ruskin, 'Modern painters, vol. IV', p.13.

29 John Ruskin, 'Modern painters, vol. IV', p.14.

30 John Ruskin, 'Stones of Venice, vol. II', in Edward T. Cook and Alexander Wedderburn (eds.), *The Works of John Ruskin*, vol. X, 1903 (1853), London: George Allen, p.214.

31 John Ruskin, 'Stones of Venice, vol. II', p.363.

32 John Ruskin, 'Stones of Venice, vol. III', in Edward T. Cook and Alexander Wedderburn (eds.), *The Works of John Ruskin*, vol. XI, 1903 (1853), London: George Allen, p.15.

33 The poet William Empson speculates on the importance of contrast in his *Seven Types of Ambiguity* ([rev. edn.] 1947 (1930), London: Chatto and Windus). The use of differing forms of contrast (contradiction, open-ended meaning, double meanings, ironic meaning, and so on) enriches language with a multiplicity of meaning. Discussing the line 'Brute beauty and valour and act, oh air, pride, plume, here/Buckle' in Gerard Manley Hopkins' poem *The Windhover, to Christ our Lord*, Empson notes how on coming face to face with the bird the poet is using the word 'buckle' with two tenses and two meanings: 'buckle' as an invitation to, or a commentary on, something having already happened; 'buckle' as in a collapsing bicycle wheel, a falling in and weakening; and 'buckle' as in bringing together in a stiff, militaristic fashion (p.225). The opposites are brought together to enrich meaning, conveying contradictory feelings of affection, recoil and doubt simultaneously,

as they are actually felt. By appreciating and absorbing the associated uncertainty, people would not only anticipate how things might be different but appreciate the manner of their own influence on meaning, writers and readers alike. Poems, like Gothic buildings, work because of what they provoke as much as what they contain and resolve. Empson gives an important caveat to this use of ambiguity. Letting contradiction and open-ended meaning stand and settle requires we respect tradition. Just as it needs creativity, literature also needs established standards and tradition that are sufficiently unspoken and engrained to act as a relief against which the 'surprise' or gestation of alternative meanings can be experienced and registered. We have to be familiar with alternative uses and tenses, and be prepared to read this awareness into our reading of the poem.

34 John Ruskin, 'Stones of Venice, vol. I', in Edward T. Cook and Alexander Wedderburn (eds.), *The Works of John Ruskin*, vol. IX, 1907 (1851), London: George Allen, p.278.

35 B. Hanson, '*Labor ipse voluptas*: Scott, Street, Ruskin and the value of work', in Rebecca Daniels and Geoffrey K. Brandwood (eds.), *Ruskin and Architecture*, 2003, Reading: Spire Books, p.125.

36 Ruskin's admiration for the great Gothic cathedrals of Europe is attributable to this recognition. For example, the achingly slender spire of Salisbury Cathedral, its defining structure, emerged as an afterthought to the work of the original masons, being finished around 1330, a century after the main building and lantern tower. Standing 404ft high, the spire tapers from a two-foot-thick base to only eight inches at its point, yet weighs about 5,000 tonnes. Recent work on restoration has revealed how the original scaffolding was retained *within* the spire as a frame, allowing the elegant external stonework to rise without effort. The entire structure has been braced, bandaged, trussed and buttressed with copper, stone, iron and wood over the ensuing centuries. Different quarries, styles, architects and crafts have all had a hand in keeping the spire breathing. The building resonates with continual amendments and trickery, a palimpsest of conservation and creative response that continues to this day (see Tim Tatton-Brown, 'Building the tower and spire of Salisbury Cathedral', *Antiquity*, 1991, 65 (March), pp.74–96).

37 Martin Heidegger, *What Is Called Thinking?*, pp.14–15.

38 For a fuller expression of this ecological sensitivity, see Charles Taylor's essay 'Heidegger, language, ecology', in Hubert Dreyfus and Harrison Hall (eds.), *Heidegger: A Critical Reader*, 1992, Oxford: Basil Blackwell, pp.247–269.

39 Martin Heidegger, *What Is Called Thinking?*, p.187.

40 Heidegger's sometimes equivocal and even contradictory relationship with technology is discussed by Hubert Dreyfus in 'History of the being of equipment', in Hubert Dreyfus and Harrison Hall (eds.), *Heidegger: A Critical Reader*, pp.173–185. Dreyfus himself has a somewhat pragmatic reading that tends to repress the inherent questionability and mystery of Being found in Heidegger's discussion of thinking about thinking. *Phronesis* is more than simply absorbed coping, as it is a steady unfurling of the there (the *da*) in *Dasein* such that we come to realize that, potentially, we are not the only ones who are doing the speaking in the world (see Jeff Malpas, *Heidegger's Topology: Being, Place, World*, 2006, Cambridge, MA: MIT Press).

41 Quoted in Martin Heidegger, *What Is Called Thinking?*, p.18.
42 Martin Heidegger, *What Is Called Thinking?*, p.33.
43 Robert Cooper, 'The open field', *Human Relations*, 1976, 29(11), pp.999–1017.
44 Martin Heidegger, 'The origin of the work of art', in *Basic Writings* (ed. David Farell Krell), p.163.
45 Martin Heidegger, 'The origin of the work of art', p.164.

CHAPTER 6

1 Edwin Hutchins, *Cognition in the Wild*, 1995, Cambridge, MA: MIT Press, cited in Tim Ingold, *The Perception of the Environment*, p.12.
2 Alfred Gell, quoted in Tim Ingold, *The Perception of the Environment*, p.236.
3 Edwin Hutchins, quoted in Tim Ingold, *The Perception of the Environment*, p.236 (Ingold's emphasis).
4 Tim Ingold, *The Perception of the Environment*, p.236.
5 Tim Ingold, *The Perception of the Environment*, p.237.
6 Tim Ingold, *The Perception of the Environment*, p.237.
7 T. E. Hulme (*Speculations: Essays on Humanism and the Philosophy of Art*, 1936, London: Routledge and Kegan Paul) suggests that in being able to isolate and specify the location and trajectory of things we have lost the sense of what it means for a human life *to be led*. This loss is significant. In thinking of life like a map and ourselves as points moving on it, we are in the thrall of determining forces to which we have no adequate, human response (pp.210–215), our lives simply movements in a plane and our theories of life simply intellectual determinations of where these movements occur with law-like regularity. Prices rise and demand falls; wages rise and labour supply increases; transaction costs increase and organizations become increasingly hierarchical; and so on.
8 Martin Heidegger, *What Is Called Thinking?*, p.62.
9 Tim Ingold, *The Perception of the Environment*, pp.228–230.
10 Tim Ingold, *The Perception of the Environment*, p.236 (emphasis in original).
11 Tim Ingold, *The Perception of the Environment*, p.242.
12 Thomas Gladwin, cited in Tim Ingold, *Perceptions of the Environment*, pp.239–240.
13 Tim Ingold, *The Perception of the Environment*, pp.239–240.
14 Alfred Gell, quoted in Tim Ingold, *The Perception of the Environment*, p.235.
15 Tim Ingold, *The Perception of the Environment*, p.237.
16 Gavin Menzies, *1421: The Year China Discovered the World*, 2003, London: Bantam Press.
17 Gavin Menzies, *1421*, p.93.
18 Gavin Menzies, *1421*, pp.123–124.
19 Tim Ingold, *The Perception of the Environment*, p.237.
20 Tim Ingold, *The Perception of the Environment*, p.231.
21 Tim Robinson, *Setting Foot on the Shores of Connemara and Other Writings*, 1996, Dublin: Lilliput Press.
22 Tim Ingold, *The Perception of the Environment*, p.234.

23 Tim Ingold, *Lines: A Brief History*, 2007, London: Routledge, pp.89–90.

24 Michel de Certeau, *The Practice of Everyday Life*, pp.120–121.

25 Tim Ingold, *Lines*, p.87.

26 For a good introduction, see Chris Bissell, 'The Moniac: A hydromechanical analog computer of the 1950s', *IEEE Control Systems Magazine*, February 2007, pp.69–74. Bissell mentions a number of the later type II machines still in existence. One is on view in the computer section of the British Science Museum, and other versions are being restored at the London School of Economics, where Phillips was a professor, at Cambridge University and at Leeds University, where Newlyn was a professor.

27 J.J. Gibson, *The Ecological Approach to Visual Perception*, 1979, Boston: Houghton Mifflin, p.198.

28 Tim Ingold, *The Perception of the Environment*, p.239.

29 Jacques Derrida describes a bricoleur as 'someone who uses the "means at hand", that is the instruments he finds at his disposition around him, those which are already there, which had not been especially conceived with an eye to the operation for which they are to be used and to which by trial and error one tries to adapt them, not hesitating to change them whenever it appears necessary, or to try several of them at once, even if their form and origin are heterogeneous.' (*Writing and Difference*, 1978 [1967], London: Routledge, p.33). Organizationally, this bricolage can be experienced out of frustration; an institutional confinement forces improvisation of the kind undertaken by disgruntled or disengaged employees redeploying the equipment of the firm for their own designs. This *détournement* can throw up surprises. Motown Records, for example, was founded by workers from Detroit's Ford Motor company, who, despite finding the production line discipline overbearing, recognized the potential of self-similar repetition in any mode of production, and simply sought to transfer the logic from the production of cars to hit records.

30 See 'The amazing Mr Musicals', *The Guardian*, 24 January 2008.

31 Graeme Obree, *The Flying Scotsman: The Graeme Obree Story*, 2004, Edinburgh: Birlinn.

32 See http://news.bbe.co.uk/sport1/hi/other_sports/cycling/6748587.stm.19th June2007.

33 Tim Ingold, *The Perception of the Environment*, p.242.

34 David Vise, *The Google Story: Inside the Hottest Business, Media and Technology Success of Our Time*, 2005, New York: Bentham Dell.

35 Gary Hamel, 'Management à la Google', *Wall Street Journal*, 26 April 2006 (emphasis in original).

36 The Fast Company website has an interesting article based on testimony from Google employees. One example is from Jessica Ewing: 'It was clear to Google that there were two groups: people who loved the site's clean, classic look and people who wanted tons of information there – email, news, local weather. IGoogle [a customized Google home page] started out with me and three engineers. I was 22, and I thought, This is awesome. Six weeks later, we launched the first version in May. The happiness metrics were good, there was healthy growth, and by September, we had a link on Google.com. When

the Google Maps team released Street View [featuring 360-degree photos], we thought, That is the coolest thing ever. We try to out-innovate each other. We asked, 'How do we take iGoogle to the next level?' Rather than using brute force to create everything, we built the tools and infrastructure to leverage the outside developer community. We couldn't believe the stuff that people came up with. There was one high-school kid who developed the periodic table in a gadget [Google's version of a widget]. We'd never have thought of that' ('Google: The faces and voices of the world's most innovative company', www.fastcompany.com).

37 Robert Hof, 'How Google fuels its idea factory', *Business Week*, 12 May 2008.
38 John Lanchester's ('The global id', *London Review of Books*, 26 January 2006) review of written accounts of the Google story is marbled by the question of privacy and its being the biggest problem facing Google both in terms of its identity (Google is trust – reliable information, protecting user information, and so on) and its business prospects (the more we – the users – worry about a lack of privacy the less valuable Google becomes as a search engine). Interestingly, in 2005 Eric Schmidt himself was the subject of some research on the personal information available about him using Google. When confronted with the data (hobbies, political allegiance, address, etc.), he initially refused to speak to the journalist who had undertaken the search for the technological website CNET News (see Andy Beckett, 'That interminable 0.9 seconds', *The Guardian*, 1 November 2008).
39 Stephen Baker, 'Google: the wisdom of clouds', *Business Week*, 24 December 2007.
40 For a more technically complete explanation, see Alex Isold, 'Reach for the sky through the compute clouds', *Read Write Web*, 18 February 2008, www.readwriteweb.com. Isold also explains how it is not just firms such as Google but others, such as Amazon, that are experimenting with the widespread provision of cloud computing.
41 Bobbie Johnson, in *The Guardian*, 29 September 2008.

CHAPTER 7

1 Victor Davis Hanson, *The Western Way of War: Infantry Battle in Classical Greece*, 1989, London: Hodder and Stoughton, p.224.
2 Polybius, quoted in François Jullien *Detour and Access: Strategies of Meaning in China and Greece*, 2000 (trans. Sophie Hawkes), New York: Zone Books, p.41.
3 François Jullien, *The Propensity of Things: Toward a History of Efficacy in China*, 1999 (trans. Janet Lloyd), New York: Zone Books, p.36.
4 François Jullien, *Detour and Access*, p.44.
5 François Jullien, *Detour and Access*, p.44 (emphasis in original).
6 *The Times*, 6 April 2009.
7 François Jullien, *Detour and Access*, p.47 (emphasis in original).
8 François Jullien, *A Treatise on Efficacy: Between Western and Chinese Thinking*, 2004 (trans. Janet Lloyd), Honolulu: University of Hawaii Press, p.47.
9 François Jullien, *A Treatise on Efficacy*, p.52 (emphasis in original).
10 François Jullien, *A Treatise on Efficacy*, p.54.

11 François Jullien, *A Treatise on Efficacy*, p.55 (emphasis in original).

12 Michel de Certeau, *The Practice of Everyday Life*, p.93.

13 Marcel Detienne and Jean Pierre Vernant, *Cunning Intelligence in Greek Culture and Society*, 1978 (trans. Janet Lloyd), Brighton: Harvester Press.

14 Hesiod, *Theogony* (trans. Richard Lattimore), in Patrick Reid (ed.), *Readings in Western Religious Thought: The Ancient World*, 1987, Mahwah, NJ: Paulist Press, pp.119–126, p.126.

15 Marcel Detienne and Jean Pierre Vernant, *Cunning Intelligence in Greek Culture and Society*, p.12.

16 The academic invisibility of Detienne and Vernant's *mētis* is discussed at length in R. Klein, 'The *mētis* of Centaurs', *Diacritics*, 1986, 16(2), pp.2–13.

17 Michel de Certeau, *The Practice of Everyday Life*, p.40 (emphasis added).

18 Marcel Detienne and Jean Pierre Vernant, *Cunning Intelligence in Greek Culture and Society*, pp.28–29.

19 I. Raphals, *Knowing Words: Wisdom and Cunning in the Classical Traditions of China and Greece*, 1992, Ithaca, NY, and London: Cornell University Press, p.5.

20 Philippe Baumard, *Tacit Knowledge in Organizations*, p.54, p.64.

21 Philippe Baumard, *Oblique Knowledge: The Clandestine Work of Organizations*, 1994, Université de Paris-Dauphine Marketing Strategie Perspective Working Paper no. 228.

22 George Day and Paul Schoemaker, 'Are you a vigilant leader?', *MIT Sloan Management Review*, 2008, 49(3), pp.42–51.

23 Basil H. Liddell-Hart, *Strategy: The Indirect Approach*, p.xx.

24 Liddell-Hart talks of the perfect military strategy being that which realizes outcomes without any fighting having taken place; the objective of good strategy is one of avoidance (*Strategy: The Indirect Approach*, p.324). This advocacy of absence meant that Liddell-Hart's ideas, somewhat ironically, met with stiff resistance from the more orthodox military strategists, for whom doing battle, demonstrations and the recognition of courage, and the conscious compliance of the vanquished were integral to their practice (see Alex Danchev, *Liddell-Hart: Alchemist of War*, 1998, London: Weidenfield).

25 Colin Gray, *Modern Strategy*, pp.288–292.

26 T. E. Lawrence, 'The science of guerrilla warfare', from entry on 'Guerrilla' in *Encyclopaedia Britannica*, 1929, 14th edn., Chicago: Encyclopaedia Britannica, p.950.

27 T. E. Lawrence, 'The science of guerrilla warfare', p.953.

28 Basil H. Liddell-Hart, *Strategy: The Indirect Approach*, pp.379–381.

29 For a fuller discussion, see I. Raphals, *Knowing Words*, p.5.

30 This episode is recounted in Wyndham Lewis's autobiography *Blasting and Bombardiering* (1937, London: Eyre and Spottiswoode, p.243). Lewis met with Lawrence on a number of occasions after the war. Lewis suggests that much of what Lawrence achieved was driven by ego, but a peculiarly abstinent one, which constantly refused to accept the judgement of anyone or anything, including itself. Thus Lawrence outmanoeuvred his colleagues, the Turks and even his own identity as a 'man of action', refusing to sit in judgement on others for fear of always wanting to be where the accused sat,

resisting authority. He also eschewed all pomp, refusing to be anointed a king of Arabia or whatever; he was shy, unprepossessing, seasonally invisible (pp.243–248).

31 François Jullien, *In Praise of Blandness: Proceeding from Chinese Thought and Aesthetics*, 2004 (trans. Paula Varsano), New York: Zone Books.

32 François Jullien, *In Praise of Blandness*, p.90.

33 François Jullien (*Vital Nourishment: Departing from Happiness*, 2007 (trans. Arthur Golorhammer), New York: Zone Books, pp.29–32) argues that even the golden mean is a trap for vitality, because any attempt to occupy the middle ground misses the constantly moving point of equilibrium. There are no banks to steer between.

34 François Jullien, *Vital Nourishment*, pp.41–42.

35 François Jullien, *In Praise of Blandness*, p.50.

36 Robert Musil, 'Monuments', in Burton Pike (ed.), *Robert Musil: Selected Writings*, 1986 (1936), New York: Continuum, pp.320–323.

37 Jullien makes mention of training a gamecock. We begin with its naïve expression of identity, of aspiration, its pride and a sense of its own ability. Over time, as its strength grows, it becomes steadily more inscrutable, and the training finishes when it become motionless. It avoids costly engagement and maintenance of positions; its gaze suffices; its defence against other prideful cocks is one of avoidance, whereby any would-be opposition is denied reactivity (*Vital Nourishment*, p.53).

38 Herbert De Pree, *Business as Unusual: The People and Principles at Herman Miller*, 1986, Zeeland, MI: Herman Miller, p.59.

39 Herbert De Pree, *Business as Unusual*, p.62.

40 François Jullien, *A Treatise on Efficacy*, p.64.

41 François Jullien, *The Propensity of Things*, p.79, pp.103–104.

42 This episode is recounted by Constable's biographer and friend C. R. Leslie in his memoirs, and is repeated and contextualized under the 'Varnishing days' entry of Evelyn Joll, Martin Butler and Luke Herrmann (eds.), *The Oxford Companion to J.M.W. Turner*, 2001, Oxford: Oxford University Press, pp.354–358.

43 See, for example, the last sections of François Jullien, *Vital Nourishment*.

44 Martin Heidegger, 'The origin of art and the destination of thinking', discussed in Walter Biemel, 'Elucidations of Heidegger's lecture "The origin of art and the destination of thinking"' (trans. Joan Stamborough), in John Sallis (ed.), *Reading Heidegger: Commemorations*, 1993, Bloomington: Indiana University Press.

EPILOGUE

1 William Hazlitt, 'On paradox and common-place', in William Hazlitt, *Table Talk: Essays on Men and Manners*, vol. I (2nd edn.), 1824, London: Henry Colburn.

2 John Keats, 'Letters to G. and T. Keats, 21 December 1817', in G. F. Scott (ed.), *Selected Letters of John Keats*, 2002, Cambridge, MA: Harvard University Press, pp.60–61.

3 Donald Sull makes a similar point in his *Made in China: What Western Managers Can Learn from Trailblazing Chinese Entrepreneurs*, 2005, Boston: Harvard Business School Press. See also his 'Strategy as active waiting', *Harvard Business Review*, 2005, 83(9), pp.120–129.

4 Konosuke Matsushita, *The Heart of Management*, 2002, New York: PHP Research Institute, p.45.

Index